D0897907

Democracy in Mexico

Democracy in Mexico

PABLO GONZÁLEZ CASANOVA

TRANSLATED BY DANIELLE SALTI

New York
OXFORD UNIVERSITY PRESS 1970

Copyright © 1970 by Oxford University Press, Inc.
Library of Congress Catalogue Card Number: 76-83043

First published in Mexico under the title *La democracia en México* by
Ediciones Era, S.A. © 1965

Printed in the United States of America

Preface to the Second Edition

The first edition of this book was sold out eight months after publication. Considering the controversial nature of its subject, the book was received even better than I had hoped. Among the criticisms that have been forthcoming, some were particularly useful for the clarification of concepts which led to confusion or analytical errors. To the corrections have been added a few more recent statistical and historical data.

I wish to thank Mrs. Ramona Ham López de Martínez for her assistance in gathering the new statistical data.

I am particularly grateful to Professor Jorge Basurto for his revision and correction of the manuscript in the light of new data.

P.G.C.
March 1970

Preface to the First Edition

This study is neither apologetic nor skeptical. It is not intended as evidence of the consummation of democracy in Mexico, or as a lament for the frustration of this universal idea. I have attempted to understand an odd behavioral pattern, while struggling against opacity, mockery, political interplay, and hatred, which impede understanding. I shall try to clarify the relationship between the Mexican behavioral pattern and development, which is our basic concern and which is closely linked to genuine democracy.

Those readers who may be seeking justifications for their skepticism or their enthusiasm will certainly be disappointed. Those who would look for arguments, facts, and judgments to confirm their prejudices will only be irritated. The skeptic will find optimistic data, and the apologist may find a critical examination, not because I should have sought eclecticism in a false attempt at objectivity, but because the subject I am dealing with is filled with contradictions. There is an essential dynamic to society, a dialectical movement between what we interpret as good or bad, as encouraging or depressing, as success or failure, as the fulfilment of duty or political sin.

The method I have followed in this analysis clarifies how the book should be read. There is a continuous flow from abstract to concrete levels, containing data which are mutually correcting and adjusting. Definitive judgments had better be postponed in the course of reading since, as the analysis proceeds, there may be complementary data explaining an essentially changing phenomenon which can only be understood in all its variations.

In the beginning, a search for objectivity leads us to a mere description of the structure of power, which appears at times as a metaphysical entity. Yet as the analysis unfolds, we shall see how power integrates into a far wider social and cultural structure, of which it is a part. One of the purposes of this study is to show precisely that the structure of power in Mexico is a function of its national society, of the classes and strata which compose it. From this national society there emerge ambitions and ideals, and with them the dissent and dynamics leading toward different forms of government and society.

This study is too brief for such a wide and complex phenomenon. It suggests the need to examine the subject in greater depth, not by relying solely on official statistics, but by undertaking research leading to more rigorous and objective analyses. I likewise hope to stimulate scientific research on national political problems, since as long as we lack a clear picture of Mexican political life, the social sciences will not have fulfilled one of their main aims, and political action will not be able to avoid serious and unnecessary blunders.

The scientific character of the book need not detract from its political intention. Let us remember that during the armed phase of the Mexican Revolution 1 million lives were lost, and that in this same period and in the twenties almost 700,000 Mexicans emigrated abroad.[1]

This is an attempt to face the facts, to put an end to simulation, to alienating rhetoric and propaganda, and to the false idea that the best way to love Mexico is to hide its prob-

1. In the 1911–30 period, 678,291 Mexicans emigrated to the United States.

lems. My main political goal is the search for a political course that will peacefully and civilly resolve the major national problems. I feel responsible for—and a bit a part of —the great movement initiated in 1910, which time and again has struggled to emerge and achieve its goals.

I wish to thank in particular Mr. Calixto Rangel Contla and Mrs. Esperanza Burguete de Fabila for their assistance in gathering data while they were my students at the National School of Political and Social Sciences. Without their help and that of many other students, this tedious chore, done in the little time available, would have delayed completion of the book considerably. I also wish to thank Dr. Frank Brademburg for having placed at my disposal some of his studies on Mexican politics. Finally, I wish to thank my brother Henrique and Guillermo Haro for their observations on the manuscript.

P.G.C.
San Jerónimo Lídice
May 1963

Contents

Foreword

Every once in a great while a book comes along that conveys the meaning of a nation. I have in mind such remarkable recent works as Ralf Dahrendorf's *Freedom and Democracy in Germany,* John Porter's *The Vertical Mosaic: Class and Power in Canada,* and Gino Germani's *Politics and Society in an Epoch of Transition.* To this slim list of outstanding works must now be added Pablo González Casanova's *Democracy in Mexico.* Part of the explanation of a great work on a nation is its initial ambition. And this is conveyed in González Casanova's choice of title—clearly a paraphrase of Alexis de Tocqueville's *Democracy in America.* For without a wide telescopic vision, one can scarcely embrace all the parts that make a nation a living whole. But at the other end of the social science panoply is an ability to capture the intimate side of national life: just as each citizen encompasses national goals, so too the national system exhibits a unique "personality" that comprises yet exceeds the individuals who make up the nation.

The trick is to avoid the extremes of caricature: the national type, on one hand; and the opposite extreme of atomism, that is, sectoral analysis, on the other. And perhaps the secret of González Casanova's book, and the others mentioned as well, is the realization that to write about a nation is uniquely a task of political sociology: an enterprise in the interpenetration of social stratification and social psychology; a cross between problems of social class and personal choice. For however powerful regionalism is to the ethnic groupings in Mexico, or however compelling foreign colonialism is to economic groupings in Mexico, the fact is that Mexico does exist—as a State even more than as a society, as a system of juridical-political constraints even more than as an Indian-ladino inheritance. We can learn from González Casanova not only the character of Mexican politics but, perhaps more important, the meaning of nationalism in a developmental context.

To the immense task of studying a nation such as Mexico, Pablo González Casanova brings an impressive background. Trained in economics, knowledgeable in epistemology, dedicated to political sociology, and sophisticated in modern computer techniques, this man is uniquely able to study his nation. But equally important, the author brings to his task a passionate concern for the less fortunate people of his fortunate land. As a leader of the student movement, and now as an equally forceful spokesman for greater educational democracy, González Casanova has those qualities of training and moral character that make *Democracy in Mexico* a major undertaking—perhaps the best book on this nation thus far produced by a social scientist.

Democracy in Mexico is a theoretically sophisticated and statistically informed study of modern Mexico. It represents the coming of age, if not of Mexican sociology, at least of one Mexican sociologist. And it can be strongly recommended for people interested in social change and economic development.

The book is a treatise in political sociology. It moves from an examination of how the Mexican political revolution was compelled to face the social problems of overcoming local *caciques* and *caudillos,* to the need to absorb the military and to accommodate a small but increasingly powerful Managerial Estate. The political structure of Mexico is defined by this unique combination of traditionalist and new economic power, neither in a position to overwhelm the other, both requiring the strong single-party State. Why the same sort of political system did not arise elsewhere, for example in England after its "Great Compromise," would make a fascinating study in contrasts.

The book reveals a frank indication of the United States influence; particularly an appreciation of the *functional* aspects of the anti-Yankee spirit. Mexico may be one of the best established countries in Latin America and perhaps the only one in which anti-American sentiments have evolved into a strategy of national independence and development. In this way González Casanova both accounts for and yet is able to discuss the rhetoric of the Left.

González Casanova contends that Mexican *society,* in contrast to Mexican *polity,* had to achieve its own resolution after the Revolution. It had to resolve the relationship of Church and State. It had to find the way to institutionalize the counterrevolution. Finally, it had to develop such means for redistributing material wealth as would not threaten the whole social system. Because of the partial and piecemeal way Mexican society handled such issues, it perfectly illustrates the incomplete revolution.

With the Revolution frozen in its incompleteness, the chances for any kind of socialist revolution or even for a fascist counterrevolution are held to be rather remote. It would seem that Mexico is thus joining those societies which Gino Germani has called fully mobilized and integrated mass societies. Mexico is becoming a country of the Non-Event, or for the more militant-minded, the uneventful. Paradoxically, this uneventfulness is itself one of the most remarkable aspects of Mexican life, stemming as it does from a nation with one of the most turbulent and violent histories in all of Spanish America.

Professor González Casanova has managed to make a virtue of eclecticism—a rare feat in itself. He has taken Marxist and liberal ideologies as a means of overcoming "the schizo-phrenia of social scientific analysis." And in a brilliant pair of chapters (10 and 11) he has shown that both Marxist and liberal premises lead to the same conclusions concerning the future of Mexico as are suggested by contemporary political sociology. Mexico is unlikely to undergo another revolution-ary upheaval in the near future despite its pronounced polit-ical problem of single-party democracy, or what I choose to call party charisma along a democratic-falangist axis. The de-velopment of a strictly middle-class vision of what the Mexican Revolution was all about has led to a situation in which the Revolution was the end for the ruling classes, and only the beginning for the rural classes.

Yet the authenticity of the Mexican Revolution of 1910–20 is as significant as its incomplete character. One finds in Mex-ico the unresolved dualisms of a popular revolution of the masses which ended by consecrating a military dictatorship of the middle classes; a very rapid growth of the industrial sector which leaves the traditional peasant sector untouched and un-absorbed; a national culture more vital than nearly anything else in Latin America wallowing in mimesis of mass cultures. González Casanova's use of the concept of democracy in Mex-ico has an ironic and biting aspect because the author is clearly aware not only of how far Mexico has come, but how far it has yet to go to realize a mature concept of democracy.

Several weaknesses cannot go unnoticed. While there is an exceptionally good analysis of the dual society in Mexico, there is no comparative analysis with the mass-class dichot-omies elsewhere in Latin America. Indeed, there is no real comparative international material. The only references are to the United States, yet comparisons with Brazil might have been more fruitful. Also, González Casanova fails to recognize the brittle, essentially unimaginative condition of present-day politics in Mexico. The Mexican Revolution was indeed prag-matic at its outset. This pragmatism has, however, hardened over the years. With the thorough determination of PRI to establish a universal consensus has come an ideological liberalism that is more rhetorical than real.

Because of this inelasticity in the social system it might well be that the delicately laced system that is Mexican society could be irrevocably undone. Further, any drastic asymmetry in the pillars of present-day power, any *political* miscalculations in terms of what sector of society needs what at whose expense, and Mexico could once again become a dramatically eventful nation. González Casanova himself, while minimizing the possibilities of further discontinuities in the process of political development, does hold open the possibility of either (or both) revolution or counterrevolution. He leans to the latter possibility, and on this I agree with him. Yet it might have been just as important to locate more precisely the sources for potential disequilibrium as the present temporary basis for equilibrium.

Democracy in Mexico is already a "modern classic" of the social sciences in the Spanish language, and I cannot imagine it would be anything else in the English language. Indeed, this version more nearly links the data and the theory than does the original edition, and hence makes the interpretation offered even more convincing.

Whether the analysis provided in *Democracy in Mexico* is correct in all its details, or for what period of time, is hard to say. González Casanova himself warns against conversion of intuitive guesses into scientific truisms. But despite these admissions and premonitions, *Democracy in Mexico* should be widely read with great profit by political sociologists and Latin American area specialists for years to come.

IRVING LOUIS HOROWITZ
New Brunswick, New Jersey
March 1970

Democracy in Mexico

Introduction

When speaking of economic development, I implicitly or explicitly think of the process of increasing the net national product or the per capita product, and also of progress toward a more equitable distribution of the national product than in the past. Without exception, developed countries have a larger and better distributed national product than underdeveloped countries.

When I speak of economic development, I think also in terms of raising the standard of living of the population with regard to food, health, clothing, and education. Further, when speaking of economic development, I am referring to a phenomenon which is far broader than the mere growth of the national product or the increase in the standard of living. I am referring to a moral and political problem. The term "economic development" is the successor of other less technical but more comprehensive terms, such as "civilization" and "progress," which expressly pointed to the same idea that is contained in the term "economic development": a type of egalitarian morality which has underlain all social ethics since the eighteenth century and which has been at the basis of all political activity since the beginning of the widespread revolution of popular expectations in that century.

3

The theory of economic development is one of the most recent responses to these moral and political mass pressures. Owing to technical and ideological reasons, however, this theory tends to bypass the essence of the problem of development and its solution. Analysis is limited to studying the growth of the national product or its distribution, and the relationship between these phenomena and the social and political fields is usually neglected.

In order to begin development (or what development really means, that is, the increase and redistribution of the national product), then, it is necessary to think not only in terms of political economy but in terms of political science and economic sociology. It is necessary to think radically, not only according to the categories used by the economist but according to the categories used by the political scientist, those which lead him to make decisions concerning investments, expenditures, salaries, markets, for example. Such decisions are often the despair of the economist, since they do not correspond with his models of development, which are usually removed from operative political problems.

A curious fact in the evolution of economics is that up to this date it has remained enclosed within its traditional limits, despite repeated experiences which ought to have long since expanded its boundaries. Efforts of men like Myrdal, Baran, Ackermann, and Perroux, aimed at breaking this isolation, are rarely made. Generally, the attempt to link economics with sociology or political science does not go further than the utterance of a series of principles, which should be only the starting point of a scientific analysis of development as an economic, political, social, and cultural phenomenon.

The more refined instruments of research for the analysis of the different elements which constitute development have seldom been used. In the scientific literature on the subject, case studies—even elementary ones—are still scarce. In general, only statesmen, ideologists, and politicians analyze particular situations in such a way that the political aspects of development are treated as the very essence of the problem.[1]

What I have said concerning economic development and the science of development generally can be applied to the case of Mexico. When I speak of development that has taken place there, I think of it in the true sense—that is, as being at the same time a process of growth and distribution of the national product, of increase in the standard of living, and a political answer to the egalitarian morality and policy of the masses. In Mexico, then, it has been a process which is at least as political as it is economic; it must be studied in all its dimensions, and not only in its economic aspects.

Within this framework, Mexico's problems of economic development lead us to ask unusual questions. In what way does the power structure of a country like Mexico condition and limit decisions regarding economic development, or lead to decisions constituting simple measures of economic growth? To what degree is it possible to modify the power structure to achieve economic development?

The same kind of questions might be asked using the term "democracy": To what degree does the kind of democracy prevalent in Mexico condition and limit economic development? To what degree can the country bring about the kind of democracy that ensures development? Since the term "democracy" is laden with value implications and lends itself more to debate than to understanding, I shall use it with reserve and postpone its analysis until the final section of this work, where it can be defined with greater precision. The analysis of the political structure of the country will enable us to form an operational concept of democracy in Mexico which might serve for deeper and clearer studies of the problems involved.

Thus provisionally setting aside the two main topics— development and democracy—and taking the power

1. The number of studies dealing with development as an integral phenomenon and using refined methods of analysis has considerably increased in the past few years.

structure as a springboard for this study, I shall consider three major phenomena: the relationship between the formal political structure—the theoretical and juridical models of government—and the actual power structure; the relationship between national power—that of the nation-state—and international power; and the relationship between the actual power structure and the social structure—that is, macrosociological groups, strata, and classes. These three sets of analyses are needed for any study of political decisions regarding economic development, but they are needed most for the study of underdeveloped or developing countries.

Theoretical models of government or of constitutional institutions have a formal character which has given rise to a *sui generis* functioning. This was not accounted for by European theoretical models, and it was not foreseen by the ideologists and statesmen who imitated and introduced these models. In any city or nation it is easy to perceive great contrasts between ideological or juridical norms and political reality. In underdeveloped nations these contrasts are even greater. Through the process of imitation, an aspect of the universalization of the West, models and constitutions have been imported into and imposed upon non-European environments since the nineteenth century.

Whereas in Europe theoretical and legislative models are the result of direct and creative interaction between experience and political and legislative thought, in the underdeveloped nations creativity is stifled by appropriated foreign ideas and by imitation and adjustment. National customs and techniques operate upon the ideas, the constitutions, giving them a civilized-savage, Western-tropical symbolic life. This no longer happens when the countries become masters of their own existence, and it is at this point that development begins. In the governmental sphere there is a process similar to one of a religious nature: the idols are hidden under the altars along with the psychology of the persecuted, the idolater.

Today, in spite of the legislative genius of the 1917 constituent assemblies and the creation of models and institutions derived from Mexico's own historical and political experience, the Constitution still embodies institutions that originated in Europe and the United States. Because these institutions are not suited to the needs of Mexico, they have a ritualistic function which is absent in their places of origin. This function is connected to national security, vernacular institutions, and *Realpolitik*.

The institutions urgently need to be confronted with the orthodox, official juridical models and forms. Every citizen of an underdeveloped country forms the habit of comparing the orthodox model with the pagan reality in which he lives, and he becomes obsessed, morally and intellectually sick of comparing. Comparison is a part of his rhetoric or criticism, of his satisfaction or wrath.

The people of Mexico, too, have the habit of comparing ideas and juridical models with reality. Generally, the comparison is made with a touch of bitterness, or irony. This attitude, the product of long-standing frustration with government, is often a barrier to making the kind of observations on which one could base a systematic analysis of Mexicans as political beings and of Mexico as a country in which the strange functioning of public rights and theoretical models deserves objective analysis.

There is also an urgent need to relate the national power of the nation-state to the international structure in underdeveloped countries. Since they gained their independence, they have regarded as a vital problem the expansion, penetration, and domination of the great powers into and upon the small nations.

The problem is not one of imperialism, for imperialism involves other kinds of values and draws our attention from the perspective of *national power*. The problem is, however, one of the political dynamics of national inequality, which affect the total complex of national economies and the contractual powers of states, and which place upon these nations the threat of becoming nominal nations with no polity of their own. This vital and empirically obvious problem is directly related to the actual normal phenomena of strength, pressure, and politics which the very ideologues of imperialism cannot deny or call rhetorical or metaphysical. This is a problem that is beyond polemics. It is a part of the political processes of these nations.

The ideologists and students of small nations have two important objectives. The first is to denounce the big powers insofar as they are domineering and exploitative, and to discover and develop national strength by trying to determine the nature of obstacles to it and how they can be overcome. The second objective, which is of particular interest is probably of the greatest importance from a practical point of view, for its goal is to change the present situation in a way favorable to the nation and to increase the capacity of the Mexican State to negotiate internationally. Besides these problems in Mexico and in other underdeveloped nations there is an urgent need to analyze the relationship between the political structure and the social structure, for stratification, mobility, and social classes and groups there differ notably from their counterparts in metropolitan societies.

In both the social sciences and the juridical field there has been a tendency to apply to Mexican society categories and concepts based upon European political experience. It seems to have been easier to force facts to conform to the models of the dominant countries than to find Mexican models. Even though underdeveloped nations are discarding European concepts and categories, now that cultural and political independence of the underdeveloped countries is progressing, actual research has only barely begun. Underdeveloped countries— poor and semi-colonial—resemble each other much more than they resemble developed countries. It is of vital importance for the analysis of Mexico's political institutions to do away with the last traces of intellectual colonialism and to attempt an analysis of the relationship between the political structure and the social structure, using categories applicable to the underdeveloped countries.

I

THE STRUCTURE OF POWER

1

The Structure of Government

MODEL AND REALITY

Mexico's Constitution, like those of the other Latin American countries, takes its inspiration from the ideas of the French Enlightenment and the United States Founding Fathers. Rousseau's concept of popular sovereignty, Montesquieu's thoughts on the separation and balance of the three powers, and the ideas about checks and balances of State power developed by Madison in *The Federalist Papers* are the theoretical political bases of the Constitution.

In fact, however, governmental structure and political practice are a far cry from these models. They will not help us to understand the actual functioning and full significance of Mexico's government structure. The parties, voting patterns, elections, the "three powers," the "sovereignty of the federal states," and the whole apparatus of traditional democracy generally operate in such a way that actual political decisions are made in a way having little or nothing to do with the theoretical models of the Constitution. The dynamics of the government, the institutionalization of change, equilibria, and controls, and the concentration and distribution of power are classical formulations that have become symbolic elements to envelop and sanction novel situations.

Elections and Shift in Power

Since its creation in 1929, the government party, first called
the National Revolutionary Party, has never lost a presidential, gubernatorial, or senatorial election. Up until the presidential election of 1964, the party, now called the Institutional Revolutionary Party (PRI), had brought to power 6
presidents, almost 200 governors, and 282 senators.[1] Since
then, these figures have increased, owing to the victory of all
PRI candidates for those positions in the 1964 elections. The
opposition parties have lacked the actual and institutional
strength to win even one of those positions. Many of these
parties exhibit characteristics essentially different from those
attributed to a party on the basis of theory or of the European
and American experience. Financed in many cases by the government itself, they have either supported the government's
candidates or provisionally fought against them in exchange
for concessions for their supporters. Thus they have participated in the political game and the ceremony of elections.

The opposition parties have continually fought to gain
strength but have achieved only the status of pressure groups.
Their leaders are fully aware that they are doomed to lose any
election for governor, senator, or president. If the parties do,
under these strange circumstances, run candidates for one of
these offices, it is because the political contest allows them to
obtain in exchange a few positions as representatives or municipal presidents (a relatively recent development). Above all,
they receive government recognition of their most important
members—a recognition manifested in the form of contracts, loans, or services. In addition, their members receive
political training for future elections when the chances of success might be greater.

The weakness of opposition parties in Mexico becomes evi-

1. Cf. Frank Brandenburg, *The Making of Modern Mexico* (Englewood
Cliffs, New Jersey: Prentice-Hall, 1964).

dent from the distribution of votes among presidential candidates. Between the last presidential elections prior to the Revolution (those of 1910) and the most recent presidential elections in the revolutionary period (those of 1964), for example, the opposition has not been able to poll more than 25 per cent of the vote, and this percentage was reached only once, in 1952. Normally, the official candidate for the presidency receives more than 90 per cent of the vote: 99 per cent in 1910 with Porfirio Díaz; 99 per cent in 1911 with Madero; [2] 98 per cent in 1917 with Carranza; 96 per cent in 1920 with Obregón; 84 per cent in 1924 with Calles; 100 per cent in 1928, when Obregón was re-elected (he was assassinated shortly thereafter); 94 per cent in 1929 with Ortiz Rubio; 98 per cent in 1934 with Lázaro Cárdenas; 94 per cent in 1940 with Avila Camacho; 78 per cent in 1946 with Alemán; 74 per cent in 1952 with Ruiz Cortines; 90 per cent in 1958 with López Mateos; and 89 per cent in 1964 with Díaz Ordaz (see Table 1).

If we consider the data in absolute terms we see that since the beginning of direct elections the winning presidential candidate received from a minimum of 797,000 votes (in 1917) to a maximum of 8,400,000 (in 1964). Opposition as a whole (exclusive of the case of the 1928 elections, in which there was no vote registered for the opposition) fluctuates between 16,000 votes as the minimum (in 1917) and 1,054,000 as the maximum (in 1964). In the 1964 elections a candidate of the institutionalized opposition, Acción Nacional, received a far greater number of votes than opposition candidates in previous elections, which might be an indication of the growth both of the party and of its absolute and proportional strength. Yet to the present there has been no indication of the emergence of a classical party system. All the data point to the absence of a party system, as well as to the considerable amount of power with which the President is endowed.

2. In 1910 and 1911 elections were indirect.

Trade Unions, Strikes, and Strikers

In the evolution of Western democracy after the Enlightenment, an organization emerged which cannot be ignored in an analysis of democratic interplay after 1850. I am referring to the trade union. Indeed, the democratic struggle in countries such as England, Italy, and the United States cannot be explained without considering the basic role played by trade unions. In Mexico the 123rd article (one of the most advanced and pioneering) of the Constitution recognizes the right of workers to organize as well as the right to strike. Trade unionism, a national political force, exhibits many of the characteristics of a dependent variable, not only of the government party but of the executive power specifically.

In the first place, two-thirds of the unionized workers belong to the Confederation of Mexican Workers (CTM), which is closely linked to the government party and to the government itself through the working-class sector of the party. Other trade unions which are not members of that organization also have strong ties with the party and the government; their leaders are able to obtain concessions. In the legislature of 1952–55, for example, there were thirty-five workers' committees, nineteen of which belonged to the main organization and the rest to other organizations and trade unions of the government party (railroad workers, mining workers, CROC, CROM, CGT).[3]

In the constitutionalist period of the Mexican Revolution, between 1918 and 1962, at least 52 senators (33 between 1940 and 1962) and more than 250 representatives (150 since 1940) were from the working-class sector.[4] An analysis of their participation in the Chambers scarcely suggests the influence and attitude considered characteristic of representatives

3. Frank Brandenburg, *op. cit.*
4. Matías Humberto González Ortiz, a student at the Escuela Nacional de Ciencias Políticas y Sociales, assisted in gathering these data.

of an independent workers' movement. (These data, however, would require close examination to expand them from an example into a proper analysis.) One indicator of the dependence of Mexican trade unionism on the government, and particularly on the President, is the number of strikes and strikers. If we observe larger trends of the different presidential regimes, we note that when the incumbent President is known to have a policy favorable to the working class, the number of strikes and strikers is higher. It is as if the trade union leaders and the workers feel protected and even encouraged by the President's power. The opposite occurs when the incumbent President generally espouses a less radical policy or one implying a more open alliance with domestic or foreign entrepreneurial sectors. Thus, although during the regime of President Obregón, who numbered the "Red Battalions" and the workers' leaders among his most ardent supporters, there was an average of 197 strikes per year, during the regime of Calles and the Maximato, the average was 41; under Lázaro Cárdenas, 478. Subsequently, the average was 387 under Avila Camacho, 108 under Alemán; 248 under Ruiz Cortines; and 472 under López Mateos. The average number of strikers per year was 64,000 under Obregón, 4,000 under Calles and the Maximato, 61,000 under Cárdenas, 56,000 under Avila Camacho, 19,000 under Alemán, 25,000 under Ruiz Cortines, and 53,000 under López Mateos.

In most countries where there are powerful trade unions and workers' unions, we find a clear correlation between strike movements and the economic cycle. In Mexico, where unions are dependent on the government, there is very little correlation, and that which exists is found in the export sectors.

There are a few exceptions to the general rule that the broader trends of presidential policy determine the number of strikes and strikers. Large strike movements which obviously did not depend on the policy of the executive power emerged in 1934, at the climax of Calles's anti-revolutionary policy; 1943–44, after Manuel Avila Camacho's first two years in office, when the number of strikes decreased to one-fourth the number in the last years of the Cárdenas period; and 1958, after a period during which there were relatively few strikes. Indeed, whereas in 1933 there were 13 strikes with 1,084 strikers, in 1934 there were 202 strikes with 14,685 strikers; whereas in 1942 there were 98 strikes with 13,643 strikers, in 1943 there were 766 strikes with 81,557 strikers, and in 1944, 887 strikes with 165,744 strikers. Finally, whereas in 1957 there were 193 strikes with 7,137 strikers, in 1958 there were 740 strikes with 60,611 strikers.

In at least three cases real upheavals, which had different meanings and effects, took place. The strikes of 1933 revealed the workers' dissatisfaction with the Maximato's anti-working-class and conservative policy; the strikes of 1943-44 came about because the working-class movement wanted to prove its strength, which was being ignored by the new government; and the strikes of 1958 signified that the working-class movement was struggling to regain its independence. Thus the working-class movement, even though dependent on the executive power's policies, constitutes a potential force which manifests itself in cyclical explosions.

We find variations in the effects of these strikes. It is obvious that the strikes of 1933 were decisive in the presidential succession which brought Cárdenas to power, and equally decisive in the popular policy of President Cárdenas. The government itself recognized the need to endow the working-class movement with greater importance and to control it by means of a pro-working-class and revolutionary policy. The strikes of 1944 brought about a considerable repression which allowed the executive power to keep control of the working-class movement and to emphasize the moderate policy initiated a few years earlier. Finally, the strikes of 1958 allowed the working-class movement to achieve partial victories in regaining its internal democracy—as it did in the telegraph, telephone, and electrical unions, for example.

When studying the problems posed by democracy in Mexico,

one must carefully analyze the strikes of 1933, 1944, and 1958 to learn how the conflicts emerged and evolved, what the strategies of the conflicting sides were, and why in some cases the strikes were successful during times of pro-working-class policy whereas in other cases they were defeated. One should investigate why in certain cases trade unions retained their independence whereas in other cases they lost it. At any rate, even though the working-class movement shows strong dependence on the policy of the executive power and particularly on that of the President, there is no doubt that it represents a potential force—and in some cases an already operational one—in Mexican political life.

The President and Congress

Government power and dynamics do not adjust to the models of the classical theory of democracy—we have seen, for instance, the almost absolute preponderance of the government party over the other parties and over the trade unions and government unions—and the power of the President within Congress is at least equally different from the formulations of the model.

The Chamber of Senators is composed exclusively of representatives of the government's party. It is very difficult to assess its power as compared to that of the President. Only in the past did the Chamber of Representatives present a strong opposition. During Madero's presidency, for example, there was a powerful group of representatives from the opposition headed by the famous "quadrilateral" (formed by Querido Moheno, José María Lozano, Francisco M. de Olaguibel and Nemesio García Naranjo), representing the ideas and interests of *porfirismo*. Madero was assassinated, and after his death the opposition became a part of the new executive, headed by Victoriano Huerta, one of the intellectual authors of the assassination. At that point the large majority of the senators and representatives who had supported Madero built up a strong opposition to the usurper. Many of them were assassinated. Finally, Huerta dissolved both Chambers.

The different revolutionary factions had representatives at the Convention of Aguascalientes and at the Constituents' Congress. The debates were conducted with great freedom and displayed a diversity of interests. This liberal climate was maintained until the regime of Obregón, when the opposition and independence of large sectors of the legislature became apparent. This opposition, in keeping with the general climate of violence, almost overthrew Obregón, but he instituted strong repressive measures, which gave him almost absolute control over the legislature. Since then, the measures taken by the executive to control the legislature have become one of the basic institutional characteristics of Mexican government. Not until 1940 did some members of the opposition, about 5 per cent of the total, re-enter the Chamber of Representatives. They were carefully selected from among the less brilliant or the less popular. It is important to note that the taboo which for eighteen years had prevented the mildest opposition within the legislature was then broken.

In comparing legislative with executive power, one does better to consider the actions of the Chamber of Representatives, where there is at least some opposition to the Executive. The Chamber is renewed every three years, and the President governs during the first three years of his six-year term with the legislature elected during his predecessor's last year in office. Thus, we should examine the differences between the behavior of the Chamber inherited by the President and that of the Chamber elected during the term of the ruling President.

If we examine the votes of the Chamber of Representatives on bills proposed by the Executive during the period 1935–59, both at the end of the first year of the presidential period (inherited Chamber) and during the first period of sessions of the renewed Chamber (third year of the presidential term), the following facts emerge. In 1935, 1937, and 1941—that is, during the regimes of Cárdenas and Avila

Camacho—100 per cent of the bills proposed by the executive power were unanimously approved. In 1943, 92 per cent of the bills were unanimously approved, 74 per cent in 1947, 77 per cent in 1949, 59 per cent in 1953, 62 per cent in 1955, 95 per cent in 1959, and 82 per cent in 1961. For bills approved by a majority, the opposing votes represented only 4 per cent of the total (1943), 3 per cent (1947), 3 per cent (1949), 3 per cent (1953), 5 per cent (1955), 4 per cent (1959), and 3 per cent (1961) (see Table 2).

On the basis of historical and political factors and the analyzed data, the following observations on the nature and characteristics of the power of the legislature in Mexico might be made.

1. During the first stages of revolutionary regimes the opposition tended to become linked to those groups and classes overthrown by the Revolution, or to factions of armed revolutionaries. Opposition within the legislative power and a rebellion or a *coup d'état* were associated phenomena.

2. When opposition became strong enough to be a threat to the Executive, there was an attempt to eliminate it from the Chambers completely. A series of measures ensued that led to the control of Congress by the Executive.

3. Complete executive control over the legislative power was broken only in 1940. This break with "tradition" was important because of its background and context. On the other hand, its quantitative and qualitative significance was very small in terms of political forces and their legal and institutional representation and performance in Congress.

4. The differences between the inherited Chamber and the new Chamber are minimal and insignificant. The President controls the Representatives elected in the course of the previous six-year presidential period and those elected in the course of his own term.

5. In the period 1934–64, we note that most of the bills proposed by the Executive were unanimously approved, but that fewer bills were unanimously approved during the admin-

istration of Ruiz Cortines than at any other time. This signifies that in Mexico a government with a popular base and policy does not necessarily encounter greater opposition in the
legislative power, and vice versa.

6. Those bills not receiving unanimous support never
face an opposition exceeding 5 per cent. If we were to examine which bills were unanimously approved and which
received the support of the majority, we would discover
that—as under multi-party regimes—essential bills were
unanimously approved.

In other words, the system of balance of powers does not
work. There is a strong disequilibrium, and it favors the Executive. Thus one cannot help but wonder what the function of
the legislative power is. It seems that the legislative power has
a symbolic function. It sanctions the actions of the Executive.
It gives them a traditional and metaphysical legitimation.
Thus they acquire the status of laws, owing to a very old yet
secular symbolic mechanism. The rulers of old governed in
the name of the law, which in turn was sanctioned by divine
powers. This had a symbolic-religious functional significance.
In Mexico today, the Chamber of Representatives fulfils a
function similar to that of the divine powers. Its theoretical
significance to the community is as a visible "sanction of
legality."

Ever since the eighteenth century, rational thought has seen
the base of legislative action not as God, but as the people and
their representatives. From an anthropological point of view,
Mexican laws and models of government are belief systems.
This becomes particularly evident from an analysis of the behavior of the Chamber of Representatives, though it can be
observed in other institutions. We shall see that the recent reform of Article 54 of the Constitution has modified both the
structure and the functions of the Chamber of Representatives
since the time of Obregón.

The President and the Supreme Court

It is quite clear that the Supreme Court of Justice is at least as different from Montesquieu's model as is Congress. It has some unexpected and interesting aspects which clarify the structure and dynamics of Mexico's political life. The Court deviates from the Enlightenment model in more than one particular; its actual performance does not correspond to the model. We analyzed the final decisions of the Supreme Court of Justice, in which the President of the Republic appears as responsible for the suit. The immediate objective was to see how many claims have been made against the President, who made them, what issue they concerned, and what the Court's decision was. The ultimate goal was to measure the power of the Court, if any.

We found the following facts [5] to be true from a study of the period from 1917 to 1960.[6]

1. From 1917 to 1960 there was a total of 3,700 rulings in which the President of the Republic was expressly mentioned as being sued. The annual average of rulings in presidential regimes varied: 20 with Carranza, 35 during the provisional six-month rule of de la Huerta, 79 with Obregón, 62 with Calles, 53 with the Maximato, 78 with Cárdenas, 126 with Avila Camacho, 110 with Alemán, 95 with Ruiz Cortines, and 131 in each of the first two years of the term of López Mateos. The averages might be an indication of the speed of the Court's work or the incidence of claims against the Chief Executive, phenomena that were not measured. At the least, however, they tell us the number of Mexicans who appealed to the Court against the President.

5. The record begins on October 19, 1917, and, for our purposes, ends on November 17, 1960. The tabulations are provisional and are only a general indication of the order of magnitude of the phenomena involved.
6. The tabulations are based on a study of the records made by Esperanza Burguete, Juana Servín, José Miller Cabrera, and Filiberto Navarrete.

2. Of all the rulings in the period 1917–60, 34 per cent are Court protections or suspensions granted the claimant. This means that of 3,700 rulings, in a little more than 1,200 the claimant's demands were satisfied. Of the remaining 66 per cent of the rulings, 34 per cent were denied protection or suspension of decision, 24 per cent were discontinued or received no ruling due to the claimant's waiving of his right or other causes, 9 per cent comprised other types of rulings.

3. In order to know who the claimants were and the nature of the contested rulings, we made different kinds of tabulations. The first tabulation included the cases from 1917 to 1940 by claimant, contested action, and ruling. Of a total of 1,470 claimants, 140 were oil companies, 186 were banks and other commercial companies, 644 were landowners, 30 were civil authorities and other public employees and functionaries, 27 were peasants, and 13 were workers. The remaining 430 are more difficult to categorize by social status or claims. From the above data it can be inferred that at least 66 per cent of the claimants are foreign and Mexican owners (of companies, banks, land, etc.), and it is very probable that a more detailed analysis would show an even higher percentage.

Of these Court cases in the period 1917–40, 44 per cent contested action taken by the Executive limiting the rights of the big owners—redistribution of latifundia (460), declarations relating to national waters (136), expropriations (42) —and 23 per cent contested the passing of laws, regulations, decrees, and agreements of the revolutionary governments, or tax levies. Claims relating to actions affecting property and utilities make up 67 per cent of the total. This percentage is the same as that of the claimants belonging to the owners category. Other motives for complaints, such as destitution from posts (23) and apprehensions and extraditions (21), have a lower rate of incidence.

The orientation of the Court in this period is reflected in its granting an average of 26 per cent rulings of protection and suspension of decisions and its denying 46 per cent. The remaining cases either were discontinued or they included diverse types of rulings that are less characteristic of acceptance or refusal.

4. Our second tabulation includes the cases in job matters for the period 1917–60. Court actions contested by employers amount to 150, of which the Court granted only 25, including both protections and suspensions. There were 24 cases of Court actions contested by workers for the whole period, and the Court granted only 4 claims. Most were discontinued, and 2 were not heard.

5. Our third tabulation sums up cases in which the claimants were farmers and covers the period 1940–60. There were 210 cases of actions contested by farmers working on public lands,* communities, villages, small landowners, landless peasants, and other farmers. Twenty-seven per cent were granted, and 52 per cent were discontinued. The most frequent reasons for complaint were orders involving restitution of property to the original owners, expropriation of public lands, deprivation or denial of public land or agrarian rights generally, rulings affecting small properties, and cancellation of plot titles.

These data indicate that the Supreme Court of Justice operates with a certain degree of independence with respect to the executive power, sometimes exercising a controlling action over the President or his assistants. The Court subjects to judgment certain acts coming from the Executive. Its main political function is to provide hope for those groups and individuals who are able to utilize this recourse to protect their interests or rights. Among those claimants who go to the Court, there is a preponderance of owners and companies, old latifundists, and the new bourgeoisie. Businesses and members of the middle class are mainly occupied with complaints concerning fiscal legislation or tax enforcements. Compared to

---

* *Ejido:* form of land ownership which is collective and inalienable. The tilling is done either individually or collectively. The term *public land* will be used throughout (translator's note).

them, workers and peasants who appeal to the Court constitute a minority.

There is no doubt that the Supreme Court of Justice is endowed with power; yet it does generally follow the policy of the Executive, and in fact it serves to make the Executive more stable.

Federation and States

The idea of a federation composed of free and sovereign states, like that envisioned by the Founding Fathers of the United States and incorporated into probably all liberal constitutions up to the present, is not embodied in Mexico, where there is a dependence of states on the federal government and of governors on the President. This dependence is political, military, and economic.

The federal government can easily depose a governor by means of diverse juridical-political recourses ranging from voluntary resignation (which is practiced through request of leave of absence) to the "withdrawal of powers." The latter, the most radical recourse, enables the federal legislature to eliminate not only the governor but also representatives and other local authorities.[7]

Governors are subjected to a system of military control by which the zone commander, designated by the federal government, fulfils political functions fundamental to the maintenance of the central power. Other political functionaries are of lesser importance, and they support the control exercised by the central government.

The power of the federal government over the states is clearly manifest in the financial sphere. The federal treasury is very powerful, both economically and politically, while the

7. The President who exercised these powers the most was General Lázaro Cárdenas, who during his term (1934–40) brought about the forced leave of absence of two governors and the resignation of another ten.

treasuries of the states are very weak. The Federation and the Federal District alone received 87 per cent of the total public funds dispersed in 1962, while the states received only 10 per cent (see Table 3).

During the period 1929–62, the states (excluding the Federal District) received as an average the following percentages of the public treasury disbursed: 16 per cent under the Maximato (1929–34); 14.5 per cent under Cárdenas (1934–40); 12 per cent under Avila Camacho (1940–46); 10 per cent under Alemán (1946–52); 10 per cent under Ruiz Cortines (1952–58); and 9.5 per cent in the first four years of the López Mateos regime.

Thus, in the last three presidential periods, the percentage of the income received by the states, always small, is even smaller than in earlier periods. From an economic point of view, the centralization of the public treasury is indicative of a low availability of funds nationally. But this concentration of resources by the Federation subsumes a corresponding concentration of public services and powers, whereas the poverty of the state resources exhibits a corresponding limitation of services and a structural political weakness.

This concentration of funds became accentuated because a high percentage of the State income—between 8 and 34 per cent during the period 1950–63—is largely income from federal participation and subsidies and loans, which depend on the federal government and the official banks (see Table 4).

Indeed, the contribution of the Federation to the states amounted to 28 per cent of their total income in 1950; 29 per cent in 1951; 34 per cent in 1952; 22 per cent in 1953; 24 per cent in 1954; 25 per cent in 1955; 24 per cent in 1956; 12 per cent in 1957; 16 per cent in 1958; 10 per cent in 1959; 8 per cent in 1960; 9 per cent in 1961 and 1962; and 10 per cent in 1963. There is a marked trend toward a decrease of the percentage contributed by the Federation, the only deviation occurring in the period from 1961 to 1963, when there was a slight increase. Of course this percentage

varies from state to state, ranging (without considering the
Federal District and the national territories), for example, between a maximum of 46 per cent and a minimum of 2 per
cent (1950); 72 per cent and 2 per cent (1951); 66 per cent
and 3 per cent (1952); 58 per cent and 4 per cent (1953); 60
per cent and 6 per cent (1954); 73 per cent and 6 per cent
(1955). In 1963 the maximum was 60 per cent and the minimum 8 per cent.[8]

The assignment of federal contributions to each state in
particular is made on the basis of economic status—that is,
in general the more advanced and wealthy states receive larger
amounts in both relative and absolute terms, although politics
is also a factor.

The total amount of the federal contribution varies by as
much as 100 per cent from one year to another. These variations seriously hinder the sustained development of the states:
the normal performance of their public functions; their
strength, weakness, or lack of popularity, which depend on
federal power and on the central government; and the governor's influence, or lack of it, on the secretary of the treasury
or the President (see Table 5).

One might suspect that a governor's political affiliations influence the federal contribution to his state. Hypothesizing
that there is a correlation between affiliation and contribution
and that affiliation can be partly inferred from whether a governor had been elected or designated in the previous regime or
in that of the incumbent President, I made a study of the contributions during the term of President Ruiz Cortines. I found
that I could not confirm the hypothesis because sometimes the
increase in contributions was considerable during the year of
the gubernatorial campaign, and at other times, it was during
the first year of rule of the new governor. Also, there were
campaign years in which federal contributions decreased and
first years of governorship during which the same thing oc-

8. The data were gathered with the assistance of Carlos Castaño, a student
at the Escuela Nacional de Ciencias Políticas y Sociales.

curred. What the study did show was that the political schedule of the succession of power in the states accounts for an increase in the power of the presidents of the republic as the date of presidential succession approaches. In addition, there is some overlapping of the former President's influence into the first years of the regime which succeeds him.

Despite the power which the President no doubt has over the governors, the fact that the governors were designated during his term and largely owe him their appointment, or the fact that they may have been designated during the former President's term and therefore are aware of his initiation of their political careers, is important in the political process, particularly with respect to presidential succession. In this sense the political order reveals the wisdom of government structure. In the first year of the term of President Ruiz Cortines, 22 governors had been designated during the Alemán regime and 7 were designated during his own regime. These figures varied from year to year in the following manner: 19 governors designated by Alemán and 10 by Ruiz Cortines in the second and third years; 13 by Alemán and 16 by Ruiz Cortines in the fourth year; 5 by Alemán and 24 by Ruiz Cortines in the fifth year; and 1 by Alemán and 28 by Ruiz Cortines in the last year.

President López Mateos had a ratio of inherited to appointed governors identical to that of Ruiz Cortines during the first four years of his government; it was also quite similar during the final two years: 4 governors designated during the previous regime and 24 during his own in the fifth year. All the governors in his last year had been designated by him.

During the presidential term of Ruiz Cortines the normal order became altered in his favor through the designation of interim or substitute governors, giving him three governors more in the first year and four more in the second and third years. López Mateos had two governors more in the first year of government, and to these one more was added the fifth year. But even the normal course of events which ensures the continuity of government accounts for the fact that at the decisive moment of presidential succession, the President is able to add to the military, political, and financial power which enables him to control the governors, the power of a schedule which allows for 95 per cent of the state governments to have been designated during his presidential term.

The dependence of the states on the central government is a political, military, and financial fact. The application of the Constitution for the ouster of governors, the political functions of the chiefs of zones, the agents of government, the deputies and senators who make their political careers in the capital city, the small finances of the states, the considerable dependence of the states' income on the federal income, the wide range of variation of federal aid, and a political timetable which gradually increases the President's power as the presidential term evolves—all of this explains why the political instruments conceived to achieve a system of counterweights and balances does not function in present-day Mexico.

Free Municipalities and Actual Local Government

The system of government which Tocqueville so highly admired in the United States and which he considered to be the pillar of democracy was incorporated into Latin constitutions in an idealized form. Free municipalities formally exist, but the political situation is such that the municipality depends on the state government and is so financially indigent that its public function is reduced to a minimum.

Thirteen of the state constitutions [9] empower the governors to depose the municipal governments. It is rarely necessary for a governor to go to such an extreme, as the state government and the party are usually sufficient to control the municipalities.[10] Frequently, municipal liberties are violated by state

9. Those of Coahuila, Colima, Durango, Guanajuato, Guerrero, Nuevo León, Querétaro, Sinaloa, Sonora, Tabasco, Tamaulipas, Tlaxcala, and Yucatán.
10. William P. Tucker, *The Mexican Government Today* (Minneapolis: University of Minnesota, 1957), p. 395.

authorities even though the Supreme Court of Justice has occasionally supported the municipal governments.[11] The feebleness of the municipal governments is, moreover, evident in the recommendations of the Fourth National Congress of Municipal Governors held in 1959: "That the municipalities themselves should designate their own functionaries"; "that the functions of the agents of the public ministry should be delineated in order that they might not intervene in the functions of municipal president and other authorities," etc. Often the municipality lacks the power to perform even the smallest acts of government.

Indigence in both relative and absolute terms is the essential characteristic of most municipalities and the surest indicator of their economic and political weakness. The percentage of total public funds that they receive has always been low, and it has decreased from regime to regime. Under the Maximato they received 8 per cent of the total treasury contributions. Under the government of Cárdenas they received 6 per cent. Under that of Avila Camacho, 4 per cent; and in the three administrations following Camacho's and during the four first years of López Mateos's regime, only 3 per cent (see Table 3).

The problem is exacerbated because the average yearly income of the municipalities is already low (371,000 pesos in 1963), but in ten states of the Republic it is even lower than 300,000 pesos, with extreme cases such as that of Oaxaca with an average of 22,000 pesos and Tlaxcala with 77,000. In the interior of many states there are municipalities which have yearly net incomes lower than 500 pesos.

In effect, the income of municipalities is reduced to meager authorized appropriations—which they do not always receive—and to the small proceeds from fines and licenses. Excises, which in an unconstitutional way prevent free transportation of goods from one location to another, are an extreme recourse having an adverse effect on the national mar-

11. Lloyd Mecham, "Mexican Federalism in Mexico—Fact or Fiction?" *Annals*, March 1940, pp. 23–38, as quoted by William P. Tucker, *op. cit.*

ket. Municipalities do acquire some funds in this manner, but at the same time they are acquiescing to illegality and thus they accentuate their political weakness.

The financial recommendations of the National Congress of Municipal Governments confirm the fact that the municipal treasury is weak, while at the same time they constitute an invitation to make the weakness even more structured politically: "It is recommended that the federal or state governments should pay the functionaries in the name of the municipalities." In the federal commission of arbitration, moreover, the federal government, the states, and even the populace are represented, but the municipalities have no representation. Their economic-political dependence tends to increase with the invasion of fiscal resources by the states, and because of the permanent desire of municipal authorities that debtors to the municipalities should be condoned by the federal government, such as was the case in 1953, when the Executive was empowered "to grant the cancellation of municipal debts." [12]

The poverty of municipalities has led the Federation to take over even their primary services. Municipalities have become politically dependent on the state and federal governments, thus entirely destroying the classical model of local government.

Municipal freedom is virtually nonexistent. Neither the local power structure nor the political activity of the neighborhood lead to anything resembling a free municipality. The political entity called a free municipality is in effect controlled by state power and the Federation.

12. *Diario Oficial,* December 26, 1953.

2

The Factors of Power

FORMAL POWER AND ACTUAL POWER

The analysis of all the institutions established in Mexico on the model of European and American political theory reveals the existence of a dominant party, both dependent on and assisting the federal government. Even the working-class movement is in a similar state of dependence. Congress is controlled by the President; the states are controlled by the Federation; the municipalities are controlled by the states and the Federation. In sum, the model of the three powers, the system of counterweights and balances, or the local government of elector-citizens conceived by the philosophers and legislators of the eighteenth and early nineteenth centuries does not obtain.

What does obtain is a concentration of power—in ascending order—in the government, the central government, the executive branch, and the presidency. With the exception of the limitations imposed by the Supreme Court in particular cases and in defense of particular interests and civic rights, an analysis of the power structure in Mexico would show the President as exercising unlimited power.

A comparison of the model with the reality not only reflects an image of a presidentialist regime, but overemphasizes the notion of unlimited presidential power, however. Only an analysis of the actual factors of power and of the international structure will lead to a delineation of presidential power in proper perspective.

The actual factors of power in Mexico, as in many Latin American countries, have been (and sometimes still are) regional and local *caudillos* and *caciques,* the Army, the clergy, and the latifundists and national and foreign entrepreneurs. In every case, these institutions have influenced (or now directly influence) governmental decisions. Their existence as political institutions are foreign to the European and American theory of democracy, and the complete liberal ideology is aimed against them.

The Regional and Local Caudillos *and* Caciques

A political geography of Mexico during the twenties would have listed every state in the Republic as governed by regional *caudillos* and *caciques.* The *caudillos,* with armies relatively obedient and loyal to the revolutionary chief, and the *caciques* of villages and regions—outgrowths of the pre-Hispanic and colonial period, but continuing through *porfirismo* or replaced in the same functions by the new men of the Revolution—dominated the national picture. Even in the early thirties, the power of *caciquismo* was still enormous: practitioners were Rodríguez Triana in Coahuila; Rodrigo M. Quevedo in Chihuahua; Carlos Real in Durango; Melchor Ortega in Guanajuato; Saturnino Osornio in Querétaro; Rodolfo Elías Calles in Sonora; Tomás Garrido in Tabasco; Galván, Aguilar, and Tejeda in Veracruz; Matías Romero in Zacatecas.

During the last thirty years, regional *caudillismo* and *caciquismo* have gradually disappeared or at least lost their influence in both national and state politics. A few remaining figures—such as Gonzalo N. Santos, in San Luis—have recently seen their absolute power become extinguished by strong pressures both within and outside of the government party, which grew into popular riots. In 1959, one year after the events in San Luis, others were subjected to similar political pressures—for instance, Leobardo Reynoso, of Zacatecas. Reynoso, now a Mexican minister in Guatemala, is gradually losing his old power. By 1966 he was probably one of the last survivors of the old state *caciquismo*.

There are, it is true, four states in which four ex-presidents of Mexico or their families have a considerable amount of power: Michoacán, Puebla, Veracruz, and Baja California. In two states—Nayarit and Hidalgo—there exist the types of personal relationships characteristic of *caciquismo*. Yet these are only partial, broken-down remnants, and they are far from having the total dominion of the *caciques* of the past, on which everything depended: wealth, position, honor of families, and the political future. These remnants of the great *caciques*—who were more powerful than the governors and than even the acting presidents, lords and masters of a whole territory and of the destiny of its inhabitants—are a thing of the past. Even the last strongholds of ex-presidents, their places of birth, where they retain personal influence characteristic of the old *caudillo,* are presently being destroyed. In the electoral struggle and in state governments, there is an increasing number of individuals who are neither relatives, close friends, nor godparents of ex-presidents.

The influence of the *cacique* does persist to some extent in local governments and the small communities of the more backward areas of the country. But his influence is not felt in decisions of state or national politics. It is evident in the concessions of the state and federal governments. Above all, his influence is felt in the communities themselves, but even there the process of dissolution of *caciquismo* is visible, and the old "subjects," frequently rebel.

The process of controlling *caudillismo* and *caciquismo,* begun during the presidency of Obregón and emphasized during that of Calles, depended partly on the professionalization of the Army, which sought to replace personalized norms of obedience with national norms of obedience. This control demanded a degree of energy and violence which often led to bloodshed.

The National Revolutionary Party fulfilled a similar function. It integrated and controlled the regional and personal "parties" of the *caudillos* of the Revolution. Indeed, when the *caudillo* was seeking an electoral position, the National Revolutionary Party saw that he conformed to the rituals and symbols of the law and created "parties." As late as 1929, 51 political parties were registered,[1] and in the 1929 elections 61 parties participated.[2] By 1933 only 4 parties were registered, while 49 applications were being processed.[3]

During all these years, the history of the government party has been one of the control of *caudillos* and *caciques*. This is one of its main functions. All the processes of concentration of presidential power originate in the tasks of the control of *caciques,* of their parties, their cronies, and their municipal presidents. This phenomenon is only indirectly related to the disappearance of the *caciques.*

Indeed, if the central government controls *caudillismo,* at the same time it enters into a sort of "political contract" with the *caudillos.* Although it removes them from the command of forces, it grants them other powers or honors or loans. From among the *caudillos* there thus emerge politicians working side by side with the President, or entrepreneurs, or a new type of *cacique*-revolutionist, with whom the same kinds of personal relationships and controls as those applied by Porfirio Díaz to his *caciques* are maintained over a long time: this can be traced back to the colonial and pre-Hispanic epoch. The revolutionary, anti-clerical, and agrarian *cacique* in turn maintains forms of government and personal chains of command identical to those of his predecessors. But in the process

1. *Memoria de la Secretaría de Gobernación* (1928–29).
2. *Memoria de la Secretaría de Gobernación* (1929–30).
3. *Memoria de la Secretaría de Gobernación* (1933).

of bringing about agrarian reform and co-operating in the development of the country, he himself is transformed. He is no longer the agrarian *cacique,* but the owner of ranches and properties and even of factories and stores. He is still a *cacique,* and he calls himself a revolutionist. The difference is that he now belongs to the rural upper bourgeoisie.

The transformation of the *cacique* runs parallel to the weakening of *caciquismo.* Indeed, the strongholds of the *caudillos* and *caciques* have been taken over by presidential power. But their real destruction depends above all on the development of the country: the expansion of roads, the market economy, the industry and capital to do away with the total and closed dominion which the *cacique* exercises in his territory. As a result of increasing mobility, people can buy elsewhere and sell their working power to other employers. The roads, stores, factories, the growing urban and rural bourgeoisie, all these destroy the power of the *cacique.* Thus, it is not unusual in the process of national development to see *caciques* who are opposed to building roads and establishing factories and who exercise influence and even violence toward this aim. But whether the *cacique* opposes development or promotes it, development ends up destroying his personal power.

The *caciques* and political chiefs are presently limited to local government and national political movements, which are linked in turn to more influential forces such as finance, banking, commerce, and industry. This intertwining in the over-all picture of the national polity represents a stage of transition from the old to the new pressure groups and from systems of personal associations to forms characteristic of interest groups in contemporary society. Personal relationships characteristic of the *cacique*-dominated polity do exist to some extent in present-day Mexico, however.

Caciquismo, having disappeared as a national system of government, leaves behind a culture of personal relationships, kinship, and godparents, which survives within a different structure and becomes intertwined as a style or form of political knowledge with the new mores and associations of modern Mexico.

The Army

Another traditional base of power is the Army. "Out of the 137 years of our existence as an independent nation," wrote José E. Iturriaga in 1958,

> during 93 years as a whole, the military exercised power, while civilians only exercised it for 44 years. That is, 70 per cent as compared to 30 per cent. And with respect to the percentage represented by both military and civilians within the total of 55 individual rulers that we have had, the 36 who wore epaulets on their uniform represent 67 per cent, while the remaining 33 per cent is made up of our 19 civilian rulers. [4]

Since the end of the Mexican Revolution, the presence and influence of the military in the national polity has been decreasing. This is shown by a series of facts:

". . . While in the period between 1821 and 1917 out of 44 individual rulers 30 were military and 14 were civilian," [5] in the period between 1917 and 1966 six were military and seven civilian. Each of the four men who were President of Mexico in the past twenty years was a civilian.

For thirty years the Army has numbered 50,000 men, and the ratio of the Army to the labor force has noticeably decreased.[6]

Perhaps the best example of the decrease in military power within the Mexican polity is the decrease in the percentage of the federal government's expenses allocated to the Army: whereas in 1925 the Army absorbed 44 per cent of the total

4. José E. Iturriaga, "Los presidentes y las elecciones en México," *Ciencias Políticas y Sociales,* January-June 1958, pp. 1–36.
5. *Ibid.*
6. Edwin Lieuwen, *Armas y Política en América Latina* (Buenos Aires: Sur, 1960), pp. 151–52.

expenditures of the Federation, in 1963 it absorbed only 6 per cent (see Table 6). From one presidential period to the next the percentage of expenditures allocated to the Army decreases: 28 per cent in the government of Calles (1925–28); 26 per cent in the Maximato (1929–34); 18 per cent in the government of Cárdenas (1934–40); 16 per cent with Avila Camacho (1940–46); 10 per cent with Alemán (1946–52); 8 per cent with Ruiz Cortines (1952–58); and 6 per cent as an average during the first five years of the López Mateos administration. Today the Mexican Army absorbs a smaller percentage of the national product than that assigned to the armed forces of any other Latin American country, with the exception of Costa Rica.[7]

It is an incontestable fact that Mexico has controlled and overcome the stage of militarism. Militarism no longer represents a permanent and organized threat of a political force imposing its own conditions by coercion and threatening to break the peace if it does not receive special grants and privileges as a chosen and powerful group within the nation.

The control of the Army and of its political participation was promoted by military men: it was General Calles, General Cárdenas, and General Avila Camacho who instituted measures of control. The professionalization of the *caudillos* and military chiefs began with Calles. Compulsory membership in the party as one of its sectors increased the control and political discipline. Disappearance of the military sector within the party and its fusion with the so-called "popular sector" was one more step toward this control, which tends to prevent distinctions between civilians and military within the polity. The organization of the peasants, who had received not only land but arms during the Cárdenas regime, was certainly another of the important steps toward the control of militarism.

If we consider the political measures together with the fiscal measures, we will understand the nature of the process of de-

7. Edwin Lieuwen, *op. cit.*

militarization of the Mexican polity. Yet we should add one more fact, little known, which accounts for the concurrence of military and entrepreneurial interests: the old, parasitical military underwent a process of bourgeoisification. In part, this was a result of certain political measures by which the financial power of the military as a whole was reduced while contracts were signed and the military chief was provided with necessities to become an entrepreneur. As a political body, the military therefore lost strength, and a number of military chiefs lost their belligerence and devoted themselves to their personal business, a development widely tolerated and even encouraged.

To all the political, financial, and commercial measures was added the economic and social development of the nation. The militarism of the Latin American countries is part of a system in which the latifundia are an essential element. When the latifundia disappear as a predominant economic and political form, militarism comes to occupy a very different position in the network of social relationships. Measures of direct control, agrarian reform and economic development, are at the root of the disappearance of the military as the principal component of the Mexican polity. The fact that this disappearance might not be definitive and that the old militarism might re-emerge in some form is another question. For the present, we can assume, as in the case of the *caciques,* a tendency toward secularization within the military sector as it withdraws from the political forum.

The Clergy

The Church—the largest Mexican landowner and money-lender of the nineteenth century—lost its immense power during the Reformation, which put an end to ecclesiastic latifundism. It recovered part of its power during *porfirismo,* saw itself threatened by the Mexican Revolution, and engaged in large-scale conflicts with the State. These conflicts reached unusual violence with the rebellion of the *cristeros* and reached their climax precisely when *callismo* was less revolutionary, substituting popular and nationalist policies for anticlerical demagogy.

With Portes Gil and especially with General Lázaro Cárdenas, a *modus vivendi* between the State and the clergy was achieved. Persecutions stopped, both changed their policies, and there were even moments of outright alliance and support by the clergy for revolutionary policies. This was the case, for instance, during the oil expropriation, when the Archbishop of Mexico exhorted the people to support the government.

Since the time of Avila Camacho—he was the first revolutionary President to declare himself a Catholic—the Church has regained its influence upon education and in the government itself. Large groups of Catholics joined organized parties and movements with conservative and even fascist ideologies. In their speeches and proclamations they deliberately manipulated religious symbols and beliefs. Subsequently, the political activities of the clergy and confessional groups —pilgrimages, public appearances, and public acts— became increasingly frequent and positive in nature.

In October 1951, the Archbishop of Mexico asked the Catholic organizations of the nation to participate in a national moralizing campaign. After that, an executive committee—headed by the Archbishop, a Jesuit priest, and the leaders of four groups: Catholic Action, Marian Congregations, the Legion of Decency, and the Knights of Columbus —carried out a vigorous campaign, climaxed in January 1953, by the largest national assembly of Catholic-leaders since the beginning of the Revolution. This assembly released information which until then had not been publicly known. The assembly represented 44 Catholic organizations with a total of 4,530,000 members. Of these groups, 24 were secular orders, and 20 were religious orders. The more powerful secular groups were : (1) Mexican Catholic Action, composed of four main units—Union of Mexican Catholics, a group of men either married or over 35 years of age, with 44,000 members; Feminine Union of Mexican Catholics, composed of teachers, urban workers, and peasants, with 198,052 members; Catholic Action of Mexican Youth, with 18,000 members; and Mexican Catholic Feminine Youth, a group of women between 15 and 35 years of age, with a total of 88,221 members; (2) National Union of Heads of Family, with 500,000 members; (3) Knights of Columbus, with 3,500 members; (4) Federation of Private Schools, composed of 112 schools in the Federal District; (5) Mexican Legion of Decency, with 25 members in each of the 32 federal entities of the Union, and additional members in the subcommittees; and (6) the National Association of the Good Press, which since 1952 has published a prodigious amount of Catholic literature (magazines, 36,971,594 copies; information bulletins, 208,030,509; books and pamphlets, 5,990,539; and other publications, 13,248,093). It regularly publishes 13 magazines, 8 information bulletins, and 2 books per month.[8]

The increasing influence of the clergy is also apparent in the number of newspapers registered since 1952: 65 in 1952; 179 in 1953; 197 in 1954; 242 in 1955; 277 in 1956; 312 in 1957; and 321 in 1958.[9] To these we should add an extraordinary number of the so-called "prayers," which contain reports and comments of a political journalistic variety and which are distributed in all the churches and parishes of the country. It should also be noted that the pulpit is being increasingly used for political ends.

The power and activities of the clergy—imperceptible at first—have also accounted for the fact that the model of the Constitution—liberal and anti-clerical—which went from

8. Frank Brandenburg, *The Making of Modern Mexico* (Englewood Cliffs, New Jersey: Prentice-Hall, 1964).
9. Dirección General de Estadística. *Anuarios.* The only data published since 1959 have been those corresponding to newspapers registered at the National Administration of Post Offices, so that the figures decrease considerably: 206 in 1960; 186 in 1961; and 181 in 1962.

the text of 1857 to that of 1917, was not affected: religious education, confessional newspapers, public manifestations, the support provided by the high ecclesiastic hierarchy to the confessional parties or groups, the organization of political religious groups such as the Christian Family Movement —all of these prove not only that there is a difference between the formal and actual structure of Mexican political life, but also that the power of the Church is increasing.

Of all the traditional powers, the Church alone has survived the large social transformation of contemporary Mexico, and it has even regained and partially increased its strength. In order to understand the political role performed by the Church within the present social context, we must consider various phenomena which deserve serious study and which are indispensable for a true sociology of religion in Mexico.

The profanation of customs is a fact in contemporary Mexico: in vast regions of the country and especially in the cities, in the private life of the proletariat, and in the urban middle and upper classes, religious holidays and ceremonies, daily practices of morals, and the religious interpretation of problems become faded or lost, giving way to profane celebrations, ceremonies, and practices, to moral concepts and interpretations removed from religious conceptions. Today the calendar of pilgrimages of the dioceses and archdioceses still extends from January to December. An average of 15,648 Mexican Catholics visit the Basilica of Guadeloupe a day.[10] Often on Sundays, the faithful worship at the doors of the churches because there is not enough room inside. Yet the pilgrimages are not necessarily a contradiction of the profanation of customs by those same believers, with the separation of the religious and the profane—which characterizes modern man and detracts from religion as an integrated vision of the world— with the mixture of modern and traditional profanity which

10. Report by Alfonso Marcué González, Curator of the Museo del Tesoro Artístico de la Basílica, 1962.

affects large peasant regions. Perhaps all of this explains why in wide sectors of the population the believer performs in politics as a "citizen" and not as a believer. Father Pedro Rivera R., a serious researcher of Mexico's religious problems,[11] states,

> Approximately 25 per cent of the Mexican population practices no religion; 30 per cent is ignorant of the basic elements of Christianism and of supernatural life and place their whole religion in the more or less orthodox cult of an image or saint, almost always motivated by the egocentric spirit of receiving the saint's protection. Among the young and adult, 15 per cent of Mexico's population which calls itself Catholic has not made its first communion. Making a conservative estimate, only 20 per cent regularly attend Sunday mass. And there are many towns and cities in which attendance to Sunday mass is 5 or 6 per cent.
>
> If from the general practice of religion we go on to certain concrete aspects, the picture is no less depressing. There are various parishes in the city of Mexico in which more than 500 common-law marriages are to be found. In many towns the so-called Catholic cult is reduced to a popular celebration on the day of the patron saint and to certain acts of manifest superstition.
>
> Of the nation's population of approximately 34 million, close to 10 million are of school age. Making a very favorable estimate, only a half million of these, that is, scarcely 5 per cent of all Mexican youth, are under the educational influence of the Church.[12]

For another thing, José E. Iturriaga notes,

> the irreligious stratum has widened during the first four decades of the present century—particularly during the revolutionary period—more than 4,000 per cent, an increase which bears no proportion to that of the population, since the

11. Pedro Rivera R., S.J., *Instituciones Protestantes en México* (Mexico: Editorial Jus, 1962), p. 122.
12. This extremely conservative estimate might refer to the *direct* influence of the Church.

latter only increased 44 per cent during the same period. . . . Indeed, while in 1900 there were 18,640 persons who practiced no religion, in 1910 there were 25,011. In 1921 this group sharply increased, with the corresponding census registering 108,049 persons in this classification. In 1930 the figure increased to 175,180. And finally, in 1940, the number of persons having no religion at all was 433,671.[13]

The process of profanation of customs has not been sufficiently studied, and the population with no religion at all was no longer counted by the time of the 1950 census, in which it was assumed that all Mexicans had a religion, be it Catholic, Protestant, or other. This assumption is unusual, and it reveals censal incongruity (see Table 7). The 1960 census registered a population of 192,963 individuals with no religion, which indicates that from 1940 to 1960 this population decreased by 57 per cent. Since the population not indicating whether or not it had any religion increased by fifty times during this same period, one might assume that there were individuals who had no religious beliefs and did not wish to state this fact out of either indifference or fear.

If we add the number of those who declared themselves to have no creed and the number of those who did not declare themselves either believers or non-believers, we obtain 414,-253. This figure is 34,000 lower than the corresponding figure in 1940, and 29,000 lower than the number of non-believers in 1940 (see Table 8).

These data can be interpreted in a variety of ways: (1) the rate of increase of non-believers might have decreased during the period of industrialization, urbanization, and modernization of the country (1940–60); (2) political and psychological pressures on census authorities might have been increased so that these subjects were not included in 1950; (3) the same pressures might have been exerted on the population to declare itself religious in the 1960 survey; or (4) the census em-

13. José E. Iturriaga, *La estructura social y cultural de México* (Mexico: Fondo de Cultura Económica, 1951), p. 146.

ployees might have automatically registered as Catholic a population that was not.

The first interpretation is highly improbable. In any sociology of religion, the absolute and relative increase of irreligiosity is a trend that naturally occurs as societies become urbanized. The other three interpretations would reveal to what degree this increase may coincide with political and psychological pressures—conscious or unconscious—which tend to hide it.

In any event, in judging the role of the clerical policy of our day, the most viable hypothesis is that traditional Catholicism is being replaced by a modern type of Catholicism: political religious fanaticism is increasingly confronted with a Catholicism which separates religious action from political action; there is an increase in the type of population which, although declaring itself Catholic, does not regularly practice all the ecclesiastic rites.

This distinction between traditional and modern Catholicism applies to the faithful and to priests and prelates. This is a fact which cannot be ignored and which prevents the interpretation that the increase in the power of the Church is leading us to positions similar to those of the past. Traditional nineteenth-century and early twentieth-century clericalism can also be explained as a function of a whole system with latifundism, *caciquismo,* and militarism as its complement. Today's clericalism is enmeshed in a very different social structure. It may, it is true, perform a few roles similar to those of the past, and if the other traditional holders of power—particularly the Army—should reassert their strength, the danger of a traditional political struggle would increase. But it is important to recognize that the modernization of the country, the consequent profanation of customs, and the emergence of a modern Catholicism increasingly removed from medieval political patterns and from Spanish obscurantist political traditions are facts of contemporary Mexico. This modernization exists to different degrees throughout the country, and in fact there still remain stagnating regions in which traditionalism is deeply embedded.

The uneven and varied development of the different regions of Mexico is demonstrated by different forms of religiosity and profanity. The more traditionalist and fanatical religious attitudes are found, with their concomitant political effects, in the central states. In other areas, such as Nuevo León, there is a political religiosity of a paternalistic variety, promoted by the entrepreneurs and linked to the factories. Large parts of the North, of the Gulf, and of the Southeast exhibit a far more limited religiosity, less linked to political activity.

One indicator that this is not a traditional society with respect to religion is the number of individuals who say they have no creed at all and are registered as non-religious— despite the obstacles mentioned. If we classify the states according to whether they have small or large proportions of manifest non-believers, we find that 13 states have a proportion of non-believers larger than the national mean (.57),[14] and 19 have a smaller proportion. The highest proportions of manifest non-believers are found in Baja California, Quintana Roo, Sinaloa, Tabasco, and Veracruz; the smallest proportions are found in Jalisco, México, and Querétaro (see Table 9).

Another indicator, which may be more important in determining geographical variation in religious feeling, is the percentage of the population (twelve years of age or over) who have marital ties but who were married in a civil ceremony only or not formally married at all. In 1960, of a total population of 11,689,960 aged twelve or over, 33.13 per cent had not been married in a religious ceremony. Half the federal entities had a percentage of their population with non-religious marital ties higher than this mean. In Tabasco this population amounted to 78.15 per cent of the total; in Chiapas 77 per cent; in Sinaloa 65 per cent; in Veracruz, Tamaulipas,

14. Ratio with respect to the total Catholic population.

and Sonora more than 50 per cent; in Hidalgo, Quintana Roo, and Campeche more than 40 per cent; and in Morelos, Nayarit, Oaxaca, Coahuila, the territory of Baja California, and Nuevo León more than 33 per cent. Only in the rest of the states of the Republic did the population number less than the national mean: 30 per cent in the Federal District, Chihuahua, and Puebla; between 20 per cent and 30 per cent in Yucatán, Guerrero, Tlaxcala, San Luis Potosí, Durango, and México; between 10 per cent and 20 per cent in Colima, Michoacán, and Zacatecas; and less than 10 per cent in those states where Catholic religion is not only more generally practiced but also more traditional—Jalisco, Aguascalientes, Querétaro, and Guanajuato.

A description of gradations—from political-religious fanaticism to modern Catholicism and laicism—may not suffice to explain the differences in religiosity in Mexico. There are more than 1 million inhabitants who speak only indigenous tongues, and there are 2 million who speak both an indigenous tongue and Spanish. In both groups we find pre-Hispanic, polytheist, totemic, and magic beliefs which in more acculturated subgroups become mixed with the religious and magic superstitions of a Hispanic variety. Both would deserve consideration in an analysis of the political action of the clergy.

Clerical policy is far from homogeneous. Among the prelates there are differences between the traditionalists and the modernists. In different groups of the clergy we find today, as in the past, cultural and ideological differences. Clerical policy differs from one federal entity to another, from one region of the country to another, and from one social class to another.

Although we are not faced with the dangers of clerical policy and clerical problems like those of the nineteenth century, and although the economic and social evolution of Mexico, with its changing structure and religiosity, does not permit us to think in terms of a return to the past, we *are* faced with the possibility—and even the fact, in certain regions of the country—of new connections between the traditional clerical policy and the new Mexican and foreign conservative forces.

In rather large areas of present-day Mexico there are close relationships between traditional clericalism and the Cold War, between political Christianity and an anti-Communism which manipulates primitive symbols representing the fears of traditional society, and those relationships provoke occurrences of panic and aggressive activity among the more ignorant and fanatical people, be they members of the peasantry or of the middle class.

These fears and phobias are connected with the Cold War and manipulated by means of rumor campaigns, accusations, and alarming statements. Stories and fantasies of fear are made to circulate in the countryside, in the towns, and even in the cities. Religious symbols—amulets, exorcisms, and alarm bells—of prophets and prophecies, of apostles and saints, along with monstrous superstitious images and popular conceptions of the demoniacal, are linked in the presentation of Communism as an infernal and diabolical force in the traditional sense of the term. These are all part of an increasingly effective political action, in which priests are gradually replacing teachers as leaders of the communities and public lands in order to formulate demands and organize protests and religious-political demonstrations. This provokes a fear among politicians—governors, congressmen, leaders—that they will be accused of being Communists in the magical-diabolical sense.

The extreme practice of this policy is rooted in the more backward regions of the country. In other areas, the magical and medieval conceptions of anti-Communism give way to a less primitive type of propaganda. The liberal and more modernizing forces still control the situation in the towns. And even in the federal entities where this magical conception is prevalent, there are large groups of landed peasants, of public

land revolutionists, who support the liberal elite and help
them stay in power. Yet today's traditionalist clergy acts as
one of the most vital forces in Mexican politics and constitutes one of the most powerful and diversified pressure groups.
Rulers must take the traditionalist clergy into account in making their decisions—sometimes as their ally against popular
demands endangering their power or interests, at other times
as their enemy attempting to overthrow and replace them.

The Entrepreneurs

The agrarian reform which began in the Revolution and
achieved its climax during the regime of Cárdenas, eliminated
the system of latifundia and with it the types of social relationships which some scholars equate with feudalism. Mexico
in 1910 was a country in which 11,000 landholders owned almost 60 per cent of the land. It has become a country with
small owners of public lands and large capitalist agricultural
enterprises. There are hardly any traces left of the old latifundia with owners and peons, nor of the plantations with
semi-slave workers. Between 1915 and 1965 the various Mexican presidents distributed 53,337,500 hectares among 2,-
240,000 heads of families, and the agrarian structure became
radically transformed. Small owners, public-land workers, and
salaried countryside workers appeared. Independent traders
and rural middle classes developed. Peasant entrepreneurs,
also called "neo-latifundists," appeared later; their role in the
community, the economy, and the State is quite different
from that of their predecessors, more like that of a high rural
bourgeoisie.

Another significant phenomenon in agrarian reform, of
course, was the industrialization of the country. With the
growth of the internal market, with industrial nationaliza-
tions—of railroads and particularly of oil—with all the
processes of original accumulation and capitalization, the
State acquired new entrepreneurial functions. The dominant

classes, which had already been reduced to very small groups, performed new roles as industrialists, traders, and bankers. Thus the entrepreneur took the place of the latifundist in the political system, and capitalism defined the prevailing types of social relationships, encompassing the whole of the developed areas of the country and dominating the rest.

An analysis of the growth of these relationships would require a general study of the recent development of the economic and social systems of the country.[15] We shall limit ourselves to delineating the current power of the entrepreneurs, particularly with respect to the government.

A study made in 1960 by the Mexican economist José Luis Ceceña of the largest enterprises in Mexico (2,040 enterprises with annual incomes of 5 million pesos or more, which as a whole earn 56 billion pesos annually and in fact control the Mexican economy) reveals the relative strength of the national, foreign, and State enterprise (see Table 10). Among the hundred largest enterprises, those with foreign control and strong foreign participation earn 50.27 per cent of the total income. The independent private sector gets 13.52 per cent, and government enterprises, 36.21 per cent. Among the two hundred largest enterprises the corresponding percentages are: 53.96 per cent (foreign or with strong foreign participation); 16.53 per cent (independent private sector); 29.51 per cent (government). Among the three hundred largest enterprises: 54.51 per cent (foreign or with strong foreign participation); 19.04 per cent (independent private sector); 26.45 per cent (government). Among the four hundred largest enterprises— with incomes amounting to 77 per cent of the total national income—the percentages are 54.06 per cent (foreign); 21.09 per cent (independent private sector); 24.85 per cent (government). The foreign enterprises and those with strong foreign participation earn more than 50 per cent of the total income,

15. For a preliminary study of semi-capitalist development in Mexico, see Pablo González Casanova, "México: El ciclo de una revolución agraria," *Cuadernos Americanos,* January-February 1962, pp. 7–29.

and the remaining private enterprises between 14 and 22 per cent. Together they obtain three-quarters of the total income of the four hundred largest enterprises, whereas the government obtains only one-fourth. Thus private enterprise, both Mexican and foreign, constitutes an extraordinary force in economic and political decision-making. Organized in confederations, chambers, associations, and clubs, private enterprise forms a very novel and vigorous network of pressure groups, which the government cannot ignore.[16]

Some of these organizations have an official and forceful character and constitute a powerful instrument for the entrepreneurs themselves. The National Confederation of Industrial Chambers (CONCAMIN) groups 51 local chambers. The National Confederation of National Chambers of Commerce (CONCANACO) groups 254 chambers. The Employers Confederation of the Mexican Republic has 7,000 members distributed among 21 centers. In addition, there are many other no less powerful organizations, such as the Association of Bankers of Mexico and the Mexican Association of Insurance Institutions.[17] In all these groups the members elect representatives on the basis of their economic and political power and their possible effectiveness in defending entrepreneurial interests. They are powerful and effective representatives of the forces of foreign and Mexican entrepreneurs, and they use highly efficient forms of pressure. "It has been characteristic of the entrepreneurial organization in Mexico," writes Isaac Guzmán Valdivia, a publicist for these organizations,

> that the more serious problems which affect the entrepreneurs are jointly studied by the directors of the main institutions representing private initiative. Whenever a situation of

16. Cf. José Luis Ceceña, "El capital monopolista y la economía de México" (Mexico: Cuadernos Americanos, 1963).
17. Cf. Arturo González Cosío, "Clases y estratos sociales," in *México: Cincuenta Años de Revolución* (Mexico: Fondo de Cultura Económica, 1961, Vol. II), p. 73.

a serious nature presents itself, the presidents of the Confederations of Industrial Chambers, of National Chambers of Commerce, of the Employers' Confederation and of the Bankers' Association of Mexico, immediately enter into consultations and if necessary their respective directive counsels and specialists take some action. In this way sound decisions are made, constituting a norm of action for the entrepreneurial class. On this basis joint declarations are made or steps are taken with the participation of representatives of industry, commerce, entrepreneurs as employers, and the banks. Upon other occasions—and this is the general rule —each organization acts within its own specific field knowing that it has the support of the rest.[18]

Other forms of co-ordination are arranged during the annual conventions, among the entrepreneurs of a particular industrial branch or among the entrepreneurs of different branches who share common activities within a particular field.

These organizations, powerful in the economic field and organized and co-ordinated in the political field, are, by law, "organs of consultation of the State for the satisfaction of the needs of national commerce and industry." [19] Actually, they function rather like a congress of entrepreneurs with decisive influence upon legislation and administration.

There is a system of chambers which enables the government to learn the attitudes toward a given arrangement before submitting to Congress any law which might prejudice or injure such a transaction. When each chamber receives a law proposal, it decides on the policy to be adopted by the interests it represents in order to make its observations. Most chambers have a body of specialized lawyers who submit to the government modifications they believe to be adequate. If the suggestions indicate that a proposal, should it be adopted, would be prejudicial not only to the interests of the chamber

18. Isaac Guzmán Valdivia, "El movimiento patronal," in *México: Cincuenta Años de Revolución,* Vol. II, p. 318.
19. Cf. Laws of Chambers of Industry and of Chambers of Commerce.

but also to those of Mexican society generally, then the government tends to reconsider the initiative. In this way business has a direct participation in the political system of Mexico, even though frequently it may not have formal representation in the party or in the government. Its influence is directly felt; action is quick and results tangible.[20]

In addition, there is a procedure, established since the thirties, in which the Secretary of the Treasury speaks on the administration's financial and economic policy. This speech is subjected to the effective—and sometimes very vigorous—criticism of the participants, usually backed by the press.

Thus we find in present-day Mexico a broadly and highly organized business sector with its own financing, with its own representatives elected through democratic vote, with its own experts and technicians who receive the best salaries in the country and who serve as consultants in the economic, juridical, and political fields. This sector has mutually co-ordinating organizations which follow—every time they deem it favorable to their interests—a common strategy. This sector, which represents .5 per cent of the population—that is, about 200,000 Mexicans, as noted by González Cosío in his study on "Social Classes and Social Strata"[21]—has effective instruments to influence legislation and administration, which modify the decisions of the Executive, after subjecting them to criticism. It can censure the economic reports sent them by the government and with the support of the major newspapers propose modifications of the government's economic and financial policy. All of this is done in a completely different form from that followed in the President's annual reports to Congress, which have symbolic meanings and routine comments preceding or accompanying their automatic and also routine approval.

An effective defense of the interests of the citizenry can be made for Mexico's entrepreneurial sector. For a long time, the

20. Frank Brandenburg, *op. cit.*
21. Arturo González Cosío, *op. cit.,* p. 73.

public sector represented more than one-third of the gross territorial investment. In 1961 its participation amounted to 46 per cent, and in 1963, 50 per cent.[22] Thus, the public sector has great influence upon private investment and economic development. Private investment, as various economists have noted, is a dependent variable of public investment. The private investor watches the expenditures and investments of the government and then invests. Sometimes—for instance, in 1961—government investment counteracts the negative effects of a low level of private investment. It then operates with relative independence to supplement occupation growth and income. In terms of industry and services, its strategic position is excellent. It produces and controls almost all of the country's available energy. All oil production is decentralized, and with the nationalization of the electric industry, the generation of electricity by the State increased from 23.2 per cent in 1959 to 83.4 per cent in 1965–66. In the sphere of communications and transportation, State units control 48 per cent of the national total. The railroads are completely nationalized, but automobile transportation, telephone services, and most air transportation belongs to the private sector. Air transportation, however, is increasingly moving to the public sector. State enterprises contribute only 3 per cent of the total national manufacturing production, but their activity is mainly in industries basic to development, such as iron and steel, fertilizers, assembly of motor vehicles, sugar refining, textiles, (especially cotton), and paper. State participation in mining industries is also very low (3 per cent of national production in 1960); it concentrates on the extraction of iron and coal.

Corresponding to this power in the field of production is power in the area of finances.

There has been a considerable increase in the financing granted by the national banks and the Bank of Mexico for

22. Cf. *Memoria de las Oficinas de la Junta de Gobierno de los Organismos y Empresas de Estado* (Mexico: Secretaría del Patrimonio Nacional, 1962 and 1963).

production and commerce. The figure has increased from 377.4 million pesos in 1942 to 16,327.6 million pesos in 1959 (excluding the securities granted by National Financing). This represents 31 and 52 per cent respectively of the total financing granted by the Mexican banking system.[23]

Government credit has significance for development: it complements the lack of private credit for broad sectors of production and commerce; it makes possible investments entailing higher risks that are basic for industrialization; and it achieves double the amount of investments in the private sector, which is also basic to national development.[24]

Then, too, there is a large number of official banking and financing institutions, such as the banks of Agricultural and Public Lands Credit, the National Warehouses, the National Union of Sugar Producers, the National Sugar Financer, the National Bank of Cooperative Patronage, the National Bank of Transportations, the Small Traders Bank, the Bank of the Army and Navy, the Patronage of National Savings, and the Institute of Security and Social Services of Public Workers, which serve much of the population. Thus the granting of credit is made a function of development and government policy.

The economic instruments at the service of the State— such as the monopoly of the production of energy, great influence in transportation and communications, and in credit —its strategic position in the extractive and processing industries, the essentially political character of many of its financial institutions, its power to effect wide-ranging economic decisions, and the fact of these being linked to the public administration and to the presidentialist regime indicate that the criticisms made by the private sector concerning excessive State intervention are correct in terms of a capitalist economy. But a few facts cast new light on this subject.

23. Octaviano Campos Salas, "Las instituciones nacionales de crédito," in *México: Cincuenta Años de Revolución,* Vol. I, p. 422.
24. Cf. Salas, *op. cit.,* pp. 420–44, for a broader study.

In the first place, Mexico's public sector produces a far lower percentage of the gross national product than that of other free enterprise countries. In 1960 it generated 9.5 per cent, whereas in that year the figures for other governments were higher: the French government, 19 per cent; the British, 20.6 per cent; and the United States government, 21 per cent.

An even more significant factor, which the critics of State intervention do not take into account, concerns the specific conditions of State intervention and the context within which it operates. State intervention is highly dependent on foreign financing, which contributed 30.8 per cent in 1959, 34.8 per cent in 1960, and 47.4 per cent in 1961. This dependence has come about because of the high level of imports from under-developed countries. In addition, when the international and domestic situations bring about a decrease in economic activity, such as took place in 1961, a search for credits abroad begins.

Foreign credits, which depend mostly on the United States, added to the power of foreign enterprises directly or indirectly supported by the economic policy and political power of the United States, considerably reduce the power of the Mexican State, of its presidentialist regime, and of its productive and financial apparatus. This casts serious doubt on the proposition that the Mexican State should decrease its economic intervention. If it did, almost as if by a physical law, the power and influence of the United States over Mexico would increase.

3

National Power and the Factor of Dominion

Mexico is located within the economic and political sphere of influence of the United States, and the factor of dominion operates in the latter's favor. Mexico's history in the twentieth century—especially during the period of the Mexican Revolution—consists of political, military, and economic measures seeking to limit United States influence and to increase its own negotiating capacity. It is a history of missteps, progress, and withdrawals, but the economics of inequality has never changed. Even though Mexico's negotiating capacity is now far greater than in the past, the same problem still exists at different levels, in the economic, political, and cultural spheres.

We will limit ourselves to the more gross indicators of the power and domination exercised by the United States at the economic and political levels. It is evident that in this brief chapter we must set aside many possible methods of measurement and analysis, but we will, at least, suggest an outline of American domination.

Even though the total foreign contribution to internal capitalization amounts to hardly 2.3 per cent of the gross national investment, we have already seen how of the four hundred most powerful Mexican enterprises—those which practically control the national economy—more than 50 per cent are either foreign enterprises or enterprises with strong foreign participation.

Among the foreign enterprises, the United States enterprises predominate, and their participation in direct foreign investment has increased in the course of the past two decades. Toward the end of the Cárdenas regime, United States investment represented 62 per cent of the total foreign investment. Under Avila Camacho (1941–46), it was 66 per cent; with Alemán (1947–52), 72 per cent; and during the first five years of the Ruiz Cortines administration (1953–57), it was 74 per cent. After 1957 the Bank of Mexico no longer published this information. But it is likely, in view of the observable trend and of national and international circumstances, that the percentage of direct United States investments in Mexico has increased further, or, by a conservative estimate, that it has remained the same (see Table 11).

The United States has the highest percentage of total foreign credits. In 1964, for example, 54.8 per cent of the credits obtained through national financing originated in that country. These credits are far more convenient from an economic point of view than direct investments insofar as they do not produce unfavorable balances or decapitalization. Nevertheless, until recently the attempt to diversify the sources of foreign credit has not altered the predominance of American sources. In 1964, Great Britain contributed 15.2 per cent and France 8.1 per cent. But Germany contributed 3.6 per cent only; Belgium 2.6 per cent; Canada 1.6 per cent; Holland 1.2 per cent; and the international organizations 8.4 per cent. The contribution of Sweden, Switzerland, and Italy was less than 1 per cent.[1] In addition, from 1945 to 1954 the yearly average of credits was $35.1 million, from 1955 to 1964 the average was $207.1 million—that is, more than five times greater.

"Fifteen per cent of internal economic activity depends on the foreign market, and this constitutes the quantitative degree

1. Nacional Financiera, S.A. *Annual Report for 1964* (Mexico: 1965), p. 49.

of external dependence of the Mexican economy." [2] The dominant external market is the United States, which in the course of the forty years from 1925 to 1965 absorbed more than 60 per cent of total imports: 69 per cent with the Calles administration; 65 per cent with the Maximato; 65 per cent with Cárdenas; 86 per cent with Avila Camacho; 85 per cent with Alemán; 79 per cent with Ruiz Cortines; 70 per cent with López Mateos; and 64 per cent during the first year of the present administration. During the same period, the percentage of the United States market of total Mexican exports is: 70 per cent (Calles), 58 per cent (the Maximato), 68 per cent (Cárdenas), 85 per cent (Avila Camacho), 78 per cent (Alemán), 63 per cent (Ruiz Cortines), 62 per cent (López Mateos), and 72 per cent during the first year of the Díaz Ordaz administration.

These data demonstrate that the major crisis of 1921 saw a decrease in the percentage of United States exports and imports. It increased during World War II. It decreased only recently, even though United States predominance is still indicated by the figure of 60 per cent for Mexican imports and exports.

Mexico's situation with respect to dependence on a limited number of export products has always been more favorable than that of most other underdeveloped countries. Dependence exists, however, with respect to a few products, mostly agricultural and mining products subject to depression in the world market, to considerable cyclical variations in volume and price and to economic-political speculations and pressures from abroad.[3]

During the administration of Calles, the three major export products accounted for 44 per cent of the total value of exports. During the Maximato the percentage was 36 per cent.

2. Cf. Secretaría del Patrimonio Nacional. *Memoria 1960*.
3. Pedro Guzmán Gallegos, Juan Antonio Mateos, Daniel de la Pedraja, María Guadalupe Puente González, and Jorge Arturo Ojeda, students at the Escuela Nacional de Ciencias Políticas y Sociales, assisted in gathering data on the main export products.

With Cárdenas it was 42 per cent; with Avila Camacho, 32 per cent; with Alemán, 32 per cent; with Ruiz Cortines, 39 per cent; with López Mateos, 38 per cent; and during the first year of the present administration, 32 per cent. During the same periods, the value of the five major export products was 60 per cent, 49 per cent, 59 per cent, 42 per cent, 44 per cent, 48 per cent, 47 per cent, and 40 per cent of the total, respectively. The value of the ten major products was 76 per cent of the total in the first of those periods (1925–28), 70 per cent in the following period (1929–34), 76 per cent (1935–40), 61 per cent (1941–46), 60 per cent (1947–52), 58 per cent (1953–58), 63 per cent (1959–64), and 55 per cent (1965, the first year of the present administration). Thus, three products account for between 30 and 40 per cent of the Mexican export economy, five products for between 40 per cent and 50 per cent, and ten products for between 50 and 60 per cent. These are largely non-manufactured products, and they are mostly sent to the United States. The proportion that these products are of the total exports varies because of a multitude of factors. A minor general decrease in exports is evident, but the foreign market is still very significant.

Some information about political and cultural influence will reinforce the impression given by the economic data. One historian, Gastón García Cantú, has counted 74 invasions, threats, despoliations, and offenses to Mexico at the hands of the United States between 1801 and 1878.[4] Subsequently there were various well-known transgressions of the same kind—the invasion of Veracruz, the Pershing expedition. These incidents terminated with Franklin D. Roosevelt's Good Neighbor policy, and they were superseded by conventional political pressures, which did not openly violate the precedent established by Roosevelt and which were applied to Mexico at a higher stage of its development.

4. Gastón García Cantú, "México en el Mediterráneo Americano," *Revista de Ciencias Políticas y Sociales,* Year VII, July-September 1961, No. 25, pp. 7–10, 16, and 23.

Between 1848 and 1958, 305 bilateral pacts and treaties were signed by Mexico, of which 94 (30 per cent) were with the United States. Between 1921 and 1958 Mexico signed 246 pacts and treaties, of which 85 (34 per cent) were with the United States. The United States is the country with which Mexico has the most political ties, partly because of geographical proximity. In order to study the factor of dominion in politics, one would have to analyze treaties, agreements, and pacts, and to reconstruct their histories. Some were imposed upon the country under conditions of inequality and strong political pressure, such as the famous treaties of Bucareli; the United States tried to impose some unsuccessfully; and some exhibited a formal equality but did not in fact operate that way.

Cultural barriers are an important obstacle to United States penetration into certain fields. Of the total number of books imported for elementary education, for example, United States books account for 55 per cent (1930), 56 per cent (1935), 85 per cent (1945), 84 per cent (1950), 78 per cent (1955), 37 per cent (1960), and 73 per cent (1964).[5] These books are used for the education of United States children residing in Mexico and for a few upper-middle-class Mexican children who attend North American schools. Their influence is relatively small, though not negligible since they influence the education of some of the future leaders.

There are similar barriers in the field of religion. Despite the many and extended attempts at Protestant catechization, the number of Mexican converts is minimal. Between 104 and 115 Protestant societies operate throughout the nation working to strengthen Protestantism in Mexico. Mexico has the fourth largest number of Protestant societies in the world; only India, Japan, and Brazil have more. There are 65 Protestant seminaries, with a percentage of the total population twice the corresponding percentages in Colombia, Argentina,

5. Cf. *Comercio Exterior. Anuarios Estadísticos.*

and Brazil. There are 2,777 Protestant educational centers (schools, educational and recreational centers, student housing).[6] Protestantism is largely subsidized by United States funds, but its influence is not large, even in politics. The increase in the number of Protestants in Mexico, in relative numbers, is far below that of the Catholics. In the period 1930–60 the Catholic population increased 48 per cent, and the Protestant population increased only 22 per cent (see Table 7). The imitation of United States techniques and even tastes and habits apparently is not practiced in Mexican cultural, spiritual, and political structures. A study of the influence of United States culture in Mexico and its various effects on groups of Mexicans is a task no less urgent than a study of the positive aspects of innovation and the adoption of industrial and administrative techniques.

There are fields in which United States influence is great because of the means at its disposal, which at times can carry strong political weight. The sources of international news in the major newspapers, for instance, are predominantly North American. In a sample covering representative newspapers over a period of a few months, we find that in February 1962, 63 per cent of the total international news items published by *El Universal* was provided by United States agencies; of that published by *Novedades* 78 per cent was North American; of that published by *Excélsior* 62 per cent was North American. In June of the same year the percentages of the total foreign news items provided by United States agencies was 75 per cent in *El Sol de Puebla,* 58 per cent in *Excélsior,* and 68 per cent in *El Universal.* In general, between 63 and 75 per cent of the foreign news items in the Mexican press is derived from United States agencies.[7] Associated Press and United Press International practically monopolize foreign news. The Agence

6. Pedro Rivera R., S.J., *op. cit.,* pp. 22, 73, 78, 87–92.
7. The gathering of data was effected with the assistance of Carlos Narváez and José Manuel Morante, students at the Escuela Nacional de Ciencias Politicas y Sociales.

Française Presse (A.F.P.) and Reuters are used only exceptionally or in a secondary capacity. Other agencies occupy insignificant positions in the large newspapers or no position at all.

A study made by John C. Merrill shows the quantitative importance of the United States regarding foreign news. The study was based on analysis of ten daily newspapers: *Excélsior, Novedades, El Norte* of Monterrey, *Diario de Culiacán, El Heraldo* of San Luis Potosí, *Diario de Yucatán, Sol de Tampico, El Fronterizo* of Ciudad Juarez, *El Occidental* of Guadalajara, and *El Imparcial* of Hermosillo. These ten newspapers were analyzed throughout January 1960. During that month their total combined circulation was 477,340 copies, and they had approximately 2,000,000 readers. Some of Merrill's conclusions shed light on our problem. He found "that in one month the ten newspapers had 4,110 new items on the United States, with a total of 34,094 column inches. This equals 213 pages of United States material in one month, a large amount considering the fact that in that same month the ten newspapers as a whole only had a *total* of 3,555 pages of information, news analysis, and editorials.

"*Excélsior* and *Novedades,* two Mexican newspapers of approximately the same size (in number of pages and circulation) as that of seven South American 'quality' newspapers studied in 1959 by James W. Markham of the University of Pennsylvania, used more space for United States material than did the seven South American newspapers for the *whole* of their *foreign* materials.

"Another index of the gigantic dimensions of the space devoted to the United States in two large newspapers of Mexico City is the fact that *Novedades* published as much material on the United States in one month as did *The New York Times* (according to Markham's study) during that same period on all foreign countries, and that *Excélsior* published more material on the United States than *The New York Times* did 'on the world.' "

Merrill observed an anti-American attitude in the Mexican press but he did not state whether it was due to the boomerang effect of propaganda. Nor did he state whether he found praise toward the United States lacking and excessive criticism present. The second interpretation is close to my view, but it is insufficiently documented, and it deserves further analysis.[8]

The importance of the direct influence of United States press in Mexico is clearly demonstrated by the fact that in 1964 three magazines published by the United States in Spanish had an average circulation greater by more than 200,000 copies (100,000 more than in 1961) than that of the ten largest Mexican magazines. One of the three United States magazines, *Selecciones del Readers Digest,* had a circulation in the interior of Mexico eight times higher than that of the largest Mexican newspaper.

Of all motion pictures shown in Mexico between 1950 and 1964, 52 per cent were North American and 24 per cent were Mexican. During that same period, 69 per cent of the total of foreign motion pictures were North American.

These economic, political, and cultural influences, which are evident throughout Mexico's history and which continue or appear in new forms even today, largely condition the political decisions of the nation, the State, the parties, and the pressure and interest groups, seriously limiting the power of the Executive. Other factors are important, such as the significance of income derived through tourism and the pay of day laborers. These are subject to cyclical variations and vary with economic and political crises and pressures—the equilibrium of the balance of payments and monetary stability, for example.

It is necessary for us to undertake a careful examination of the structure of the Mexican State and its limitations, of the external causes which determine its weaknesses, of its own economic and political limitations, and of a way in which to

8. John C. Merrill, "The United States as Seen from Mexico," *Journal of Interamerican Studies,* January 1963, pp. 53–66, particularly 55 and 56.

perfect its structure in order to increase its negotiating capacity and break the dynamics of inequality.

The Mexican presidentialist State has the capacity to use the vital instruments of the national economy. This explains how, despite difficult international circumstances today, Mexico is able to continue a policy of liberation and nationalization (such as the recent purchase of electrical industry) and to pursue an independent international policy based on its national traditions. It has not lost its economic negotiating capacity, evident in its refusal of military pacts with the United States and of servile alignment with the United States policy against Cuba.

Consequently, Mexico has received an insignificant amount of aid from the United States as compared with that received by other Latin American nations ($3,500,000 in the decade of 1950–59, compared with $424,000,000 received by Latin America as a whole). But it has also meant the existence and survival of the Mexican State. In the midst of difficulties and pressures, Mexico is one of the most stable countries in Latin America and perhaps the only one in which "anti-American" sentiment has given way to a strategy of national independence and development.

II

THE SOCIAL AND POLITICAL STRUCTURE

4

From the Political Structure to the Social Structure

Speaking generally of the actual holders of power and the structure of the Mexican government, the *caciques* and the Army have lost power and importance. The *caciques* have practically disappeared and the Army has become an instrument of the modern State. The power regained by the Church in the political sphere operates in a new context; although it is still important, there is no indication that the Church might once more assume a role like the one it held in the past. Finally, a relatively new power in Mexico has become apparent—that of native financiers and entrepreneurs. They, along with the large foreign enterprises and the great power that supports them, hold the real power which the Mexican State must take into account in its important decisions.

The State itself, however, is the largest entrepreneur in the country. It has economic power which is reinforced on the political level by the presidentialist regime, in which power is concentrated in the central government and the Executive Chief. This arrangement has a functional character that maintains both the political stability and the economic development of the country. It is true that it has upset classical political and economic theories, but the arrangement has contributed to the development of a nation-state that emerged in an international environment very different from that in which bourgeois Europe and the United States developed.

The entrepreneurial State and the concentration of power in a presidentialist regime function in several ways to promote stability and development. For instance, they make possible the concentration of scarce resources for rational utilization within a free-enterprise or capitalist framework. They increase the political stability of a nation threatened by intervention of large enterprises and great powers. They give Mexico the scope to move in the international field and to exert pressure in order to increase its capacity for negotiation and gradually to break down the external forces against equality that are typically felt by underdeveloped countries.

These functional qualities of the Mexican State must be understood in terms of underdevelopment. The presidentialist regime put an end to the conspiracies of the legislative power, the Army, and the clergy. The dominant party put an end to the *caudillos* and their parties. The centralist regime put an end to regional feuds. Intervention in local government not only eliminated free municipalities, but served to control the local *caciques*. The entrepreneurial State formed the basis for a national policy of economic and industrial development when large investments were needed for roads, dams, and centers for production, and when private initiative, both Mexican and foreign, was too backward or indifferent to invest. Limitations placed upon ownership effected agrarian reform and the oil expropriation, establishing the basis for an internal market and national capitalization in a country in which the number of customers was very small and national entrepreneurs practically non-existent.

All these experiences demonstrated that it would have been senseless to apply literally the classical theories of democracy and economics. Respect for the balances of power would have been respect for the conspiracies of a semi-feudal society. Respect for political parties would have been respect for the *ca-*

ciques and the military parties. To respect the "system of checks and balances" would have been to tolerate the regional *caciques* and *caudillos*. To respect free municipalities would have been to tolerate the freedom of local *caciques*. The observance of the principle of non-intervention by the State in the economy would have meant the abandonment of the country to underdevelopment and to intervention by foreign monopolies and their nations. To maintain unrestricted rights of ownership would have meant to maintain semi-feudal and foreign ownership and a status quo that could not allow for the creation of an internal market and national capitalization.

The detractors of the Mexican State do not perceive these obvious facts, and the rulers and ideologues of the Revolution often distort them. They claim that they have been faithful to the classical theories of democracy and economics, even as they twist and obscure the facts, misinterpreting their own history in order to place their loyalty to Montesquieu and Madison beyond doubt. At the same time, they have a guilt complex and they delude themselves; this prevents them from seeing the real problems.

The Mexican State and its institutions have been an effective instrument, within a capitalist system, for controlling the external pressures of inequality, for confronting and negotiating with the large monopolies and great powers with decreasing inequality, and for promoting the takeoff of national development. But there is no doubt that the State and institutions are limited and that their limitations are apparent in implementing the policy of independent development, especially in dealing with underdevelopment as an internal phenomenon and with the internal forces of inequality. What is functional with respect to a given end can be dysfunctional with respect to another, and what can be useful in terms of a given national goal may be prejudicial in terms of another national goal. The real problem that the country is facing is not that it has violated the classical theory of economics and democracy, but that it has been as yet unable to break the external and, more important, the internal dynamics of inequality. Using government power to deal with internal dynamics of inequality drains vital energy from national development and national power itself. In order to analyze this problem, we must examine the relationships between the political structure and the social structure.

There are many possible ways to analyze the relationships between the social and political structures of Mexico, but we shall limit our study to those relationships affording an international perspective and to those which are more directly linked with political actions: the relationship between social marginality and political marginality; the relationship between plural society, internal colonialism, and political manipulation; the relationship between social stratification and political nonconformity; the relationship between mobilization, social mobility, and political conformity; and the relationship between the forms assumed by nonconformity and civil struggles.

5

The Plural Society

MARGINALITY AND DEVELOPMENT

Marginal national development, lack of participation in economic, social, and cultural development, a large sector of have-nots—these are characteristics of underdeveloped societies. Not only do underdeveloped societies have an unequal distribution of wealth, income, culture, and technology, but, as is the case in Mexico, they often contain two or more socio-cultural aggregates, one which is highly participating and another which is quite marginal; one which is dominant— be it called Spanish, Creole, or Ladino—and another which is dominated—be it called native, Indian, or indigenous.[1]

These phenomena—marginality and non-participation in the growth of the country; dual or plural society; cultural, economic, and political heterogeneity which divides the country into two or more sectors with different characteristics— are interrelated. They are in turn linked to the much deeper problem of *internal colonialism,* or the domination and exploitation of certain groups by others. "Colonialism" does not, as is commonly believed, pertain only to relationships between

1. Cf. Pablo González Casanova, "Sociedad Plural y Desarrollo: El caso de México," *América Latina* (Centro Latinoamericano de Pesquisas em Ciências Sociais), October-December 1962, No. 4, pp. 31–51.

nations. It also pertains to relationships within a nation, insofar as a nation is ethnically heterogeneous and certain ethnic groups become the dominant groups and classes and others become the dominated. Despite the long years of revolution, reform, industrialization, and development, inheritances from the past—marginality, plural society, and internal colonialism—persist in Mexico today in new forms. Those factors determine the characteristics of the society and the national polity.

Marginality can be measured in various ways. Mexican censuses gather general and specific data which are quite useful for analysis of marginality. They register the illiterate population. They estimate the size of the population which does not eat wheat bread because it eats only corn or eats neither, a distinction closely linked to standards of living and marginality. They enumerate the population which does not wear shoes because it wears sandals or no footgear at all, the school-aged population which does not attend school, the population which does not drink milk, and that which does not eat meat or fish.

Some of these indicators of marginality have been traced in all the censuses since the beginning of the century; some have not. From those that have been, we can get an idea of the problem as it is today and of how it evolved.

Although marginality occurs in the cities in forms characteristic of slum life, it is a phenomenon which nonetheless tends to become closely associated with rural life. Marginal society is predominantly rural.

According to the 1960 census, Mexico has a rural population of 27,980,000 aged six or over. Of these, 17,410,000 are literate and 10,570,000 are illiterate. Among the urban population the number of literate individuals is 10,750,000, whereas that of illiterate individuals is 3,430,000. Among the rural population the number of literate individuals is 6,-660,000 and that of illiterate individuals is 7,150,000. Whereas in urban areas 76 per cent of the population is literate, in rural areas only 48 per cent is literate, and whereas the urban population only has 24 per cent illiteracy, the rural population has 52 per cent (see Table 14).

According to the same 1960 census, of a total population of 33,780,000 aged one or over, 23,160,000 ate wheat bread, and 10,620,000 did not. Among the urban population 14,-940,000 ate wheat bread, and 2,180,000 did not. Among the rural population 8,220,000 ate wheat bread, and 8,430,000 did not. Whereas in urban areas only 13 per cent did not eat wheat bread, in rural areas 51 per cent did not (see Table 15).

In 1960, according to the census, 25,630,000 Mexicans one year of age or over had one or more of the following foods—meat, fish, milk, and eggs—whereas 1,840,000 did not have any of these foods. Among the urban population 14,970,000 inhabitants ate one or more of those foods, and 2,160,000 ate none. Among the rural population 10,660,000 inhabitants ate one or more of these foods, whereas 5,990,000 ate none. That is, of the urban population, 87 per cent ate meat, fish, milk, or eggs, whereas 13 per cent ate none; of the rural population 49 per cent ate these foods, whereas 51 per cent ate none.

In 1960, 21,040,000 inhabitants of one year of age or more wore shoes, 7,910,000 wore sandals, and 4,830,000 went barefoot. That is, 12,740,000 did not wear shoes. Of the urban population, 14,450,000 wore shoes, and 2,680,000 did not. Of the rural population, 6,590,000 wore shoes, and 10,060,000 did not. Thus, 84 per cent of the urban population wore shoes and 16 per cent did not, whereas of the rural population only 40 per cent wore shoes and 60 per cent did not.

The statistical analysis, then, reveals that illiteracy, not eating wheat bread, meat, fish, milk, and eggs, and going barefoot are more usual in rural life. They also occur in the cities, but not to the same extent.

Analysis of the same data also reveals that those who do not eat wheat bread are often those who do not drink milk. Those who do not drink milk are often those who do not wear shoes, those who are illiterate, those who do not eat wheat bread, and so on. There is a kind of integral marginality. The population which is marginal in terms of one factor is highly likely to be marginal in terms of all the others. Thus there is an immense number of Mexicans who have nothing of nothing.[2]

Despite the fact that the percentage of marginal population has decreased in the past fifty years—this demonstrates a process of national integration—the marginal population has increased in absolute numbers, and should present trends continue, it will increase in the future.

We should note that certain indicators of marginality have varied relatively. For instance, the rural population constituted 71.3 per cent of the total population in 1910, 69 per cent in 1921, 66.5 per cent in 1930, 64.9 per cent in 1940, 57.4 per cent in 1950, and 49.0 per cent in 1960. The illiterate population (aged eleven or over) was 75.3 per cent of the total age group in 1910, 65.7 per cent in 1921, and 61.5 per cent in 1930. After 1910 the censuses registered illiteracy in the population aged six or over. In 1960 the illiterate population aged ten or over constituted only 33.49 per cent (see Table 16).

These data show significant integration of the country in the course of the Mexican Revolution. Unfortunately, it is difficult to find other data which would allow us to establish historical theories of that magnitude. Limiting ourselves, therefore, to a shorter period (1930 to 1960 and in some instances 1940 to 1960), we find a similar process of integration and development through other indicators. The illiterate population aged six and over was 66.6 per cent of the total in 1930, 58.3 per cent in 1940, 44.1 per cent in 1950, and 37.8 per cent in 1960. The school-aged population between six and fourteen years old which did not receive schooling constituted

2. Isabel H. de Pozas and Julio de la Fuente, "El problema indígena y las estadísticas," *Acción Indigenista* (Mexico: Instituto Nacional Indigenista, December 1957).

48.7 per cent of that age group in 1930, 54.7 per cent in 1940, 49.5 per cent in 1950, and 36.6 per cent in 1960. The population which does not eat wheat bread constituted 56.5 per cent of the population of one year of age or over in 1940, 45.6 per cent in 1950, and 31.4 per cent in 1960. The population which did not wear shoes constituted 51.5 per cent in 1940, 45.7 per cent in 1950, and 37.7 per cent in 1960 (population of one year of age or over).

From analysis of these figures and their relative values we can conclude that both the Mexican Revolution and the economic development of the country coincide with a process of national integration, homogenization of the population, and a relative decrease in marginality in its various aspects. On this basis we can derive very optimistic conclusions.

Some other facts come to light, nonetheless, about the magnitude of the marginal population in absolute figures and general trends. The rural population was 10,810,000 in 1910; 9,870,000 in 1921; 11,010,000 in 1930; 12,760,000 in 1940; 14,810,000 in 1950; and 17,220,000 in 1960. The illiterate population aged eleven or over was 7,820,000 in 1910; 6,970,000 in 1921; 7,220,000 in 1930; and 7,980,000 in 1960.[3] The illiterate population aged six or over was 9,020,000 in 1930; 9,450,000 in 1940; 9,270,000 in 1950; and 10,570,000 in 1960. The school-aged population between six and fourteen years old which received no schooling was 1,690,000 in 1930; 2,550,000 in 1940; 2,970,000 in 1950; and 3,120,000 in 1960. The population which did not eat wheat bread was 10,800,000 in 1940; 11,380,000 in 1950; 10,620,000 in 1960. The population which did not wear shoes was 9,850,000 in 1940; 11,410,000 in 1950; and 12,740,000 in 1960.

Thus, each census in the past fifty years has shown Mexico's marginal population to have increased or remained numerically unchanged. The magnitude of the problem of the mar-

3. This last census includes the population ten years of age and over.

ginal population in 1970 will be as follows: the illiterate
population will be 10,700,000 (± 660,000); the school-aged
population receiving no schooling, 3,650,000 (± 360,000);
the population which does not eat wheat bread, 10,600,000
(± 940,000); and the population not wearing shoes, 14,130,-
000 (± 120,000). Should the same trends be maintained, Mexico in 1970 will have an illiterate population of about the
same size as it had in 1960. It will have a school-aged population (between six and fourteen years old) not attending school
larger than it had in 1960. It will have a population which
does not eat wheat bread about the same size as in 1960.
And it will have a population that does not wear shoes larger
than it had in 1960.

The above facts and trends lead to a pessimistic interpretation of the social process. Yet, they must be related not only
to the problem of integrating the marginal population (a problem that, from the analysis in terms of relative figures, is
clearly difficult to solve) but also to the absolute numerical
growth of the population which does not participate in development. The linear growth or stagnation of the marginal population occurs along with an exponential growth of the general population and of the population participating in development. The rate of increase of the participant population is
far greater than that of the general population and, of course,
than that of the marginal population. For example, the total
population was 15,160,000 in 1910; 14,330,000 in 1921;
16,550,000 in 1930; 19,650,000 in 1940; 25,790,000 in
1950; and 34,920,000 in 1960. The urban population was
4,350,000 in 1910; 4,470,000 in 1921; 5,540,000 in 1930;
6,900,000 in 1940; 10,980,000 in 1950; and 17,700,000 in
1960. The literate population aged eleven or over was 2,-
990,000 in 1910; 3,560,000 in 1921; 4,530,000 in 1930;
15,850,000 in 1960 (aged ten or over). The literate population aged six or over was 4,530,000 in 1930; 6,770,000 in
1940; 11,770,000 in 1950; and 17,410,000 in 1960. The
population which ate wheat bread was 8,320,000 in 1940;

13,590,000 in 1950; and 23,160,000 in 1960. The population wearing shoes was 9,260,000 in 1940; 10,770,000 in 1950; and 21,040,000 in 1960. The population aged six through fourteen attending school was 1,790,300 in 1930; 2,110,000 in 1940; 3,030,000 in 1950; and 5,400,000 in 1960. These data explain the relative decrease of the marginal population. Despite the fact that in absolute figures it has remained unchanged or even grown, the population participating in development has increased simultaneously and at a far higher rate.

The following chart shows the rates of growth of the marginal and participant population and clarifies their general dynamics and trends from a different perspective.

Thus we see that the rates of growth of the participant pop-

RATES OF GROWTH OF THE MARGINAL AND PARTICIPANT POPULATION (1910–60)

Rates of growth of the population	1910–21	1921–30	1930–40	1940–50	1950–60
Total	−5.44	15.47	18.73	31.22	35.40
Rural	−8.71	11.57	15.84	16.07	16.27
Urban	2.69	24.07	24.47	59.25	61.19
Illiterate (11 years old or over)	−10.78	3.58	3.49	3.49	3.49 *
Literate (11 years old or over)	19.14	26.93	83.41	83.41	83.41 *
Illiterate (6 years old or over)			4.79	−1.87	14.02
Literate (6 years old or over)			49.62	73.79	48.00
Do not eat bread				5.44	−6.72
Eat bread				63.33	70.38
Do not wear shoes				15.79	11.66
Wear shoes				16.28	95.28
Do not receive schooling			50.55	16.54	4.86
Receive schooling			18.33	43.41	78.16

* Eleven years of age or over (1910, 1921, 1930) and ten years of age or over (1960). From 1930 to 1960 an average rate is considered.

ulation, considered by decades, are increasingly higher among the urban population (1910–60), the literate population aged eleven or over (1910–30), the literate population aged six or over (1930–60), the population eating wheat bread (1930–60), the population wearing shoes (1940–60), and the population receiving schooling (1930–60). The rate of growth of the marginal population is always lower (and sometimes many times lower) than the rate of growth of the participant population, except for the population receiving no schooling during the period 1930–40.

Furthermore, the rates of growth of the marginal population are negative—that is, they presuppose an absolute decrease of the marginal population—only during the period of the Revolution when the Civil War made large inroads into the rural and illiterate population (1940–50); and during the decade 1950–60, for the population not eating wheat bread.

The rates of growth of the marginal population exhibit a trend to increase in the case of the rural population (1910–60) and in that of the illiterate population (1940–60); they exhibit a trend to decrease among the illiterate population (1921–40); the population not eating wheat bread (1940–60); the population not wearing shoes (1940–60); and the population receiving no schooling (1930–60).

These rates of growth reveal the processes of national integration and economic and social participation during different decades, and demonstrate that decade by decade the rate of growth of the participant population is increasingly greater. They also reveal that the rates of growth of the marginal population are decreasing in most cases (among the major exceptions is the rural population, which has a growing rate). Finally, these data reveal that the rate of growth of the participant population is higher than that of the marginal population. Nonetheless, the absolute number of marginal Mexicans did not decrease for the illiterate population in 1940–50 or for the population not eating wheat bread in 1950–60.

The integration of the country, the relative decrease of the marginal population, and the absolute increase of the participant population amount to an absolute increase of the marginal population. That is, if the percentage of marginal population in Mexico today, for example, is smaller, in absolute figures there is nonetheless a greater number of marginal Mexicans. They constitute a national economic, cultural, and political problem of magnitude. Our integral marginal population, which lacks all the minimum products of development, is the most vigorous challenge to the development of the nation and of the national policy. It is one part of a social structure which is divided into two large sectors, the one of Mexicans who participate in development and the other of those who are marginal in terms of development. Here we see the internal dynamics of inequality, one of the major national problems.

Marginality and Plural Society

The dual or plural society in Mexico is made up of the Ladinos and Indians. The Indians constitute the super-marginal population; they almost have the attributes of a colonial society. The division between the two Mexicos—participant and marginal, haves and have-nots—scarcely indicates the existence of a plural society, but reveals the residue of a colonial society. The relationships between the Ladinos and the Indians exemplify far more precisely the problems of plural society and internal colonialism. Unfortunately, when we analyzed these phenomena we found very few correlations. For the analysis of plural society we have a single indicator, language. For the analysis of internal colonialism, we have only indirect indicators, which reveal the existence of semi-colonial discrimination and exploitation.

The percentage of Mexicans aged five or over who speak no Spanish but an indigenous language or dialect was 8.4 per cent in 1930; 3.8 per cent in 1940; 3.6 per cent in 1950; 3.8

per cent in 1960. In absolute numbers, these figures are: 1,-190,000 in 1930; 1,240,000 in 1940; 800,000 in 1950; and 1,104,000 in 1960.

The population which speaks an indigenous language or dialect, also "gibbers" some Spanish and is predominately Indian in culture. It is not integrated with the national culture, and was of these percentages: 7.6 per cent in 1930; 7.5 per cent in 1940; 7.6 per cent in 1950; and 6.4 per cent in 1960. In absolute numbers, the figures are: 1,070,000 in 1930; 1,-250,000 in 1940; 1,650,000 in 1950; and 1,930,000 in 1960.

The monolingual and bilingual indigenous population is in simple, conservative terms, the indigenous population which is not integrated with the national culture. Its percentage of the total population aged five and over has varied as follows: 16 per cent in 1930; 14.8 per cent in 1940; 11.2 per cent in 1950; and 10 per cent in 1960. In absolute numbers the figures are: 2,250,000 in 1930; 2,490,000 in 1940; 2,450,000 in 1950; and 3,030,000 in 1960.

Meanwhile, the population which represents the national culture constituted 83.9 per cent of the total aged five and over in 1930; 85.1 per cent in 1940; 88.8 per cent in 1950; and 90 per cent in 1960. In absolute figures, 11,790,000 people in 1930; 14,300,000 in 1940; 19,370,000 in 1950; and 25,970,000 in 1960 (see Table 16).

We should note that the percentage of monolingual indigenous population decreased from 1930 to 1950, and increased from 1950 to 1960. The total of the monolingual indigenous population remains practically the same during those thirty years. In absolute figures it decreased only between 1940 and 1950, but it increased from 1950 to 1960; in 1960 it was practically identical to what it had been in 1930.

The percentage of the bilingual indigenous population remained practically unchanged from 1930 to 1950 and decreased between 1950 and 1960. In absolute figures, there was a sustained increase decade by decade throughout the period.

The percentage of the monolingual and bilingual population—that is, the total indigenous population—decreased in every decade throughout the period 1930–60. In absolute figures, it increased from 1930 to 1940, decreased from 1940 to 1950, and increased again in 1960.

The population representing the national culture increased in absolute terms, both by decades and throughout the whole period. The character of this change will become evident if we analyze the rates of growth of the national population and those of the indigenous population, as shown in the following chart.

RATES OF GROWTH OF THE NATIONAL AND INDIGENOUS POPULATION (1930–40)

Rates of growth of the population	1930–40	1940–50	1950–60
Total	18.73	31.22	35.40
Rural	15.84	16.07	16.27
Monolingual	4.36	−35.72	26.47
Bilingual	17.66	31.79	16.52
Monolingual-bilingual	10.66	− 1.73	23.80
National culture	18.42	35.49	34.04

These figures lead us to several conclusions. For the monolingual population and the total of the monolingual and bilingual populations, the rates are only negative—and therefore imply an absolute decrease—between 1940 and 1950. It is unlikely that during that decade there was a decrease in birth rates or an increase in death rates among the Indians, so it seems that this is the only decade in which the absolute number of Indians who learned Spanish and became integrated with the national culture increased. Or there may have been an underestimation of the monolingual population in the 1950 census. Both changes may also have taken place simultaneously. During 1940–50 the bilingual population and the national population reached their highest rates of growth. This is particularly significant with respect to the bilingual population, insofar as it seems to grow at the expense of the monolingual population, because it indicates that large groups of Indians learned Spanish and still maintained their own languages and dialects. Among the rural population, in the decade from 1950 to 1960, the monolingual group grew at a much faster rate, the monolingual-bilingual group grew at a faster rate, and the bilingual group had the same rate of growth as did the total rural population.

All these data point to a very simple conclusion: although the percentage of Indians decreased between 1930 and 1960, the absolute number of Indians increased. The situation is particularly notable during 1950–60, for which the censuses registered both a relative and an absolute increase of monolingual population, an absolute increase of the bilingual population, an absolute increase of the Indian population generally, and an extremely high rate of growth among the monolingual and Indian population generally. It is possible that the 1950 census underestimated the size of the indigenous population. This would imply that the condition and evolution of the Indian problem in the past decade is not as serious as it seems—that the Indian problem did not become greater, but rather that there was an improvement in the census procedures. Even so, we cannot deny another incontrovertible fact: the solution to the Indian problem, although that was one of the major goals of the Mexican Revolution and although Mexico has distinguished students of anthropology, is still a problem of national scope. It is true that there has been a decrease in the percentage of Indians in the total population. But it is no less true that in absolute figures the number of Mexicans who do not belong to the national culture has increased from 2 to 3 million between 1930 and 1960. The Indian problem, therefore, far from being lesser, is in absolute terms greater by one-third than it was in 1930. Should the same trend be maintained, in 1970 there will be a monolingual population of 910,000 ($\pm$ 20,000) and an Indian population (monolingual-bilingual) of 3,130,000—that is, the situation will be approximately the same as it is now.

All these estimates are conservative; they are based only upon census data and linguistic criteria. The facts reach far beyond. As the anthropologists Isabel H. de Pozas and Julio de la Fuente noted: "It is frequently found that census data regarding language highly differ from reality, and that the decrease of the monolingual Indian population is only apparent, since Indians who hardly speak a few words of Spanish are registered as speaking that language." Using the linguistic criterion, the Indian population was 10 per cent of the total in 1960; using other indicators, such as the awareness of belonging to a community which is different and isolated from the national culture or to the tribal or pre-Hispanic spiritual and material culture,[4] we find that the percentage of Indians is between 20 and 25 per cent, and thus numbers between 6 and 7.5 million.[5]

This problem is far more significant and pervasive than has been previously thought. It is not merely an Indian problem, but a problem of national structure. As such it explains not only the behavior and condition of the Indians, but also that of Mexicans generally, and with far greater precision than a simple analysis of the nation's class structure.

PLURAL SOCIETY AND INTERNAL COLONIALISM

The ideology of liberalism, which considers all men to be equal before the law, is a great advance from the racism prevailing in colonial times. Similarly, the ideology of the Revolution is a no less important advance over the social Darwinist and racist ideas of *porfirismo*. Today the Indian problem is approached as a cultural problem. No Mexican scholar or ruler believes that this is an inborn, racial problem. Social and political mobility in Mexico has allowed Indians to occupy the highest positions and to achieve the highest social status in Mexican society since Independence, and particularly since

4. A. Caso, "Definición del indio y de lo indio," *Indigenismo* (Mexico: Instituto Nacional Indigenista), 1958.
5. *Ibid.*

the Revolution. Even national history and its pantheon of heroes have viewed Cuauhtémoc, the leader of the resistance against the Spaniards, and Juárez, the Indian President and builder of modern Mexico, with highest regard. The same equality has been recorded at national and local levels by anthropologists. Indians who participate in the national culture are able to achieve the same status as mestizos or whites in economic, political, and interpersonal and family relationships. An Indian participating in the national culture is in no way an object of racial discrimination. He may feel the consequences of discrimination because of his economic status, his occupational role, or his political role. But that is all. For these reasons, Mexican anthropology views the Indian problem as a cultural problem. This affirmation represents an ideological advance over the racism prevailing in the social sciences of the Porfirian period. From a scientific point of view, the statement corresponds to reality. Yet it does not explain all the basic characteristics of this reality.

The Indian problem is essentially one of internal colonialism. The Indian communities are Mexico's internal colonies. The Indian community is a colony within the national territory, and it has the characteristics of a colonized society. This fact has not been recognized by the nation. Resistance has been multiple and will be powerful. The habit of thinking of colonialism as an international phenomenon has caused people to overlook internal colonialism. The habit of viewing Mexico as an ex-colony or a semi-colony of foreign powers, and of seeing Mexicans generally as subjected to foreign colonization, has blocked the development of the view that Mexicans are colonizers and colonized. The past and present national struggle for independence is a factor in this problem, and it has made the men involved in this struggle national heroes. Another fact which has contributed to obscuring the situation is that both internal and international colonialism manifest their more extreme characteristics in typically colonial regions far from the metropolis. Although in the city there are no colonialist prejudices or struggles, but rather democratic and egalitarian styles of life, quite the opposite obtains in the outlying areas. Here we find prejudice, discrimination, colonial types of exploitation, dictatorial forms, and the separation of a dominant population, with a specific race and culture, from a dominated population, with a different race and culture. This is what occurs in Mexico. In the conflict areas, in those regions in which both Indians and Ladinos live, we find prejudice, discrimination, colonial types of exploitation, dictatorial forms, and the racial cultural alignment of dominant and dominated populations. From a social point of view, the most striking difference from international colonialism is the fact that a few members of the Indian communities can physically and culturally escape from these internal colonies. They can go to the cities and find a job, and they have the same chances of mobility as the members of the lower classes who have no Indian cultural background. Yet this mobility has limitations and does not end internal colonialism. Internal colonialism exists wherever Indian communities are found. Research done by Mexican anthropologists reveals the existence of a way of life that corresponds to that of the historical definition of colonialism. This is true among the Amuzgos, Coras, Cuicatecos, Chatinos, Chinantecos, Choles, Huaxtecos, Huaves, Huicholes, Mayas, Mayos, Mazahuas, Mazatecos, Nahoas, Mixes, Mixtecos, Otomíes, Popolocas, Tarahumaras, Tarascos, Tepehuanos, Tlapanecos, Tojolabales, Totonacas, Tzeltales, Tzotziles, Yaquis, and Zapotecos—that is, among several million Mexicans.

One form assumed by internal colonialism is when what anthropologists call the "ruling center" or "metropolis" (San Cristóbal, Tlaxiaco, Huauchinango, Sochiapan, Mitla, Ojitlán, Zacapoaxtla) exercises a monopoly over Indian commerce and credit, with relationships of exchange unfavorable to the Indian communities. This is manifest in a permanent decapitalization of the Indians at the lowest levels. The commercial monopoly isolates the Indian community from any other center or market, promoting monoculture and dependence.

Another form of internal colonialism is the exploitation of the Indian population by the different social classes of the Ladino population. This exploitation, as is the case in all colonies of modern history, is a combination of feudalism, capitalism, slavery, forced and salaried labor, share farming and peonage, and demand for free services. The despoliation of Indian lands performed the same two functions it fulfilled in the colonies: it deprived the Indians of their land, and it transformed them into peons or salaried workers. The exploitation of one population by another manifested itself in different salaries for the same jobs (in mines, sugar refineries, coffee plantations); in the over-all exploitation of Indian craftsmen (workers with wool, *ixtle,* palm, willow, ceramics); social, verbal, and dress discriminations; and, as we shall see, juridical, political, and trade-union discriminations. Such discrimination demonstrated colonialist attitudes on the part of local and even of federal functionaries, and of course on the part of the Ladino leaders of political organizations.

Still another form of internal colonialism is shown by cultural differences and differences in standards of living according to whether the population is Ladino or Indian. Observable differences, however, are not sharply divided between people speaking Indian languages and those who do not, because a large sector of the nearby non-Indian peasant population has standards of living as low as those of the Indian populations.[6]

6. Cf. Julio de la Fuente, "Población Indígena" (unpublished); Alejandro D. Marroquín, "Problemas Económicos de las Comunidades Indígenas de México" (mimeographed course program), Mexico, 1956; Miguel O. de Mendizábal, "Los problemas indígenas y su más urgente tratamiento," *Obras Completas IV* (Mexico, 1946); Moisés T. de la Peña, "Panorama de la Economía Indígena de México," *Primer Congreso Indígena Interamericano* (Pátzcuaro, 1946); Jorge A. Vivó, "Aspectos Económicos Fundamentales del Problema Indígena," *Revista América Indígena,* Vol. III, No. 1, January 1947; Gonzalo Aguirre Beltrán and Ricardo Pozas, *Instituciones Indígenas en el México Actual* (Mexico: Instituto Nacional Indigenista, 1954).

Indian communities have the following characteristics: a predominantly subsistence economy, with minimal money and capitalization; lands unsuitable for crops or of low quality, unfit for agriculture because of hilly terrain, or of good quality but in isolated locations; deficient crop-growing and cattle-breeding because of low quality seeds and inferior animals smaller than the average of their kind and pre-Hispanic or colonial techniques of land exploitation; a low level of productivity; standards of living lower than those of peasants in non-Indian areas, exemplified by poor health, high rates of mortality, including infant mortality, illiteracy and the presence of rickets; lack of facilities and resources, such as schools, hospitals, water, and electricity; promotion of alcoholism and promotion of prostitution by hookers and Ladinos; aggressiveness among communities, which may be overt, or expressed through games or dreams; magic-religious culture; economic manipulation through the imposition of taxes and a status-bound economy; and, as we shall see, political manipulation.

All these conditions are basic to colonial structure and are found in the definitions and explanations of colonialism from Montesquieu to Myrdal and Fanon. They are also mentioned in the works of foreign writers and the anthropologists of Mexico. Together they demonstrate the existence of internal colonialism, which is characteristic of those regions where Indians and Ladinos coexist. Internal colonialism is *also* characteristic of the *national society,* in which there is a continuum of colonialism from groups exhibiting the entire range of colonial characteristics to regions and groups in which only traces are visible. Internal colonialism affects an estimated 3 million Indians using the criterion of language, 7 million using the criterion of culture, and almost 12 million according to the Index of Contemporary Indocolonial Culture created by Whetten.[7] In fact, internal colonialism encompasses the whole mar-

7. Cf. Nathan L. Whetten, "México Rural," *Problemas Agrícolas e Industriales de México,* Vol. V, No. 2 (Mexico, 1953), pp. 245 ff.

ginal population and penetrates the entire culture, society, and polity of Mexico in different ways and intensities, depending on the groups and regions.

The Indian problem is one of national scope; it defines the nation itself. It is the problem not of a small sector, but of many millions of Mexicans who do not share in the national culture and also of those who do participate in the national culture. The concept of internal colonialism explains the national structure as a whole better than the concept of social classes in a pre-industrial society, in terms of ideology, political affiliation, and class consciousness.

MARGINALITY, PLURAL SOCIETY, AND THE POLITY

Social and cultural marginality are obviously related to political marginality; they mutually influence each other. In order to understand the political structure of Mexico, one must bear in mind that a large sector of the population is marginal with respect to the polity. To put it another way, marginal people are political objects for those who participate in the polity. They are not political citizens in terms of information, consciousness, organization, or action.

We shall examine two indicators of this political marginality—information and voting—postponing an analysis of membership in parties and trade unions.

The three main cities of Mexico, which in 1964 had approximately 19 per cent of the population, have 57 per cent of the total number of copies of newspapers. Mexico City, which has 15 per cent of the population, has 48 per cent of the copies of newspapers. In other words, of a total of 4.2 million copies of newspapers for the country as a whole, 2.4 million were sold in Mexico City, Guadalajara, and Monterrey. Mexico City alone originates 2 million copies. The rest of the country, with 81 per cent of the population, has 43 per cent of the newspapers. And although it is true that the large newspapers of the capital city—*Excélsior* and *Ultimas No-*

ticias, Novedades, La Prensa, El Universal, El Sol (morning and evening editions), and *El Heraldo*—circulate in the interior, their provincial circulation is, as an average, one-fourth of the total.

Circulation is for the most part limited to the urban population, so that 50 per cent or more of the population lacks the basic national and international information that would enable them to be politically aware. Although some may agree with those who have said that people are almost better off without the kind of newspapers Mexico has, the truth is that isolation, lack of communication, and absence of the ills that accompany modern alienation only encourage the kind of alienation and political ignorance characteristic of a closed, traditional, and peasant—even archaic—society. Thus the problem of the struggle for political knowledge comes to rest at a far lower and more rudimentary level.

The problem of marginality in disseminating journalistic information is even more serious than we might infer. If we hypothesize that each copy of a newspaper reaches at least one family, of the total of 8 million families in Mexico in 1964, only 4.2 million had a newspaper, and 3.8 million did not; that is, 52.5 per cent had a newspaper, and 47.5 per cent did not. The percentages, of course, vary from one area to another; in the highly urbanized Federal District there was an average of five newspapers for every three families, whereas in Campeche, Hidalgo, Oaxaca, and Zacatecas, for example, more than 90 per cent of the families had no newspaper.

Voting abstention is a phenomenon characteristic of all democratic regimes. There is always a group of non-voting citizens, be it for lack of interest, because of sickness, or as a form of protest. The percentage of voting population with respect to the total national population is nonetheless lower in Mexico than that of other more advanced countries. In 1917, 5 per cent of the Mexican population voted, whereas of the United States population in the presidential elections of 1916, for example, 18 per cent voted. In 1920, in Mexico and the

United States, respectively, 8 per cent and 25 per cent voted. In 1924 and 1928, 11 per cent voted in Mexico, and 25 and 31 per cent voted in the United States. In 1929, 1934, and 1940, 13 per cent voted in Mexico, and in 1932, 1936, and 1940, 32, 36, and 38 per cent, respectively, voted in the United States. In Mexico in 1946, 1952, and 1958, 10, 13, and 23 per cent, respectively, voted, and in the United States, in 1948, 1952, and 1956, 33, 40, and 37 per cent voted. In the Mexican presidential elections of 1958, the percentage of votes increased considerably owing to the granting of voting rights to women (in the United States women were granted voting rights in 1920).

These data provide only a crude idea of voting marginality. A more accurate estimate, which eliminates the distortion caused by including the population under voting age, would be based on the figures for the population twenty years of age and over. The Constitution specifies that voting rights are acquired at age twenty-one, age eighteen for married persons. Taking as a basis the male population twenty years of age and over, which is enumerated by the censuses, we can estimate fairly accurately the population which has voting rights and does not vote, and thus is marginal in terms of the basic act of the democratic process. Using these figures, we note that marginality decreased throughout the revolutionary period. In the 1917 election, approximately 75 per cent of the citizens did not vote; in 1920, 65 per cent did not vote; in 1924, 56 per cent; in 1928, 57 per cent; in 1929, 47 per cent; in 1933, 44 per cent; in 1940, 42 per cent; in 1946, 58 per cent; and in 1952, 42 per cent. In the elections of 1958 and 1964, the point of reference must be changed because women gained the vote. Women's lack of voting rights had previously been the legal justification of the political marginality of 50 per cent of the population. Thus we take as a base the total number of men and women. Here we find that political participation began with far lower percentages. Indeed, from this point of view, political marginality was 88 per cent in 1917; 83 per cent in 1920; 79 per cent in 1924; 80 per cent in 1928; 75 per cent in 1929; 74 per cent in 1934; 72 per cent in 1940; 79 per cent in 1946; 72 per cent in 1952; 51 per cent in 1958; and 46 per cent in 1964 (see Table 18).[8]

In 1917, seven out of ten citizens did not vote, but in 1964 only five out of ten citizens did not vote. Bearing in mind the fact that women did not vote until 1958, we find that of the potential voters, men and women, in 1947, only one out of ten actually voted, whereas in 1964, five out of ten did. Although these data may seem encouraging, there are other considerations which reduce optimism, such as the level of information and political consciousness in voting. Without taking these elements into account, the absolute figures reveal that although marginality tended to decrease—a trend which became reinforced when women became a part of the voting population—the total number of non-voting citizens stood at approximately 2 million since the 1917 elections and increased to 3 million and 2.5 million in the elections of 1946 and 1952, respectively. But if we count not only the male population but the total—that is, non-voting men and women twenty years of age and over—marginality increased from 6 million in 1917 to 9 million in 1946 and 1952, and decreased with the women's vote to a little more than 7.5 million in 1958 and to 8 million in the presidential elections of 1964.

The ruling class cannot ignore the fact that democratization is the basic and indispensable prerequisite of development. It must remember that possibilities for democracy have increased insofar as per capita income, urbanization, and literacy have increased; that there remain serious obstacles such as the plural society and that the foremost goal must be one of national integration; that the pre-fascist condition of those regions which have lost status calls for special plans for their development; that those culturally traditionalist areas, with a

8. For a more accurate computation of marginality in the 1964 elections, compare Table 30.

considerable marginal population, no political rights, no political freedom, no functional political organizations, are the very sources of violence, and make the special effort necessary for democratization and political representation. There must be legislative, political, and economic reforms in order to ensure the integration of the marginal strata into full economic and political citizenship. Emphasis must be laid on the unity of the Mexican secular political culture, and on the constitutional principle that political alignment must not be linked to religious faith. There must be a redistribution of income and popular pressures, and *national* discipline must be organized and maintained. The majority party must be maintained and democratized. Simultaneously, there must be an intensification of democratic interplay among the remaining parties. This would set the internal democratization of the majority party as a primary goal, and it would earn the respect of, and serve to encourage, the opposition parties. It would compel the immediate revision of the electoral law. The democratization of the party must be linked to the democratization of trade unions and to the reform of many labor laws and institutions. Sustained economic development is the minimum requirement for a guaranteed public peace.

In order to achieve all of these goals, the correct personal style of the President, planning of a technical character, and democratization of the party are indispensable prerequisites. Mexico is a country in which the President holds an extraordinary amount of power; this is a time when technical plans must not be distrusted or used demagogically; and we have arrived at a stage where popular pressures must be channeled to unify the country, to ensure the continuity and acceleration of development, and to allow for free expression and organization of dissent to gain peaceful and democratic solution of conflicts.

Women's suffrage represents an obvious advance. Of the total number of citizens, men and women, there are more than 7.5 million non-voters. Absolute voting marginality decreased only in the elections of 1946 and 1952, in which there were 9 million and 9.4 million non-voting men and women, respectively. Despite the achievement of high rates of development, which in relative terms reduced political marginality, there has not been a decrease of the socially marginal population. Today there are more non-voting citizens and, insofar as voting is representative of political participation, more politically marginal citizens.

Depending on which sets of data are used, we might make either a sympathetic or a critical demagogic interpretation. Yet if we carefully examine the meaning of the figures, we note that the two following statements are entirely compatible.

First, Mexico has undergone cultural and political development; it has become integrated as a nation and its social and political culture has become more homogeneous than it was in the past. The percentage and number of voting citizens rose from 12 per cent in 1917 to 54 per cent in 1964—from 812,928 in 1917 to 9,400,000 in 1964.

Yet, second, the rate of growth of the national population has been so high that today the absolute number of marginal people—socially, culturally, and politically—is greater than in the past.

It is possible to take either point of view. The first emphasizes the resolution of problems; the second indicates the magnitude of the problems to be solved. Among the problems to be solved are the fact that almost 4 million families do not have access to political information; that more than 50 per cent of the total population does not have access to direct national political information, but instead has only local or verbal information (this group also largely lacks national consciousness); that in the last presidential elections approximately 8 million citizens who should have voted did not do so, and that an even larger number did not vote in the elections for deputies and in those for other representative positions, which raises the percentage of non-voters to about 50 per cent. These are straightforward facts which do not lend themselves even slightly to a demagogic interpretation. They indicate the existence of a social structure in which at least 50 per cent of the population is marginal with respect to a democratic polity.[9]

These figures may be subjected to a rigorous criticism. The indicators we used are the number of newspapers and of votes, which should indicate the level of information and of actual voting. The statistics we used are those provided by official organizations, publications, and archives. How much truth is there in them all? How much objective information remains hidden? What of the absence of a dialogue in which opposing views might be considered? It is not even necessary to consider these questions in order to know that in Mexico, a large part of the population is structurally marginal with respect to income, culture, information, and power. Using the official statistics alone, the existence of political marginality affecting the whole national society is readily demonstrated.

INTERNAL COLONIALISM, PLURAL SOCIETY,
AND THE POLITY

No serious and systematic studies have been made of the political manipulations of the citizens of Mexico. In the press and in everyday experience, through public debates in which truth, passion, and demagogy are mixed, we vaguely apprehend that there is such a thing as automatic voting, collective voting. We also know that electoral fraud exists—that votes are sold, that ready-made votes are fabricated, and that the dead "vote." Yet we do not know to what extent these phenomena are generalized or localized: nor do we know whether they occur at certain times rather than at others.

It is very difficult to provide statistical information on electoral fraud or to compile a stratified analysis of fraud in terms of regions, cultures, groups, or classes. Analysis of political

9. To study electoral marginality by district, compare Tables 29, 30, 31, and 32.

phenomena generally presents considerable obstacles, and the sort of research that would enable us to provide reliable generalizations is even more difficult. We shall deal with the problem indirectly through the analysis of political opposition in Mexico, of how and where it is manifested. Here we shall limit ourselves to sketching the form in which certain citizens are manipulated by certain others in a typically plural society, the form in which Indians and Ladinos often "intersect" within the polity. The effects on the national consciousness and national culture as a whole may serve to clarify the political condition of Mexicans and to encourage more precise and general studies in the future.

Over the indigenous people of Mexico there are two types of authorities, traditional authorities and constitutional authorities.[10] The traditional authorities are the indigenous government, which is not recognized by the constitutional system; the constitutional authority is the "municipal governments" [11] —that is, "colonial and contemporary systems." [12] Under certain circumstances, the duality is more complex: there are chiefs of clan, *caciques,* and "juridical" authorities.[13] Somewhat further from the Indian political consciousness is the State government; further still, the government of Mexico City, which supports the boarding school system,[14] sends attorneys and teachers, soldiers, and even airplanes. Yet among these and many more authorities (governors, mayors, constables, chiefs of police), two main kinds may be

10. Alfonso Fabila, *Los huicholes de Jalisco* (Mexico: Instituto Nacional Indigenista, 1959), p. 112.
11. Gonzalo Aguirre Beltrán, *Formas de Gobierno Indígena* (Mexico: Imprenta Universitaria, 1953), pp. 83–92.
12. F. Cámara Barbachano, *Cambios culturales entre los indios tzeltales del Alto Chiapas: Estudio comparativo de las instituciones religiosas y políticas de los municipios de Tenejape y Oxchua* (Mexico: Escuela Nacional de Antropología, 1948), p. 246.
13. Cf. Calixta Guiteras Holmes, "Organización social de Tzeltales y Tzotziles," *América Indígena,* Vol. III, No. 1 (Mexico, 1948), pp. 45–48.
14. Francisco M. Plancarte, *El problema indígena Tarahumara* (Mexico: Instituto Nacional Indigenista, 1954), p. 34.

distinguished: those of the Indians and those of the mestizos. The former are bound by tradition, the latter take power from the law.

The traditional authorities are elected democratically, on the basis of merit, in a series of meetings which sometimes go on for days. The Tarahumara Indians fulfil their political careers with abnegation, honesty, loyalty, and intelligence, up to the position of governor, and finally they become relatively retired. Authorities receive no pay. The people elect them "for their abnegated, honest, loyal and intelligent services to the community. . . ." [15] This was the case in Sayula, where the people chose their traditional authorities from among the most outstanding citizens,[16] and is the case for the traditional authorities of Tarahumara where "every Tarahumara citizen is a potential functionary, the elections depending upon the reputation enjoyed within the community." [17] The elections are direct, and a majority vote carries. The government holds assemblies, tribal meetings, trials; it debates possible courses of action regarding cases for which there are no juridical records; it revokes power when it is not efficiently or honestly exercised; it holds meetings among the chiefs, who pledge loyalty and honesty and discuss the people's problems; it manages plebiscites.

When reading the works of anthropologists on the subject of the traditional Indian government, one cannot help but think that they must have been influenced by the image of the noble savage. The system of government they describe is idealistic. Only when we view the complete picture of the Indian polity can we understand that this primitive democracy has a functional character. Indeed, it serves to defend the tribes and communities, which have hardly any stratification, as a whole against Ladino harassment. In the more stratified regions that

15. Alfonso Fabila, *op. cit.*, pp. 109–12.
16. Calixta Guiteras Holmes, *Sayula* (Mexico: Sociedad Mexicana de Geografía y Estadística, 1952), p. 112.
17. Wendell Clark Bennett and Robert M. Zingg, *The Tarahumara, An Indian Tribe of Northern Mexico* (Chicago, Ill.: The University of Chicago Press, 1935), p. 202.

have Indian *caciques* the situation is different. The Ladino uses the *cacique* as his mediator, consults him regarding decisions, and uses him for political and economic control of the community generally. Yet in both cases the Indians are confronted with formal, constitutional Ladino power and perceive their intermediaries or representatives as a sort of foreign authority.

"Indians do not like to deal with municipal authorities, who are always whites or mestizos. That is why they resolve issues as best they can, only having recourse to municipal presidents and other authorities when they have complaints against a white man." [18] The Yaquis "do not recognize any state but their own. They consider themselves an autonomous nation, yet circumstances—enforced by power, not theory—have brought them to expect a certain amount of interference by Mexican institutions." [19] Constitutional authorities represent whites and mestizos.[20] They are designated by the governor in accordance with the preferences of the whites. When there are elections for these authorities, the results are fabricated by delegates of state power.[21] These elections obviously make no sense: the "constitutional representative" does not even remotely represent the community. The constitutional authorities serve the interests of the Ladinos. The notaries public of the Chamula region represent the interests of the Ladino state.[22] The local authorities, "generally represented by mestizos are for the Tarahumaras the machinery used in order to legalize abuses and send them to jail. . . . There is no other choice but to obey." [23] As to the municipal government, "it would be ridiculous to deny that it is in the hands of the

18. Carlos Basauri, *Monografía de los Tarahumaras* (Mexico: Talleres Gráficos de la Nación, 1929), p. 43.
19. Alfonso Fabila, *Las tribus yaquis de Sonora: Su cultura y anhelada autodeterminación* (Mexico: Primer Congreso Interamericano, Departamento de Asuntos Indígenas, 1940), p. 159.
20. Ricardo Pozas, *Chamula: Un pueblo indio de los Altos de Chiapas* (Mexico: Instituto Nacional Indigenista, 1959).
21. Calixta Guiteras Holmes, *Sayula,* p. 118.
22. Ricardo Pozas, *op. cit.,* p. 152.
23. Francisco M. Plancarte, *op. cit.,* p. 34.

chabones, the sectional presidents and police commissars. This is why the Tarahumaras avoid discussing their problems with the *chabones.*" [24] Among the Tzeltales "a few free municipalities can elect representatives. There are also representatives in the municipal agencies. These important positions are generally for the Ladinos." [25] Among the Yaquis, a few governmental agencies place unconditionally loyal natives at the head of the municipal commissariats. The problem is a simple one: all these authorities are under the jurisdiction and control of the Ladinos. They ignore and humiliate the Indian authorities and inflict all kinds of thefts, attacks, injustices, humiliations, exploitations, military provocations, and acts of violence, ranging from the most arbitrary to the most rational, by motivation ranging from caprice to the desire to sanction the theft of lands or to eliminate native leaders.

There are few anthropological studies, whether descriptive or lacking in detail, that do not record acts of this nature. Indian life is the life of colonized peoples—so much so, that even the public services provided by the central government are acts similar to those exercised by any metropolitan power. In the Indian communities there are educational organizations, small programs for social change, and even Mexican and especially foreign religious groups practicing charity. None of this is foreign to colonial life. The fact that these institutions are producing indirect effects, which establish a foundation for more positive attitudes, and that from their social service, educational, and charitable activities result the indirect effects of acculturation and liberation, are characteristic of colonial development. The roads, the opening of markets, the expansion of the national economy, although less than what Ladino areas have, are setting the pace for change. This situation is similar to that in the old African and Asian colo-

24. Cf. Gonzalo Aguirre Beltrán, *op. cit.,* pp. 83–92.
25. Alfonso Villa Rojas, *Sobre la organización política de los indios tzeltales del Estado de Chiapas* (Mexico: Congreso Indigenista Interamericano, Pátzcuaro, 1940).

nies. In the case of Mexico, this problem is more complex because Mexicans view themselves as revolutionists and anti-colonialists. Mexican schools and Indian communities teach the people about Juárez. Mexican textbooks say that Juárez was Indian, knew no Spanish, and was one of the greatest presidents of Mexico. This is good: the Mexican Indian child differs from the colonial African, who was taught the cult of the conqueror heroes. Yet at the same time it prevents Mexicans from seeing themselves as colonialists; they are able to ignore the fact that all the development programs in the Indian area are politically weak in the metropolis, compared with local interests there. Thus, the colonial exploitation of the Indian communities continues, broken only by occasional acts. *137958*

From contacts between the two governments, the traditional and the constitutional, the Indian and the Ladino, emerge images of man and the polity. The Indian image of the white man and his policy is "They have a system and it is right; their municipal presidents achieve their positions by means of politics, and their judges often sell justice, especially when dealing with us who have no protection from above." [26]

> The Tarahumaras . . . says Plancarte . . . are legally Mexican citizens with all the rights and obligations established by the laws. Yet on the whole they are unaware of their legal position. To them only the members of their group are their people. The rest are *chabochis,* foreign people, who have invaded their territory and brought them innumerable grievances and prejudices. They are robbers who have dispossessed them of their best lands, abused their women, stolen their cattle, and who, in the best of cases, conduct commercial transactions with them in which they always artfully take for themselves more than they give.[27]

In view of this, there is nothing surprising in the Indians' lack of interest in formal, constitutional, and national politics.

26. Gutierre Tibón, *Pinotepa Nacional: Mixtecos, negros y triques* (Mexico: Universidad Nacional, 1961), p. 125.
27. Francisco M. Plancarte, *op. cit.*

These are not their laws, nor their constitution, nor their nation. Their indifference toward politics is due to the fact that their destiny is decided outside of it.[28] "Their abstention in municipal, state, or national elections is total, since these have nothing to do with their interests."[29] There is an explanation for everything: their voting abstention, and the automatic way in which they vote, performing the Ladino "ceremony"; their conformity; their ignorance of "national" politics, of "national" laws; their submission to paternalism when they humbly beg. Under prevailing conditions, they cannot be demanding citizens.

The image of the white man inspires the deepest mistrust: "The efforts of the authorities (when they occur) find no response in the community, due to the great mistrust that the Indians feel toward the mestizos, who have always exploited and humiliated them iniquitously."[30] The Indian himself has "a profound skepticism with respect to peace . . . and has even developed a philosophy of poverty and humility."[31] His world is one of insecurity: "These good and hardworking people suffer the worst of torments, that of insecurity . . ."[32] says Blom about the Lacandones. The self-imposed judgment of the Zapotecas is highly significant: "I am Indian, a worm who finds shelter in the grass: all hands avoid me and all afoot crush me."[33] His reactions to the harassments, dispossessions, and humiliations of the mestizos and their authorities vary: "They are unable to take revenge and remain quiet,"[34] they "submit without a word," "they learn Spanish in order to defend their friends,"[35] they run away and become migratory or extinct,

28. Calixta Guiteras Holmes, op. cit., p. 120.
29. Alfonso Fabila, op. cit., p. 48.
30. Pavía Crespo, "Los Mixtecas de la Costa Chica," El Maestro Rural, Vol. VIII, No. 6, p. 14.
31. Alfonso Fabila, op. cit., p. 150.
32. Franz Blom and Gertrude Duby, La selva lacandona (Mexico: Editorial Cultura, 1955), p. 154.
33. Lucio Mendieta y Núñez, Los zapotecos: Monografía histórica, etnográfica y económica (Mexico: Imprenta Universitaria, 1949), p. 228.
34. Francisco M. Plancarte, op. cit.
35. Calixta Guiteras Holmes, "Organización social de Tzeltales y Tzotziles," op. cit., pp. 45–62.

like the Lacandones,[36] and they retain a traditional, imperceptible rancor toward "the men of the white government." [37]

This is the image that the Indian has of the Ladino and of Ladino or constitutional authorities. We must add the image that the Ladino has of the Indian—not in the view of anthropologists, Mexico's historians, politicians of the Center, teachers of good will, or modernizing priests, but in that of the authorities confronting the Indian, manipulating him, dominating him, and using the coercion of the local government for colonial exploitation. The image of the Indian these people have is one of an inferior being, a being-thing: "The authorities say of the inhabitants of Jicaltepec: They are bad people . . ." [38] they are "lazy," "robbers," "liars," "good-for-nothing." [39] The image is different when the Indian is acculturated, when he learns the language and dresses like a Ladino.

> The ladinos who live in Indian villages or make their living by exploiting the Indians always accuse them of being liars, bandits, and shameless. They never participate in Indian festivities, or when they do it is on the pretext of getting more drunk than usual. There is strong discrimination against the Indian, and he is treated in a contemptuous and even insulting manner. When an Indian has learned Spanish and returns to the village in ladino attire, the others respect him and are very careful not to abuse him. If his wife and children adopt the ladino style of dress, and abandon their Indian group, the ladinos will treat him as an equal and will recall his Indian past only when wishing to insult him.[40]

Matters are different when an Indian rebels and comes to grips with the situation. It is said that mestizos are able to maintain their political hegemony by means of force or arms,

36. Franz Blom and Gertrude Duby, *op. cit.*
37. Alfonso Villa Rojas, "Los mayas del actual territorio de Quintana Roo," *Enciclopedia Yucatanense*, Vol. VI, 1946, p. 36.
38. Gutierre Tibón, *op. cit.,* p. 125.
39. Franz Blom and Gertrude Duby, *op. cit.,* p. 154.
40. Calixta Guiteras Holmes, "Organización social de Tzeltales y Tzotziles," *op. cit.,* p. 61.

or even by murdering Indian leaders. In general terms, whites and mestizos (both citizens and authorities) consider their Indian fellow citizens as inferior, and treat them with a roughness comparable to that of the Spanish conquerors. The way in which the authorities view the Indian, how they make him suffer, amuse themselves at his expense, feel more intelligent than he, humiliate him, make him uneasy, attack him, treat him with excessive familiarity, these are all forms linked to the violence of domination and to colonial exploitation.

Mexican anthropology—which has taken a humanistic view of the Indian problem, but has never had an anti-colonial spirit—has been unable to concentrate on the Indian problem as a colonial and eminently political problem. The distance between present studies and those which may emerge in the future is the same as that between two famous anthropologists, Malinowski and Kenyatta. Kenyatta became the leader of his people and found the need to study systematically the problem of exploitation and politics.

Perhaps a serious study of relationships among Mexicans will enable us in the future to attain a deeper knowledge of the Indian problem, especially as it concerns the entire Mexican polity. Although it is true that when an Indian adopts the Ladino style of dress and learns Spanish the authorities treat him differently, it is also true that authority-citizen relationships generally exhibit varied nuances of violence and contempt, and elicit reactions that are most typical of the relationships between the Ladino authority and the Indian citizen. A study of the Sánchez family, conducted by the anthropologist Oscar Lewis, illustrates the treatment of the urban poor by the authorities. The phenomena of political vendettas and of polemical insult in the press, in which people are sharply attacked, of the politicians' attitudes of feeling quite wise in their manipulation of people as if they were things, and on the other hand, the violent offense taken by the authorities when confronted by individuals or groups of inferior status who protest and demand instead of supplicate; these are the counterparts at the national level to the treatment given the Indian. Indeed, conformity, abstention, depersonalization, paternalism, skepticism, insecurity, lack of a rational dialogue with groups organized for protest, all the political ills that thwart Mexico's democratic development are certainly not limited to the relationships between Ladinos and Indians. Just as in the Indian regions the Indian is the subordinate and the Ladino represents the "principle of authority," so in Mexican politics, men take the roles of Indians and Ladinos, depending on their circumstances and social classes. That is why studying the Indian as a political being, and the Ladino authority in the Indian villages, is the best way to learn about the Mexican citizen as a political being, with his passive or undemocratic traits.

6

Stratification and Social Mobility

Another approach to the problem of the relationship between social structure and the Mexican polity is the study of stratification—that is, the way in which a society is differentiated in terms of income groups, salary levels, and standards of living. From such a study new conclusions about social and political marginality might emerge. Indeed, those groups in Mexico with lower income and salaries would doubtless exhibit—as has been the case universally—a higher percentage of illiterate people, children without schooling, families without newspapers, and the like. But our study of social stratification will more directly concentrate on the problem of radicalism and conformity, of the revolutionary and conservative attitudes of the Mexican population, and of structural conditions. We shall study the general trend of stratification and social mobility in Mexico. We shall use the few data available, which have been provided by economists, because Mexican sociology has lacked the financial and technical resources needed to undertake field study basic to the understanding of national problems.

STRATIFICATION

Mexico, as is characteristic of all underdeveloped or developing nations in general, is a society exhibiting large inequalities. These inequalities are apparent in all areas—economic, social, and cultural.[1] The range between those who have little and those who have much is far wider than it is in more developed democratic nations. For this reason, we have added to the usual study of stratification the two categories basic to the understanding of Mexico's social dynamics—those who have and those who have not. On the basis of typical studies of the economy and society of developed nations—distribution of income, occupation, standards of living—the contrasts appear sharp.

A comparative study of the distribution of income in about 1950 showed that the percentage derived from salaries and wages was 49 per cent of the total national income in France, 59 per cent in Canada, 59 per cent in Switzerland, 65 per cent in the United States, and 67 per cent in England.[2] At about the same time, the working sector in Mexico received only 24 per cent of the national income. This figure must be compared with the others with reservation, because it is not from the same series and has not been adapted to it, yet it does reveal that there are large differences involved. Eleven years later, in 1960, the percentage earned in wages and salaries in Mexico was 31.4 per cent of the national income. This figure is still far lower than that of any developed country, and it is characteristic of Mexico's present state of underdevelopment (see Table 19).

The income per employed man and per job is less than half the mean product in agriculture (1957), whereas it is nine times less than half the mean product in the oil industry, two times in commerce, and four times in the electric energy industry.[3]

1. Francisco M. Plancarte, *El problema indígena Tarahumara* (Mexico: Instituto Nacional Indigenista, 1954), pp. 22–23.
2. Cf. *National Income and Its Distribution in Underdeveloped Countries* (New York: United Nations, 1951, Series E, No. 3).
3. Ifigenia Martínez de Navarrete, *La distribución del ingreso y el desarrollo económico de México* (Mexico: Instituto de Investigaciones Económicas, Universidad Nacional Autónoma de México, 1960).

Differences also exist between the city and the countryside: the per capita annual income of the rural sector in 1960 was 1,500 pesos as compared to the 6,300 pesos of the urban sector.

The monthly income per family exhibits very large differences. Research done during 1961–63 by the Sampling Office under the direction of Ana María Flores shows that in Mexico only 23 per cent of families have monthly incomes higher than 1,000 pesos, and only 3 per cent have incomes higher than 3,000 pesos. The differences between the countryside and the city are once more apparent. Among rural families only 8 per cent have more than 1,000 pesos per month, and among urban families, 35 per cent do. And whereas 5 per cent of urban families have monthly incomes higher than 3,000 pesos, only .4 per cent of rural families do. The differences among higher strata are presumably very large, yet they are rarely, if ever, analyzed. The percentage of the population earning more than 3,000 pesos and less than 5,000 pesos, more than 5,000 pesos and less than 10,000 pesos, and the like, is not known.

In the lower income groups, 26 per cent of families receive up to 300 pesos per month; 50 per cent receive up to 500 pesos; 77 per cent up to 1,000 pesos. The differences between income in the city and income in the countryside are equally large. In the city, 10 per cent of the families receive up to 300 pesos, whereas in the countryside, 45 per cent do; in the city 31 per cent receive up to 500 pesos, whereas in the countryside 73 per cent do; in the city 65 per cent receive up to 1,000 pesos, whereas in the countryside 84 per cent do.

In 1963, experts from the Bank of Mexico conducted a study based on a representative sample and reached conclusions similar to those of Ana María Flores. In that year a little over 29 per cent of all families had incomes lower than 400 pesos per month. This situation, serious in itself, was extreme in rural areas, where the income of more than 41 per cent of the families was below this amount. For urban families this percentage was 10.8 per cent, far lower.

At the other end of the scale, according to the same study, in 1963 only 28.8 per cent of all families had incomes higher than 1,250 pesos per month (15.8 per cent in the countryside and 48.2 per cent in the city); 5.7 per cent had incomes higher than 4,000 pesos (1.8 per cent in the countryside and 11.6 per cent in the city); and 1.2 per cent had incomes higher than 9,200 pesos (0.3 per cent in the countryside and 2.6 per cent in the city).

The study made by the Bank of Mexico also reveals that 29.2 per cent of the families had only 6.1 per cent of the total income, whereas 1.8 per cent (4.1 per cent in the city and 0.4 per cent in the countryside) of the high-income families had 15.5 per cent of the income.[4]

To the social differences we have observed we must add the regional and state differences. Mexico's regional development is profoundly unequal, as is that of all underdeveloped countries. In 1960, for example, an area containing one-third of the country's population had more than three-fourths of all the industry; in Mexico the area in which the remaining two-thirds lived had less than one-fourth of the industry. Here as anywhere else, these differences in industrialization are directly related to differences in standards of living.

The Federal District and the northern states have standards of living higher than the national average by percentages ranging from 35 to 100 per cent. In contrast, Chiapas, Oaxaca, Guerrero, Tlaxcala, Hildalgo, Guanajuato, San Luis, and Zacatecas all have standards of living two-thirds lower than the national average. The report made by the Bank of Mexico states,

> This percentage increases. In 1940 the difference in the per capita gross national product between the wealthiest areas

4. "Distribución del Ingreso Familiar," Mexico, 1963 (Unpublished document).

and the ten poorest states was close to 4,500 pesos (monetary value for 1960). In 1960 the difference was of 6,500 pesos. Even though the rate of productivity per capita is increasing more rapidly in the poor states than in the rich ones—4.3 per cent as compared with 2 per cent—with these rates of development it will take more than seventy years for the poor states to catch up with the rich states.[5]

A comparison of the lowest and highest standards of living in the regions and states would show that the poor have a death rate more than twice as high as that of the rich, an illiteracy rate more than twice as high, a student-teacher ratio almost four times as high, almost four times as many dwellings without running water; furthermore, minimum salaries are almost five times lower, sugar consumption more than four times lower, and so on. Many of these are rough estimates, but they do demonstrate an undeniable fact: the observed differences are not between individuals or families with a relatively high standard of living and those with an extremely high standard of living. Rather, there is a scale ranging from poverty to wealth, from misery to splendid living. This is confirmed by other indicators, such as malnutrition, ignorance, general and infant mortality, poor health, and bad housing. Some of these were analyzed earlier; others confirm the research done on these problems.[6]

We have thus a series of facts which have been confirmed by statistical analysis. Martínez de Navarrete states,

> If we assume that the average income of 700 pesos per month per family for the whole Republic was barely sufficient to satisfy the minimum requirements for food, clothing, housing, and entertainment, we can deduce that in November, 1956, the following were needy: 33 per cent of the families in the Federal District and North Pacific; 60 per

5. For all the previous data, see Paul Lamartine Yates, *El Desarrollo Regional de México* (Mexico: Banco de México, 1962).
6. See Ana María Flores, *La magnitud del hambre en México* (Mexico, 1961); and *Investigación Nacional de la Vivienda Mexicana, 1961–1962* (Mexico: Instituto Nacional de la Vivienda, 1963).

cent of the families in the Gulf of Mexico and the northern region; and 80 per cent of the families in the central and south Pacific states. In the country as a whole, approximately two out of three families lacked economic means in the sense that they had a lower than average (already low) income.[7]

Such were the findings too, of a survey conducted during 1961–62. If we accept the premise that 1000 pesos per family per month is a minimum for a modest standard of living, then during 1961–62 only one out of every five Mexican families had a modest or better standard of living.

These factors, which reveal and confirm the existence of a highly differentiated society whose strata and standards of living exhibit the sharpest contrasts, might lead us to the conclusion that politically Mexico is a profoundly discontented nation, in which large sectors of the population have an aggressive and even revolutionary attitude and in which everything tends to a violent explosion. In a more systematic study analyzing these conditions over a period of time, however, they acquire a different meaning which equilibrates the trends and conclusions that might emerge from a static analysis.[8]

SOCIAL MOBILITY

Mexico has indeed developed. There has been an increase in the per capita product, a more rational utilization of resources (through industrialization), and a modification of the social, economic, and political structure through constant processes of unification and integration toward a national State. This development has made possible an increase of more than four times of the gross national product (with prices remaining constant) over the past twenty-five years,[9] together with a two-

7. Ifigenia Martínez de Navarrete, *op. cit.,* pp. 74–75.
8. Here we did not specifically study other factors which account for the fact that social inequality is not necessarily and automatically linked to nonconformity or radicalism, such as the different forms of alienation in traditional and contemporary societies.
9. The gross national product was 22,600 million pesos in 1940 and reached 98,200 million pesos in 1965.

fold increase of the per capita income. At times the country achieved the highest growth rates in Latin America. Even today, in the midst of the economic recession of the area as a whole, Mexico is one of the few countries that are steadily advancing.

Mexico's economic and social development has had political repercussions. In order to understand the state of mind of the population we cannot study merely the present state of the social, economic, and cultural inequalities, but we must also examine the national dynamics and the processes of development, mobility, and mobilization of the population.

Unfortunately, these two types of analysis seem to be at odds with each other for ideological or strategic-political reasons: some see and point out the country's large· inequalities; others emphasize and extol the progress. To the conservative who, irritated by "the demagogy of the Mexican Revolution," denounces existing ills, we might counterpose the establishmentarian politician viewing with satisfaction the accomplished works. To the impatient radical, who already envisions the next socialist revolution, or to the honest, old revolutionist who feels disappointed and thinks that the time has come to "go again to the mountains," we might counterpose the functionaries and executives who watch the country's progress—the electrification of Mexico, the building of schools, the opening of new roads, and dams—and who feel that they have the agreement and the support of a large sector of the population. Both sides have a natural tendency toward political strife, and a certain perspective biased by subjective and rhetorical attitudes, yet at the same time inequality and development are compatible perspectives. It is a two-sided image, having to do with the disconformity and conformity of the leaders but also with the disconformity and conformity of the different social strata.

In order to study the phenomena of disconformity and conformity, we must first study their dynamics to understand their operation and their major tendencies. We shall begin by studying to what degree development, mobilization, and mobility in Mexico coincide with conformity, adaptation, and moderation. We shall also analyze what might be called the "hope" factor of national development—that is, the notion of individual salvation, that the individual can resolve his personal and family problems within the framework of development without substantial changes or radical attitudes.[10] Later, we shall see to what extent this notion can be validly applied at decisive times and if it may stop being applied in the immediate future.

The development of Mexico presupposes a major redistribution of wealth, most particularly of agricultural property. The revolutionary governments distributed 53 million hectares among 2,240,000 family heads (see Table 20). The peasant population was encouraged by ownership or by hope of land ownership.

The development of the country brings about constant emigration by the rural population to the urban centers and the building of new urban centers, with the usual effects on the standards of living. The percentage of rural population has gradually decreased—from 80 per cent in 1910 to 47 per cent in 1964—and the percentage of urban population has increased accordingly. Large numbers of peasants entertain

10. Although the nineteenth-century processes of accelerated industrialization, urbanization, and development in Europe coincided with the processes of radicalization in Mexico and other Latin American countries, the "hope" factor does not necessarily obtain. The variety in working-class stratification, the different statuses of the skilled and unskilled worker, the shift from a closed society to an open society—which do not appear markedly in the industrial development of the nineteenth century but are characteristic of twentieth-century development in advanced nations—are present in certain underdeveloped countries such as Mexico and Brazil, giving way to attitudes of hope and conformity in these highly differentiated and underdeveloped societies which have not achieved the standards of living of developed countries. Yet these societies have undergone changes in their conceptions of social policy, differentiating treatment, salaries, services, and loans for workers depending on their branch, region, skill, etc. This has destroyed the general concept that every worker is a "proletarian" and is a member of a "class." See my study "L'évolution du système des classes au Mexique," *Cahiers Internationaux de Sociologie* (Paris: Presses Universitaires de France, 1963).

the hope for a better life through migration to the cities. The differences in income and standards of living in the city and the countryside are attractive as leaps from a lower to a higher status. Other peasants experience the urbanization of their own environment.

The development of the country causes a growth of secondary and tertiary economic activities two times and even two and one-half times that of primary productive activities, which receive a smaller remuneration. The annual growth rate of the population engaged in secondary and tertiary economic activities was 5.5 for 1940–50, whereas that of primary activities was 2.6 (see Table 22). Occupational movement from low-paying jobs, such as agricultural work, to higher-paying jobs, such as industrial, commercial, and service activities, is constant throughout the process of industrialization. Higher-paying jobs were held by 30 per cent of the total work force in 1930, as compared to 47 per cent in 1964. This situation strengthens conformity and hope among large numbers of peasants and workers (see Table 24).

Movement of population, dealt with by Germani, is a fact of no less importance. We have seen the rates of growth of the participating population—how millions of people who did not speak Spanish do so today, who were unable to read now read, who had no schools and today send their children to school, who wore no shoes and who have shoes today, for example.[11] The transition from not having to having is critical in any man's life. Millions of Mexicans have made this transition. Their hope factor is necessarily very strong.

The development of the country brings about large movements between social strata. According to estimates by Iturriaga and Cline, between 1895 and 1960 the upper class grew from 1.5 per cent to 6.5 per cent of the total population; the middle class grew from 7.8 per cent to 33.5 per cent; and the lower class decreased from 90.7 per cent to 60 per cent. Cline

11. Cf. Pablo González Casanova, "Sociedad Plural y Desarrollo: El caso de México," op. cit.

indicates the emergence since 1940 of a "transitional" stratum or class, which rises from the lower levels toward the middle class; it was 6.5 per cent of the population in 1940 and 20 per cent in 1960.[12] In another breakdown, González Cosío estimates that between 1900 and 1960 the percentage of the upper class scarcely varied. (It was .6 per cent and .5 per cent, respectively, for 1900 and 1960, whereas the middle class doubled, rising from 8.3 per cent to 17.1 per cent, and the lower class decreased from 91.1 per cent to 82.4 per cent.[13]) In yet another kind of breakdown, Ifigenia Martínez de Navarrete estimates that between 1950 and 1957 the lower class decreased from 70 per cent to 65 per cent; the middle class shifted from 18 per cent to 19 per cent; the upper middle class increased from 7 per cent to 11 per cent; and the upper class remained stable at 5 per cent.[14]

The variety of these data exhibits a certain anarchy in the choice of intervals between classes, and there are serious obstacles in the way of considering the figures themselves definitive. Nonetheless, they all express a definite characteristic: the vertical mobility from the lower to the higher strata, the upward mobility from one class to another by large sectors of the population.[15] This fact encourages individual hopes for improvement, within the over-all national patterns.

Another aspect of mobility is the considerable internal migration from the poor states to the rich states. In 1960 the ratio of Mexicans who had moved to rich states to Mexicans born in them was 157 to 100 in Lower California, 69 to 100 in the Federal District, 40 to 100 in Tamaulipas; the ratio is generally above the mean in all the more developed states of the country. The percentage of internal immigrants increased

12. Howard F. Cline, *Mexico: From Revolution to Evolution, 1940–1960* (London: Oxford University Press, 1962), p. 123.
13. González Cosío, *op. cit.*, p. 55.
14. Martínez de Navarrete, *op. cit.*
15. Gino Germani, "Classes populares y democracia representativa en América Latina," *Desarrollo Económico*, July-September 1962, Vol. 2, p. 29.

from a national average of 13.2 per cent in 1950 to 17.6 per cent in 1960.

The hope of improving their standards of living encourages large sectors of the population to move, particularly from poor areas to rich areas. (In 1960, 5 million Mexicans were not living in their places of birth.) Between 1950 and 1960, 2 million Mexicans moved from their places of birth to other places.

Finally, many Mexican peasants hope to solve their problems through provisional emigration to the United States. This has enabled a few million individuals, leaving Mexico either temporarily or for good, to become liberated from their most pressing problems. We do not know exactly how many Mexican workers have emigrated to the United States under such conditions. Suffice it to say that between 1942 and 1957 the total number of workers hired in the United States and of wetbacks caught was more than 7 million. This is a conservative estimate, because during periods of heavy immigration, United States police is not able to apprehend wetbacks efficiently.[16] Many wetbacks were not apprehended in times of heavy immigration or in times of crisis (see Tables 25 and 26).

All of these movements—from rural to urban areas, from agricultural to industrial activities, from lower-paying to higher-paying jobs, from poor regions to developed regions, from the status of landless peasants to that of small owner and public land worker, from having nothing to having something, from lower class to middle class—are powerful palliatives of inequality. They are also channels to moderation, to conformity; they bring about hope of resolving personal problems through individual effort, education, luck, or merit in the view of leaders, employers, and authorities.

The dynamics of Mexican development contain elements of

16. Cf. Richard H. Hancock, *The Role of the Bracero in the Economic and Cultural Dynamics of Mexico: A Case Study of Chihuahua* (Stanford: California Hispanic-American Society, 1959).

patience, conformity, and even conservatism. In its uneven-
ness or stagnation, Mexico has elements of radicalism and
structural disconformity of a nation not exempt from profound political crisis. Given these conditions, the functionary
may view with alarm how each of the data mentioned above
has a structural counterpart of a dangerous trend.

"At present more than 2.5 million farmers have land problems. Among these, more than a half million have plots
smaller than a half hectare, while the rest have either no lands
at all or land inadequate for agriculture." [17] This is a conservative estimate; others indicate that 3 million peasants have
land problems.

The annual rate of growth of the gross national product has
shown great variation. In 1940–45 the rate was 8.7; in
1945–50, 5.4; in 1950–55, 4.8; in 1956–60, 5; and
in 1961–65, close to 6. Although there was one year
(1964) in which it was 10—indicating the possibility that
the country was entering a stage of recuperation—the fact
can hardly be ignored that post-war rates of growth, after having decreased, seem to have become stagnant (see Table 22).

The rate of per capita production went from 4.4 in the decade of 1940–50 to only 1.7 in the period of 1959–61.

Even though agricultural growth rates have been remarkable in the past twenty-five years (from 1940 to 1950 production doubled, and there was an additional 40 per cent increase
by 1958), by 1958 there was a loss of impetus. By 1961 it
was difficult to maintain the level of 1954, and during those
seven years the population increased by 25 per cent; so the
per capita product was the same as in the period 1945–47.
For another thing, the rates of growth of the gross national
product per working person in agriculture were generally
lower than the mean national rate.

The annual rate of growth of the population in the fourteen

17. Ramón Ramírez, "Tendencias de la Economía Mexicana," *Investigación Económica*, Vol. XXII, No. 88 (Mexico: Universidad Nacional
Autónoma de México, 1962).

largest cities, which is 6.8, is higher than the rate of growth of secondary and tertiary activities, which is only 4. This indicates that the cities are growing, and so is the rate of unemployment, urban poverty, and neo-marginality in the city itself.[18]

Since 1960 the number of wetbacks emigrating to the United States has decreased, and in 1964 it was less than half the figure for 1959 (40.35 per cent). Economic and legal obstacles to immigration have recently increased.

In absolute figures, the number of illiterate people, schoolless children, and barefoot men is still increasing by hundreds of thousands and even by millions. They witness Mexico's development, but no corresponding improvement in their own lot.

To all these social factors, which are the basis of and channels for disconformity, we should add the economic and political factors of colonial exploitation, usury in the countryside, dispossession of the peasants, abuse by authorities of the lower classes, the formation of new latifundia, and the like, together with the struggles conducted by the leading groups in order to take over the State. Then we have a far more accurate view of Mexico's political panorama, which would at least moderate any excessive optimism.

It is difficult to interpret such opposing tendencies. For many of these phenomena we lack adequate data, and when they exist, they can be used in a game of false rhetoric, with polemical adjustments which, rigorous as they may seem, are nonetheless highly debatable. The political and ideological interpretations of perspectives on the future are mainly of two kinds. Some believe that there is a definite trend toward the solution of problems, with only slight downfalls from which it is easy to recuperate. Others believe that there is an inevitable

18. See the excellent analysis in *Memoria de la Secretaría del Patrimonio Nacional.* Mexico, 1962, pp. 42 ff.; and Horacio Flores de la Peña, "Reflexiones sobre el Plan General de Desarrollo Económico," *Ciencias Políticas y Sociales,* April-June 1963, pp. 127–42.

tendency toward depression, which recuperations are never able to overcome. Since Mexico's political evolution is vacillating in nature, at every crisis the radicals claim that they were right, but as soon as stability returns or recuperation occurs, the conservatives or reformists confirm their conviction that all ills tend to be naturally and necessarily resolved.

Generally, both the leaders and the masses fail to perceive the ups and downs of development, but rather adopt preformulated attitudes, as though the development of the country were a purely rational phenomenon, directed either toward the solution of major social problems or toward chaos. The expectations of the different political groups are a cause for mutual mistrust. Predictions based on the course taken by the country provoke the suspicions of opposing groups and are viewed as forms of deceit, when they are really modes of partial understanding—of a situation that is imprecisely defined, of a country which is neither in a state of stagnation or regression nor in a stage of accelerated growth, but rather advancing within fluctuations of development–stagnation, revolution–counterrevolution, social justice–social injustice, individual improvement by large sectors of the population–over-all marginality by others, land distribution–land despoliation, employment–unemployment. Under these circumstances it is difficult to interpret the prevailing trend of development and to make an accurate prediction regarding the immediate future which might transcend polemics, rhetoric, subjective estimates, and to guarantee that the country is headed toward stable development with minor stumbles or toward an increasingly acute and violent crisis. For this, other elements of judgment are needed.

In the times of political crisis which Mexico has undergone during the past few years, both groups, the discontented and the conformist, or the revolutionist and the reformist (within which group especially the ruling elite), have inevitably come to agree on one point: that they can gain power and lose power. On this there has been a consensus, and expectations that under normal conditions are widely different and opposed, have been almost identical in times of conflict.

It is only natural that this should have been so. In times of crisis both groups are aware of one fact: that all the economically and politically marginal population can become active and that, in combination with the different political groups of the participating classes, this makes possible a struggle or brings a real danger, depending on one's perspective.

It is impossible to predict with accuracy Mexico's trends of economic development, and recuperation and crisis are both a possibility. But the country is developing at a very low level and has a very small margin of national and international economic security. The secular trends toward a decrease in the prices of raw materials, the cyclical movements of the United States economy, the political measures adopted by the United States and Europe in order to protect their own producers, for example, may bring about a social structure in which a few million human beings are marginal with respect to development and are hungry. On these facts both groups of rulers are likewise in agreement, but particularly those with optimistic and conservative outlooks, those who become alarmed when coffee prices, cotton prices, the dollar reserve, exports, or tourism go down, or when purely civic and democratic protest movements arise. Not to speak of movements of outright rebellion seeking to overthrow a municipal president, a governor, or a trade union representation: this has recently occurred frequently, from the lynching of the municipal president of Ciudad Hidalgo through the strike movements of 1958; the problems of violence in Guerrero, San Luis, Nuevo León, Baja California; the frustrated rebellion of Gasca and various peasant groups; the bloody mutiny of Huajuapan de León; the armed incidents in Chihuahua; the take-over of the first floor of the Palace of Government in Mérida; to the accusation of conspiracy and the imprisonment of Víctor Rico Galán.

At present even the most optimistic are worried, and with

cause. Yet after the legal or illegal sporadic agitations and the electoral or labor or religious conflicts are over, the ruler, pleased with having resolved them, becomes once again distracted by his daily activities and returns to congenital optimism. The leaders of the opposition, who constantly await events to deplore, who are mentally in ambush for the economic or political catastrophe, become animated and active in times of crisis. Once the crises are over, they recoil and wait once again.

Although in times of crisis, disconformity is readily perceived, how do we perceive it under normal conditions? How is disconformity manifested in Mexico? How does it become organized, and what form does the struggle take? Who organizes it, and for whom does the struggle act? In other words, to what degree does there appear in Mexico's political structure an organized consciousness pressing for the solution of the problems of the population which is marginal with respect to development—that is, more than 60 per cent of the Mexican population? The crux of the problem is to discover how disconformity is manifested in Mexico under normal civic democratic conditions.

7

Disconformity and Civic Struggle

Confronting the organized Mexico of government, with its presidentialist system, its party, its labor unions, and confronting the equally well organized factors of power, such as the Army, the Church, the national and foreign entrepreneurs, is a Mexico which is not politically organized.

Confronting the interest groups and pressure groups which utilize with greater or lesser efficiency the Constitution, the Presidency, the Congress, the court, the local and state governments, the parties, the trade unions, the industrial and commercial chambers, the embassies, and the press, is a Mexico which is civilly unarmed, for which institutions and laws are not instruments to be manipulated, to be used to struggle, or to exercise pressures.

Confronting the political Mexico there is an apolitical Mexico, which does not struggle in the civil sphere and lacks political power. Apolitical Mexico is not the subject of politics but the object of politics. It is not comprised only of that sector of the population which, due to a lack of culture and experience, is dominated and manipulated within its own organizations by the ruling classes, and which, effectively organized in trade unions, leagues, and associations, is a witness of the control of these groups either from outside or from above. The Mexico which is manipulated within organizations certainly exists.

But there is another Mexico which is manipulated by the organizations and yet is outside of them. For this Mexico, organization is a foreign element, an institution for others—for the Ladinos, for the government, for the trade union leaders, and for the politicians.

In Mexico's politics, there are two types of control: control of popular organizations and control of the unorganized population by governmental or para-governmental organs and by working-, middle-, and upper-class organizations of the participating population generally. The numerous popular organizations are controlled in order to suppress the disconformity of their members, but the large majority of citizens do not even have organizations through which to manifest their political disconformity.

In 1964 for instance, according to official statistics, of the total working population, which was 13,216,000 only 1,388,260 were unionized—that is, 10.5 per cent. Although in the electrical industry close to 90 per cent of the workers were unionized and in transportation and communications 57 per cent were, in agriculture of a total of 6,909,000 peasants only 129,868 were unionized—that is, 1.9 per cent. In other words, of the total working population, 89.5 per cent were not unionized, and of the population working in primary activities, 98 per cent were not unionized (see Table 27).

These figures may seem too large considering that in Mexico 1,200,000 public-land workers and 1,500,000 farmers and small owners work on their own (1960 census), and that the National Peasant Confederation and other organizations claim to include through collective membership all the public lands and farming communities. But if we accept these statements, which tend to coincide with the structure of ownership and political organization of the Mexican countryside, we are faced with the following facts: of the total number of workers in industry, commerce, and services, which in 1960 was 1,200,000, 76.56 per cent were unionized; of the total of agricultural workers, which in 1960 numbered 1,900,000, only

6.5 per cent were unionized. The percentage unionized is only 6.4 per cent if we consider all the rural day laborers, 1,945,000 in 1960. A more rigorous estimate thus shows that 23.44 per cent of the workers in industry, commerce, and services were not unionized, and that 93.5 or 93.6 per cent of the agricultural workers and day laborers were not unionized.

This situation has hardly changed between 1939 and 1963. In 1939 there was one unionized worker in the labor force for every 8.6 not unionized. In 1963 there was one unionized worker for every 8.3 not unionized. There were not many variations during that interval (see Table 28). Under these conditions, the large majority of workers and peasants lack even the kind of organizations or labor unions which are vertically controlled. The problem is particularly severe in the marginal Mexican countryside, where there are no trade unions, leagues, or federations for the expression of economic or political disconformity.

Then too, the political parties have a much smaller membership than the workers' unions. Even though the Institutional Revolutionary Party claimed 6,621,000 members in 1964 and announced that it would have more than 8 million at the end of 1966, these figures are not for individual members, but represent a highly arbitrary figure based on collective membership estimates. The fact that sometimes the number of members claimed by PRI in a given federal district is higher than the number of votes obtained in that same district is proof of this situation. These claims thus do not permit analysis of membership.

It is impossible to determine the membership of the other parties because they either keep no records or they do not make them public. Both reasons are symptomatic of the situation regarding party membership in Mexico.

Political parties in Mexico cannot be assessed in terms of membership. Each party has a group of politicians, administrators, and supporters which it mobilizes by means of governmental or ecclesiastic organizations or through major and minor traditional leaders. There are no mass parties. There are politicians and sympathizers, and the parties by themselves cannot mobilize; mobilization is carried through by the government and the real holders of power.

The parties are not organized, subsidized, and controlled by the citizens. The power groups organize, subsidize, and control the parties; they are the juridical-political instruments which are constitutionally sanctioned for civil struggle. Therefore, when disconformity is manifested through the parties, it is the expression of their leaders or promoters rather than of the "masses" which they claim to represent. Likewise, when the government party manifests public satisfaction, this represents the satisfaction of its leaders, or of the government itself. These judgments are not entirely accurate, since political parties function as agents for the expression of public opinion. Yet because the parties are not organized, subsidized, and controlled by the citizens, their leaders have a freedom which enables them to manifest their conformity or disconformity without necessarily representing the citizenry. For another thing, much of the masses' disconformity takes place outside of the parties and does not determine the parties' struggle, and much of the citizens' conformity and disconformity is manifested in their very abstention from membership and lack of participation in the parties.

The large majority of Mexicans are outside of the parties. Very few are within them exercising control, subsidizing them, organizing them as instruments of civic struggle. Found especially within the urban middle or upper class are "party men" —lawyers, bureaucrats, "millionaire workers" who function as politicians and mobilize and manipulate the people during elections. The people regard them as metaphysical entities, or let themselves be led by them as intermediaries of the government, the Church, and the entrepreneurs. The most extreme levels of this passivity are found in the most backward agricultural regions of the country, inhabited by men who do not have the political culture of the citizen.

Any possibility of an analysis of the political disconformity of the marginal masses by means of the parties and their members is barred by these facts. At the most, the parties as civil and political channels reflect the disconformity of different sectors of the ruling class and the more advanced middle strata, particularly in the cities.

The third way to study civil manifestations of disconformity is by analysis of voting patterns. We have already seen that the percentage of votes received by opposition candidates is relatively quite small.[1] What are the characteristics of this opposition, which appears in presidential and legislative elections? How does it function? To what extent does it express the disconformity of the poorer regions or sectors of the nation? Official data are perfectly valid to provide an answer to this question, even in those cases in which the opposition vote registered is smaller than the actual opposition vote. Indeed, the fact that the existence of opposition can be officially ignored indicates that civil life has not reached the level at which authorities become compelled in their own interest to register carefully the votes of the opposition—that is, the level at which not doing so would provoke serious conflicts.

Thus the question now is to find out whether in the poorer districts there is more officially recognized opposition, and whether in the more underdeveloped and marginal districts the voting patterns express greater disconformity.

In one of the most contested presidential elections, that of 1929, we find that in five of the poorest states the government party candidate obtained the highest percentage of votes and the least opposition: in Chiapas the opposition was .32 per cent of those voting, in Guerrero .53 per cent, in Hidalgo 5.05 per cent, and in Tlaxcala 5.24 per cent. The states in which the government candidate obtained a smaller percentage of votes and encountered greater opposition were some of

1. Cf. Tables 1 and 19.

the richest and most developed: in Coahuila the opposition gained 19.63 per cent of the votes, in Durango 15.89 per cent, in Sinaloa 24.06 per cent, in Sonora 13.16 per cent, and in Chihuahua 21.11 per cent.

If we consider the presidential election of 1964, for example, we find that in the five poor states mentioned above, the opposition candidate obtained a small percentage of votes. In Chiapas only 1.1 per cent of the voters favored the opposition, in Guerrero 3.1 per cent, in Hidalgo 1.6 per cent, in Oaxaca 3.4 per cent, and in Tlaxcala 1.6 per cent. The highest opposition was encountered in some of the more advanced states of the country: in Baja California and Chihuahua the opposition received 21.3 per cent of the vote, in the Federal District 25.1 per cent, and in Nuevo León 15.7 per cent.

In elections for representatives something similar occurred. In 1961, the candidates of the government party found the least opposition in some of the poorest states: in Chiapas 0.73 per cent, in Guerrero 7.37 per cent, in Hidalgo 1.25 per cent, in Oaxaca 5.17 per cent, and in Tlaxcala 0.27 per cent. In the 1964 elections the percentages in favor of the opposition candidates were: in Chiapas 1.81 per cent, in Guerrero 4.55 per cent, in Hidalgo 1.14 per cent, in Oaxaca 6.41 per cent, and in Tlaxcala 6.22 per cent. In the most prosperous states, on the contrary, the opposition was highest: in 1961 the opposition candidate obtained in northern Baja California 33.01 per cent, in the Federal District 35.32 per cent, in Morelos 26.90 per cent, and in Chihuahua 18.09 per cent. In 1964 they obtained in northern Baja California 28.78 per cent, in Chihuahua 23.29 per cent, and in the Federal District 34.01 per cent.

In the poorer states, then, opposition is either weak or not computed in the ballots, while it is either stronger or duly computed in the more advanced states. There are states with an intermediate level of development that express opposition in elections, showing a relative recognition of such opposition.

Generally these are central states, where the Church is very powerful; there civil opposition tends to be identified with opposition toward one of the traditional holders of power.[2]

A few more points bear upon civil manifestations of disconformity or exercise of pressures through the channels provided for in the Constitution and the law. The agricultural population and particularly the working-class people of the countryside, who are the poorest among the working population, has the lowest rates of membership in workers' organizations. Political parties, which anywhere in the world are predominantly urban organisms, in Mexico do not have either the characteristics or the size of urban organizations in highly developed countries. The citizens, especially those of the countryside, are marginal with respect to the parties, which are passive instruments of their leaders. The rural population—that is, the poorest people—is the most marginal with respect to voting. The illiterate population has equally low rates of voting participation. The voting rural population expresses the lowest opposition. The poorest states likewise express the least opposition in voting.

If the economically and culturally marginal population is also politically marginal, the least organized, and the one expressing the least opposition in elections, one might ask where and how it expresses its disconformity.

A channel for disconformity which would seem reasonable and even obvious might be violence. Not necessarily political violence, but a violent aggressive malaise, as is generally found in backward colonial societies in which politics has not replaced primitive forms of struggle. We tried to determine whether there was a higher rate of crime—attacks, murders, thefts   in the poorer areas of the country. Contrary

2. Another fact worth mentioning is that in the presidential elections of both 1958 and 1964, the opposition was the National Action Party (PAN), since the other parties—Authentic Party of the Mexican Revolution (PARM), Mexican National Party (PNM), Popular Socialist Party (PPS) —supported the Institutional Revolutionary Party's (PRI) candidate either overtly or covertly.

to our expectations, we found that the rate of delinquency among the peasantry—that is, the poorest and most marginal people of the country—is lower than the national average. Although the rate for the nation as a whole is 3 for every thousand inhabitants,[3] the rate among the peasants is 2 for every thousand. Yet among groups with higher standards of living, the rate of delinquency reached 8 per thousand in 1960. Confirming these figures, we found that the rate of those presumed responsible is 1.67 for every thousand literate inhabitants, and only .51 for every thousand illiterates. The rate of delinquency is 1.42 for every thousand literate individuals and .42 for every thousand illiterate individuals.

Among Mexico's marginal people there is no manifestation of disconformity. Under normal conditions the marginal "citizen" does not express his disconformity even by violence or unusual aggressiveness. Any act of violence, individual or collective, carries a far higher price for the marginal population than for others, so it seems that there is more to lose than there is to be gained. Such a contemplative and patient attitude is the result of long experience. The marginal citizen may be on the verge of violence or despair; he may express himself in dreams, stories, and dances filled with phobias, insecurity, and aggressiveness. Yet while no explosion occurs, he is patient; as long as he does not lose all, he is the most acquiescent religiously, courteous, and quiet of beings. As in Agustín Yáñez's novel, he asks himself: "What good does it do for the poor to get angry? We will only be hit harder."

The disconformity of Mexico's marginal population does not take a consistent and continuous form as a collective, institutional, or natural phenomenon. Disconformity does not appear either civilly or in a continuing mode. A great part of Mexico, disorganized, uninformed, and lacking the means to become informed, is still and silent. These people are not, in the true sense of the word, citizens. Those who are not citizens

3. Of the working force.

are least engaged in economic, social, and cultural participation. Those who are citizens have higher standards of living, higher incomes, and live in the more prosperous, urbanized, and industrialized cities. Whereas citizens find limitations to becoming organized and they express their disconformity or demand the fulfilment of their rights, the marginal people have no organization, no information media or juridical instruments, and not even minimum participation in the system by which disconformity is expressed in the electoral struggle.

The disconformity of the marginal population is not expressed through constitutional channels; its demands are made in the traditional forms of supplication, petition, and complaint. The humbler and more marginal the citizen, the humbler the supplication and the more bitter the complaint. This is a very old system, which has become combined with republican forms of petition and struggle. In this connection we find characters popularly called "godfathers," "defenders," "*Tatas*," * "coyotes," ** "influentials," names which indicate the stereotypes of both the good and the bad mediator. These intermediaries can be in or outside the government; they may have either revolutionary or conservative ideas. But they perform old roles in a society in which the new forces of public and private entrepreneurs dominate the forms of conflict and possess the instruments of modern society while maintaining some traditional forms of political control.

The disconformity of the marginal population is thus expressed only through mediators—negotiators from the leading groups in Mexico. This is a curious system of control and political action. The intermediaries can be divided into two main kinds: those within the government or government organizations, who have a more or less radicalized official ideology, and those operating on their own as friends of the government, who take ideological positions more moderate than either the extreme left or the extreme right. The first type con-

* Popular name for one's father (translator's note).
** Illicit broker (translator's note).

duct personal transactions or take care of their protégés during periods of stability. Only when the scheduling of elections or the constitution of a new regime creates a conflict for positions within the revolutionary groups do they become active in organizing protests, exerting pressures, and even mounting movements of a fair size. Within the Institutional Revolutionary Party or in other revolutionary organizations, these leaders paternally conduct a class struggle which has by now become both their style of rule and political action and a means to gain the support of large masses of the population. Many of these "popular leaders" obtain grants for their protégés and for themselves, and they even threaten agitation when their simplest demands are not met.

This system places the mediators in a privileged position, and it is relatively effective for those citizens who are under the mediators' protection. Yet the grants benefit mainly the lower classes of the participating groups—who are the most demanding of their own "godfathers" and of the government —whereas the marginal lower classes, more patient and civilly harmless, obtain far less under this system. The marginal population often lacks "godfathers" to protect it, and the claims of those it has, assume a moral rather than a political character. Often marginal people lack even paternalistic machinery for their continuing defense which could exert the sorts of pressures which would elicit concessions from the leading groups.

The mediators outside of the government or related organizations are priests, lawyers, physicians. They profess left- or right-wing ideologies, and they operate as intermediaries for the "needy," declaring themselves "conservatives," "Catholics," or "Marxists." They consider themselves friends of the government because they seek to help the government by helping those it represents.

Whether they are "Mexican style" revolutionists, or simply conservatives and socialists, they all have paternalistic and authoritarian attitudes. They know that they belong to high-ranking organizations, that they are not controlled by the masses, and that the masses will never demand explanations of their behavior. This permits them to enjoy a freedom of maneuver and negotiation for personal ends.

True, there are among them extraordinary men with undeniable humanitarianism. Yet it would be absurd to believe that the institutions they form—a citizen's political party, a workers' trade union, or a peasants' union in an industrialized society—are representative. Republican ideas are alien to the system in which they operate, and it is difficult or impossible to control the intermediary politically. The masses see intermediaries as a manifestation of providence; rather than being representatives, they are "godfathers"—moral beings who can be good or bad, deserve hatred or love, and produce benefits or misfortunes at will. Here there is no notion of the type of reasoning that characterizes the pressures and negotiations of modern political society, but rather of the type of reasoning which in a religious weltanschauung would correspond to prayer, expectation of miracles and addressing prayers to a divinity or saints, and use of signs and symbols to drive away demons. The culture of political reasoning and political judgments has not overtaken the culture of ethical reasoning and moral judgment.

The exceptions to this paternalistic system in a republican structure generally occur among social strata with a higher level of participation in the development of the country. They have achieved representative and ideological forms of political activity similar to forms of advanced nations.

This system, republican in form and traditional in content, has its own rules of the game, many of which are based upon a system of interpersonal relationships. These rules deserve a sociological analysis of their function in and relationship to constitutional institutions.

It is understood and accepted within the system that before elections the government intermediaries should present protests, formulate popular demands, and exercise pressures. This

is one form of participation in governing the country, channel-
izing the struggle in moments of danger; it is also a way of
demanding concessions in the new administration. It is likewise understood that the government intermediaries should
demand the fulfilment of popular claims, thereby preventing
the masses from seeking leadership among the enemies of the
government. Thus they satisfy the demands of those sectors of
the population—skilled workers, organized farmers, and
public-land workers—who already have an incipient political organization and a political culture. What is neither under-
standable nor acceptable within the system is that when they
have achieved their goals, or the election or political crisis is
over, the same leaders do not continue demanding and pro-
testing, or do not attempt to organize and politicize the marginal sectors of the country, exercising pressure among those
people.

The rules of the game are also very clear for the intermediaries with ideologies opposing those of the Revolution, and
they are directly linked to the logic of interpersonal relationships. Whether a right- or left-wing ideology, every ideology
with considerable mass support brings out a distinction between two types of leaders: one is the friend of the masses and
becomes the intermediary procurer; the other is the enemy,
who is uncommitted and never allowed to resolve any social,
economic, or political problems of the masses. Thus every *ideological* group of the opposition has a group of declared
friends and a group of enemies, who fulfil the task of resolving
the problems of the masses.

This system derives its nature from the social and political
structure of the country. It has functional significance as part
of a policy of "national unity" within a transitional culture
and political regime. It is thus also at the root of the national
political bottleneck, the obstacle to political development, and
the source of the paternalistic and providentialist culture
which impedes the development of the country toward more
advanced forms of government.

The system has an educational effect, for the masses learn that the best way to solve their problems is to have recourse to the official, revolutionary intermediary or procurer. In the event that he should be unsuccessful or unable to fight, the next best way is to have recourse to those procurers— conservative or radical—who are friends of the government. The masses also learn that the opposition parties solve the problems of the opposition politicians, not those of the masses, which they approach only in the case of sheer desperation when all other channels are closed. But even this learning process takes place only among those lower- or middle-class masses which participate in the process of development. Among the marginal classes, all that remains is the supplication to the authority, "godfather," or representative, if any.

To act politically when one belongs to the marginal sectors is viewed as presumptuous, as a transgression of the principle of authority, or as an attempt at rebellion. The marginal Mexican waits without demanding or supplicates without expecting too much, lest he provoke the irritation of the procurers and of the functionaries or leaders. At this level the Mexican political tradition is very clear; it defines no concept of organizations of the masses or political protest. Both rulers and ruled view the act of organizing for protest and demand as delinquent.

Within the participating sector, organization and protest must observe the rules of the game. They must exist within the government or among its friends, whatever their ideology, and allow the latter to control protest, pressures, and demands, establishing times for action no less than for tranquility. In the marginal sector, organization is inconceivable and protest is intolerable. The rulers view any act of organization or civil protest as an attempt at agitation or rebellion which must be controlled at its roots by means of different types of political manipulation, including violence. The marginal population considers that it is best to remain silent, quiet, in a supplicating attitude, without manifesting the least sign of opposition or protest, or without even trying to think of organization.

Supplication and silence are of little use, whereas protest and organization are the traditional roads to imprisonment, exile, and even death. Thus, a most elementary sense of survival dictates against seeking a leader, becoming organized, or voting. This does not mean that conformity is necessarily present among the marginal groups, or that conformity increases with marginality. It does mean that there is no disconformity that is civilly organized and represented or constitutionally formulated; there is not even a type of disconformity manifested through the intermediaries in order to conduct a traditional civil struggle.

The marginal man may think of fighting, but he does not view it as even a traditional type of civil struggle, since his whole experience is that peaceful struggle is impossible and counteractive. He thinks even less of struggling with leaders and votes. At this level the leader and the vote have no significance. If a struggle is to be conducted, the only remaining road is that of the masters themselves, the Ladinos and authorities. It is not a method foreseen in the Constitution; it is the road of violence. Yet this road itself seems very remote, and all that is left is patience, courtesy, silence, and at the most supplication, conducted with great restraint and full of apologies and circumlocutions.

In Mexico, as in any civil society, there is a political pact and commitment. The pact and the commitment have the characteristics common in a plural society and a pre-democratic state. Its forms are a combination of legitimacy and violence, of republican law and traditional institutions. The Constitution, the law, organizations, parties, and voting belong to the participating sectors, and in this group the dominant classes recognize the right of the dominated classes to exercise the Constitution, to have the protection of the law, to become organized, to have parties, and to vote as they increasingly participate in Mexican development and culture.

Even for the lower classes within the participating population, a combination of republican law and traditional institutions obtains. Solution of popular problems is effected by a compromise on grounds of friendship or political alliances. This permits a certain liberty to political enmity and civil disconformity by the parties and organizations, as long as they do not solve popular problems.

But for the marginal population, the pact demands that it not be touched, that it not be organized by either the friends or, even less, the enemies of the government; that it be left the way it is, without organizations, without effective public rights, in a silent and supplicating attitude and utterly dependent upon the nation's leaders.

The marginal sector has no organizations, no parties, no rights, no voting, and, most serious of all, *no effective intermediaries to exercise continuing pressure* aiming to solve its problems as part of Mexico's political activity. Ahead of the marginal population are the participating masses, poor but able to utilize the combination of traditional and modern political life. These masses must be taken account of and taken care of, for they constitute groups that act in the civil sphere, are a political problem, and are a party to the pact, even though they are the worst off of those who are on the inside. Those who are on the outside do not count as citizens. The politician does not view them as political subjects. In the best of cases he views them as subjects for charity. Anything he does on their behalf amounts to a generous act, morally satisfying yet having nothing to do with a public servant's obligations to his demanding and severe fellow citizens.

The ruler and the politician have eyes only for active forces and organizations. Under normal conditions, they see no danger in that civilly quiet Mexico, no reason for political preoccupation with or for peaceful action toward a collectivity that is politically nonexistent, a force that does not manifest itself and is not structured in either constitutional forms or the traditional forms for political pressure. Thus a large part of Mexico—50 to 70 per cent of the population—remains unorganized and silent.

III

POLITICAL STRUCTURE AND
ECONOMIC DEVELOPMENT

8

Political Decisions and Economic Development

It is relatively easy to understand how political decisions regarding economic development are made, and how the power structure sets conditions for and limits to those decisions. But it would be desirable to conduct an analysis to gain a more precise understanding. With the ideas we have already developed we can eliminate the kinds of abstractions upon which the economist *usually* bases his works and subject to objective criticism the types of promises and plans politicians make about development. What is more, analysis we've already conducted makes possible an appraisal of the viability of technical-political studies which are being issued as programs or plans for economic development. These studies, conducted by specialists in charge of national and international organizations, neither deal with the real problem of development nor analyze the political obstacles to its realization.

The level of political reasoning on the subject of development is so poor and its connection to reality so tenuous, that the elements analyzed so far sufficiently demonstrate that current economic designs for development are obsolete and that actual, operative political decisions do not necessarily deal with the kinds of technical decisions which those plans, programs, and projects involve and which take into account everything except the social and political structure in which they are to operate.

137

If we analyze the technical literature of Mexican economists, we find certain recurrent themes and within them certain kinds of economic measures, the efficacy and even applicability of which are open to doubt. Economists inveterately repeat the need to apply these measures, and the facts prove that they are either not applied or only partially applied because they meet with powerful and sometimes insurmountable political obstacles. It is a fact that many of these measures of economic policy are necessary to development. That they are not applied is also a fact. Yet economists keep proposing these measures without realizing that any research on political economy regarding programs or planning which does not consider the political element—especially after so many clear-cut experiences—is meaningless.

Development as a goal requires a special set of political decisions, without which purely economic measures cannot be achieved, programs cannot be realized, and plans remain on paper. As a result, development of the internal and external dynamics of egalitarianism is not accelerated and is even slowed down.

In order to present this problem more accurately, we shall briefly analyze some of the main policies of political economy that Mexican economists have proposed to achieve development. That these projects did not achieve their goals is a result of political decisions. Their accomplishment similarly depends on political decisions.

Economists have insisted that a redistribution of income is necessary to ensure continuity of development. They have shown that the capitalization of the country depends on the conditions of its internal market, and that capitalization does not necessarily require working-class saving, as has been claimed by some foreign economists. They have also shown that the underproduction of many Mexican factories is due to a lack of market; that large amounts of Mexican currency are either hoarded or sent abroad owing to a lack of market; that the spirit of enterprise develops with the market; and that the broadening of the market largely depends on the redistribution of income.

To bring about income redistribution there are—among others—two classical measures of political economy: increases of actual salaries and redistribution of taxes. This has been stated time and again by economists. Yet what has actually happened?

The average salary in 1960 was 6 per cent less than in 1940, and the minimum agricultural salary in 1960–61 had decreased 45 per cent from that of 1938–39. Yet during that same period, individual productivity had increased 120 per cent, and agricultural productivity had increased 100 per cent. Horacio Flores de la Peña has noted that the rate of exploitation of labor increased 134 per cent and that during this period there was an increase in loans (which today are equivalent to between 10 and 15 per cent of the average income of salaried workers). In some branches of production, such as electricity and oil, salaries did increase, but both the loans and the salary increases benefited only the urban workers who are in the service fields and better organized.

This situation is verified by analysis of income distribution over twenty-two years. The percentage of salary income in the national income, which was already very low in 1939 (30.4 per cent), had hardly increased in 1960, whereas the percentage of national income from natural utilities, which in 1939 was already very high (34.4 per cent of the total), reached 42.6 per cent in 1960 (see Table 19).

What has taken place in the way of building a more rational and equitable tax system? After many years of pressures for tax reform, a very moderate system has been adopted. Its redistributive effects do not affect the high-income groups; among them, tax evasion is still practiced by up to 75 per cent. Rather, the burden has been placed on fixed-income groups—this in a country where private brokerage, insurance companies, and loan companies make profits ranging from 12 to 46 per cent of invested capital.

Thus, what Nicolás Kaldor wrote some time ago still holds true today.

> The growing economic inequality between the different classes in Mexico and the regressive nature of the present tax system threaten to undermine the whole social structure, endangering the prospects for peaceful and constitutional evolution. In Mexico, owing to both legislative measures and administrative errors, the actual rate of taxation upon high derived incomes seems to be very low. The only high rates of taxation are those placed on high salaries. The system is unjust because it favors income derived from capital property over that derived from work. This is due to a number of omissions and exemptions unparalleled in other countries with economic and social objectives like those of Mexico.[1]

Such political decision-making is natural in Mexico because the democratic working-class movement is limited, there are no large unions or political parties, and the majority of the population has no representative organizations. Under these conditions, measures ideal for income redistribution geared toward economic development are likely to remain good intentions or to benefit small sectors only.

Mexican economists have correctly insisted for years that to have a developmental foreign policy, Mexico needs a law stating a policy on foreign investments and diversification of markets. But no such law has been passed. Foreign investments represent a slightly higher percentage of all investments than in the past (16 per cent in 1952 and 17 per cent in 1961).[2] In almost every year between 1941 and 1965, the profits derived from foreign investments have been far higher than the initial investments.[3] There has been a decrease in utilities reinvested by foreign enterprises, and

1. Nicolás Kaldor, "Las reformas en el sistema fiscal en México," *Revista Fiscal y Financiera* (Mexico); Vol. XXXIV, No. 202, April 30, 1964, p. 21.
2. Ramón Ramírez, "Tendencias de la Economía Mexicana," Investigación Económica, Vol. XXII, No. 88 (Mexico: Universidad Nacional Autónoma de México, 1962), p. 128.
3. *Ibid.,* p. 43.

profits shipped abroad have increased in the successive presidential periods. Transfers abroad regarding interests, exemptions, and other payments have likewise increased. For certain periods, the two categories reach an amount which almost equals the annual rate of foreign investments in the same years, while in other periods the amounts shipped abroad exceed by far those of the original investments.

For example, in the period 1941–46 the average amount of foreign investments was 26.2 million dollars; the average amount of natural profits shipped abroad was 34.6 million dollars. In subsequent periods the respective amounts were as follows: in 1947–52, 60.4 million dollars, with 54.5 shipped abroad; in 1953–58, 99.8 million dollars, with 80.8 million dollars shipped abroad; and in 1959–64, 84.2 million and 121.2 million dollars respectively.[4]

Other sources note that from 1941 to 1946 the average of direct foreign investments was $26.2 million. The average of "deinvestments" (profits from foreign investments returned to the "home" country, technical services, etc., paid to foreign companies) was $62 million. In successive periods the respective amounts were as follows: in 1947–52, $60.4 million against $111.7 million; in 1953–58, $99.8 million against $116.6 million; in 1959–64, $114.1 million against $164.4 million; and in 1965, $155.7 million against $225.9 million. Should the trend remain constant, then, direct foreign investment during the present presidential period (1965–70) will reach $186.8 million per annum, and "deinvestments" will reach $301.6 million. In the period 1971–76 they would be $261.6 million and $483.2 million, respectively.[5] To put it another way, during the presidential regime of Manuel Ávila Camacho the average annual deficit of direct foreign investments was $35.8 million; during the regime of Miguel Alemán, $51.4 million; under Ruiz Cortines, $16.8 million; under López Mateos, $50.3 million; and, in the first year of the administration of Díaz Ordaz, $70.2 million. If the trend

4. *Ibid.*, p. 44.
5. *Informe Semanal de los Negocios.* Inversiones Extranjeras Directas (Mexico), Years 1939–65, Nos. 693–96, Year XV.

continues, the losses for the country will be $114.7 million per annum under the present administration, and $221.8 million per annum during the successive six-year period.[6]

It is true that between 1940 and 1965 the diversification of Mexican markets improved somewhat, especially in the last few years,[7] but it is also true that in the period before World War II, the percentage of Mexico's imports from the United States increased, whereas the percentage of exports to the United States was almost unchanged. The degree to which Mexico's foreign trade is dependent upon the United States market is roughly equivalent to the degree of dependence of the old French colonies in Africa on their metropolitan markets. In our enthusiasm for recent measures of the diversification of markets, we tend to forget that these measures do not alter the secular trend of dependence on a dominant market. These measures are as limited in their effect on economic foreign policy as is the new taxation law in its effect on domestic policy. Thus, profits from foreign firms sent abroad are higher than private investments, and decapitalization results. United States products sent to Mexico become increasingly expensive while Mexican products sent to the United States become cheaper. This combination accounted for a loss of $20 billion for Mexico between 1957 and 1961, a far higher amount than estimated by the Alliance for Progress.[8]

It is difficult to take measures to control foreign investments and to diversify foreign trade in ways that will change the economic structure and the secular trend when, for example, from 1942 to 1960, United States banks issued credits to Mexico in the amount of $1.5 billion, and year after year those credits increased: [9] to maintain the equilibrium of its balance of payments, Mexico is dependent on those loans, on private investments (which amounted to $1.4 billion in the

6. *Ibid.*
7. In 1940, /9 per cent of imports were from the United States, and in 1965, 64.2 per cent were. In 1940, 89.5 per cent of exports were bound for the United States, and in 1965, 71.2 per cent were. Cf. Table 12.
8. Ramón Ramírez, *op. cit.*, p. 110.
9. *Ibid.*, p. 51.

same period), on tourism, and on income of wetbacks. After all, Mexico is a heterogeneous country, highly differentiated, and the participating sector and the State itself cannot ignore political realities. Only by emphasizing and strengthening a popular policy and, through that policy, strengthening the Mexican State, will the government be able to pursue a national policy on foreign investments and diversification of foreign trade that will place Mexico on equal terms with the United States. We might advocate additional measures pertaining to domestic credit, investments by states and regions, agrarian reform, nationalization of credit, control of exchange, reduction of the apparatus of distribution, intervention by the States, and the like, all of which have been discussed by the country's economists and progressive groups. In every case we would see that the country's political structure, as well as the laws of the market which influence economic decisions, is impeding the breakdown of the dynamics of inequality both internally and externally and is creating bottlenecks for a developmental policy.

In a free enterprise or capitalist regime, decisions regarding development derive from two historic and empirically recognized sources: the laws of the market, and the organizations, trade unions, and political parties, which are the instruments of the popular masses. In the development of Great Britain, the Scandinavian countries, the United States, France, and Italy, these two factors are always present. The first determines the decisions of private enterprise; the second, in relation to the first, determines governmental decisions. Although the laws of the market alone play into the dynamics of inequality, popular organizations bring about what Seymour Martin Lipset has called the "process of egalitarianism of capitalist democracies."

In a country like Mexico, decisions bearing on development are made in a similar fashion. The laws of the market operate as anywhere else; they serve to channelize credits and investments toward the more developed and sounder sectors, to minimize costs (by cutting salaries), to minimize tax burdens on the utilities and the income from capital, and to maximize concessions, subsidies, and tax exemptions. The self-adjusting mechanism which characterizes the European and American development of capitalist countries is aided by democratic interplay and the democratic organization of trade unions, and it forces the State and the entrepreneurs to make more and greater concessions to the masses, to make social investments, to increase salaries, to enact tax laws that will bring about a dynamics of egalitarianism, as exists in Great Britain, the Scandinavian countries, and the United States. In Mexico, this mechanism does not operate with the same efficiency. Government decisions regarding development are made on the basis of a far more limited view of equality—which is, in fact, a view far closer to inequality. Then there is also the paradoxical situation in which the satisfaction of the demands of private and foreign enterprise or of their governments do not result in an increase of private investments, a multiplication of enterprises, and the growth of national and foreign business, but rather cause economic and social instability by increasing economic and social inequality. The flight of Mexican capital in 1961, for example, equaled approximately one-third of the country's currency reserve. Between 1958 and 1961 this flight of capital from Mexico was almost the same as the amount of loans for which the government contracted abroad. At the same time, private foreign investments decreased both in absolute figures and in comparison with government foreign investments; Mexican private investment decreased with respect to previous years (in 1961, it was 16 per cent less than in 1960); and its percentage as compared with public investment likewise decreased (in the period 1953–58 public investments represented 37.5 per cent of the total and private investments represented 62.5 per cent; in 1959–61 the corresponding percentages were 43.6 per cent and 56.4 per cent, respectively).[10]

10. Ramón Ramírez, *op. cit.*, pp. 30–31 and 126.

In the face of all these facts, there are those who would come up with moral exhortations to capitalists and entrepreneurs that they should invest in Mexico and not abroad and those who insist that the government should provide greater incentives to national and foreign investment, as though the capitalist's motives for investment were of a moral order, and as though he had not already found in Mexico exactly the types of incentives which he had demanded and exactly the types of exorbitant profits which in the last few years have provoked cycles of contraction, instability, and even agitation in the economy.

The capitalist's sole incentive is the market; the capitalist goes where there is a market. The market's motor is moved by the increase in ultimate consumption, and the ruler's decision to create the market is carried out by liberating the democratic forces of a capitalist country, by not extinguishing them with violence typical of the pre-capitalist State, and by taking into account the fundamentals of capitalist development, which invigorates the internal market, national cohesion, and power.

If economic decisions are to be made in terms of economic and political forces, the alternatives are either to continue present policies and undertake development with the previously described structural limitations or to change economic and political conditions. The change—*in theory*—could be of two kinds: a change in the economic and social system which would lead to socialism, or a policy change within the prevailing capitalist economic system. If the country is to be developed and present problems resolved, one of these changes must be brought about. Under present political conditions, inequality prevails both in the international sphere and at domestic levels. Yet even the more moderate type of change, the reform of the political regime, encounters serious obstacles. In European and United States development, the force for the growth of the domestic market has been a system of parties and trade unions which were close to the classical model. In Mexico, the rate of development so far achieved is due to a *sui generis* system of government. This compels us to believe that the democratization of the country within the prevailing capitalist regime requires a special political imagination, a true democratic creation, not imitation of the forms of government of classic democracy or stagnation in the parademocratic forms now prevailing. This transformation would not necessarily require the creation of a two-party system or a parliamentary system; in fact, these are in the process of decaying and no longer meet the needs of neo-capitalist politics. The transformation does demand forms of internal democracy within the government party itself; parliamentary institutions in which the economic power of the public sector is necessarily controlled; representative institutions for national decolonization; institutions for the expression of ideas by political and cultural minority groups, including Indian groups; institutions to encourage party newspapers and Indian representation; institutions to bring about internal trade union democracy and authentic forms of conciliation and arbitration. In other words, the transformation requires new forms of government that would make the most of past national experience while moving forward in an act of political creation. The responsibility rests with the ruling class, and especially with those political and ideological groups which are most representative nationally.

As long as there are no new forms of government, we may speak of decisions for growth, but not for development. The only basic decision for development possible at present would be for an effective democracy which would expand the internal market, accelerate national decolonization and integration, and intensify those measures encouraging national independence and negotiation at a level of equality with foreign powers, particularly the United States.

As long as this basic decision is not made, any decisions regarding development will have the same limitations that have held true in the immediate past.

The problem lies in the fact that the ruling class and the conformist sectors of Mexico do not view the democratization of institutions as an urgent necessity. An opaque screen of political and rhetorical habits, of partial and actual successes, of demagogic deceit, hides the need of decolonization and effective democratization from public consciousness.

It is difficult to understand that Mexico is both a developing and underdeveloped nation, one that has only partially corrected internal and external inequality. After all, the decisions that correct inequality are compatible with those that emphasize it. Mexico still has, at a higher level of national independence, a structure of foreign trade and finances which reveals its dependence upon the United States. Although the sector participating in development has grown, structural inequality within the developed sector still exists, especially in the relationships between that sector and the marginal and semicolonial sectors.

Mexico's successes have blinded many. They have produced a parochial satisfaction which places a taboo on serious criticism of national policy and makes heretics of critics. Mexico has had relative successes, meaningful within the framework of underdeveloped countries, but from these successes comes only slow progress, and there is an enormous number of miserable human beings. An important goal for national criticism is a firm understanding that although problems have been solved in the past, the solution was insufficient.

Mexico's economic growth is a fact; Mexico's development is only partly so. The rate of mortality, even infant mortality, has decreased; the urban and industrial population has grown; the population participating in development has grown; highways have unified the nation, which had previously lacked communication; agrarian reform has expanded the internal market; the nationalization of oil has trebled its production, with favorable over-all effects upon the national economy; the Federal Commission of Electricity has multiplied its production six times in twenty-five years; and the State has nationalized electricity, thereby increasing the country's economic independence. The State has developed, and the country has become more integrated. Yet the marginal population still represents between 50 and 70 per cent of the total; in absolute figures the marginal population has increased; the distribution of income is typical of an underdeveloped country; and dependence upon the United States goods and capital market is still structural in nature.

It is evident, on the other hand, that in Mexico's development there is a series of economic decisions which are counterparts of a policy of national integration and growth. These decisions may produce a moral satisfaction among rulers and entrepreneurs.

Certain decisions have, in effect, led to national integration—for instance, agrarian reform, the fight against illiteracy, the expropriation of oil, and the nationalization of the electric industry. In the same category are decisions regarding structural investments, which allow for a national policy of development; so too other less spectacular but no less effective decisions which have given priority to production over services, and have allowed—unlike decisions in other underdeveloped countries—control of inflationary processes, increases of production, and training people for work in production. Other decisions—necessarily contradictory —have given priority to investment for production in the more developed rather than in the less developed regions; a different policy would have involved large structural investments with scarce returns. There have been decisions involving investments in undeveloped regions with readily exploitable natural resources and communications networks that made production and distribution possible. Finally, there have been decisions that have brought in new types of functionaries, better qualified and better paid, who are dedicated to the tasks of financing and production in the public sector. These decisions have enabled the public sector to become one of the most active instruments in the development of the country.

In the development of the nation there has been a series of decisions which are consistent with a rational policy of growth and development. Thus in the past thirty years the country has achieved a level of growth and economic and social integration far higher than that of other similar countries in Latin America. But economic rationality of growth is not enough; subsumed in it are measures that contradict its very goals, and inequality has not been overcome at a rate which would ensure the continuity of economic development in a peaceful form.

It is true that in present-day Mexico, decisions are made in the national interest. But when we analyze their impact upon the over-all structure, we see that they have been insufficient to eliminate dependence, internal inequality, and underdevelopment. We also find a different breed of decisions alongside: the "realistic" decisions, which are taken as a function of the economic and political power of beneficiary groups. These decisions are a direct product of existing organizations and their political power. These political decisions favor the more organized part of Mexico; and the more organized the level, the more favorable the decisions become, whereas in the poorly organized or disorganized sectors, the opposite obtains. In the realm of credits, contracts, and investments, a considerable number of decisions tend to control, and ensure the co-operation of, the various pressure groups within the public sector. There are contracts for projects paid for yet never carried through, building contracts for zone chiefs, and public investments whose returns determine the private incomes of functionaries. There are no strong popular organizations, nor is there the traditional party interplay, carrying with it the possibility of losing power in elections. The leniency with which those acts are committed is doubled by the liberty of parties and journalists to denounce or invent or hide them. As a result, nothing happens. The functionaries are never removed, subjected to judgment, or forced to prove their honesty publicly.

Other decisions tend to control and ensure the co-operation of the organized private sector—those dealing with contracts, credits, tax exemptions, salary decreases, for example. They bring about not only the co-operation and appeasement of the private sector, but oftentimes the "legal" enrichment of public functionaries who are also entrepreneurs.

Some decisions are made in view of a wider social perspective. They tend to control and ensure the co-operation of employees and workers belonging to the party or to official trade unions by means of social investments, services, and salary increases. Some are decisions to seek negotiations with the few independent workers' and peasants' organizations in order to satisfy the demands of the organized masses, as long as they do not present any kind of political opposition. These kinds of decisions partially diminish inequality in classes and unions of the participating sectors, as well as in the areas where these people live; this is a function of their participation or political integration. But these social decisions satisfy only a small part of the population: the middle classes and the organized workers, the urbanized and the industrialized. But under this visible segment, the disorganized urban and particularly rural masses, the marginal urban and rural population, and, above all, the Indians remain. Their impoverishment is increasingly profound and sharp in contrast.

Decisions that tend to satisfy the needs of the marginal and disorganized population are social charity, not social justice and development. Institutions serving this immense sector receive and merely assist their clients. They do not correct the structural situation of the marginal population, nor have they the economic and political power to do so.

Thus inequality continues, both in the domestic and in the international spheres. Those political decisions which oppose it have not been sufficient to eliminate it. The slow rate of economic growth during the past few years, the depressed conditions in the world raw-materials market, the limitations of the internal market, and the awakening of the masses in large areas of the country demand one fundamental policy: the democratization of national institutions. Research as one may, time and again the same conclusion is reached: either an effectively democratic constitution, with which there should be no violence, or the danger of economic contraction and an expansion of violence. Without an effectively democratic constitution, there would not be a more radical solution under present conditions, but there would necessarily be a period of stagnation and dictatorship similar to what many South American countries are now undergoing. Let us, however, examine the possibility that a decision will be made to carry through democracy.

IV

THE FUTURE OF DEMOCRACY

9

Value Judgments and Politics

In policy choices, utopian and moral ideas are combined with technical or common realism. These combinations are not always felicitous. They do not convey the idea that politics is the logical and scientific expression of analysis of the social structure, of historical trends, of human resources.

Divergent yet authentic interpretations, deep convictions that a given choice is correct despite others' beliefs to the contrary, complicates the problem. Rhetoric and demagogy, opportunism and sectarianism, prejudice, and the decision to take a stand and not fall prey to the neurosis of contemplation: all seem to lead inevitably to the idea that politics is not the logical product of scientific analysis, but is rather a form of action emerging from individual and class circumstances.

The function of ideologies and their very nature—they are relative and useful to the interests of different classes and groups—seem to remove politics even further from a logical and scientific basis. This confusion is not universally sustained and does not necessarily lead to skepticism, but accepted political truth always remains within the purview of a particular school of thought or party, especially if it is a truth dealing with the most adequate road to be followed by a nation. When someone tries to go beyond polemics and propose neutral choices, they remain in the realm of fantasy, ridiculous prescriptions to which no one pays any attention. And rightly so, because the solution necessarily lies within the political climate itself, in past and present social reality. In politics, no one can produce unexpected solutions. The task of the political scientist is confined to analyzing expected solutions, subjecting them only to the logic of those who submit them, and testing those solutions with facts. To speak of political possibilities is to speak of facts. Any other approach is unrealistic.

Therefore, when considering the possibilities for democracy in Mexico, we shall assume that the existence of polemics is an inescapable fact. We shall analyze the possibilities for democracy in the light of the two conflicting ideologies, Marxism and liberalism, that are at the base of any discussion of international and internal problems. What is the Marxist position on the possibility of establishing a capitalist democracy in Mexico? What is the liberal position—or the position of liberal sociology—on the subject?

In this day perhaps all scholarly works should present every problem from both the Marxist and the sociological perspectives in order to deal with the social-science schizophrenia which affects modern man, or, at least, to clarify the underlying assumptions.

Our purpose is to outline both analyses and present a kind of scientific dialogue. This is not intended as either an ironical comment or an act of disrespect for the social sciences. In Mexico the two most opposite philosophies of our time point toward the same road: the development of democracy and capitalism. In theory, this is encouraging, and it may serve to prevent unnecessary political struggles. But if both philosophies indicate the same objective, what possibilities of achieving it do they each see? What means do they indicate? What obstacles do they find? It is necessary to carry the analysis from its sources to its ultimate logical and political consequences.

By merely indicating that two conflicting ideologies arrive at the same conclusions, we do not expect to bring about a felicitous harmony and thereby end the struggle. Political battles are not so simple as their images may seem. Political reality is not the result of a logical sequence of thought, and struggles are frequently conducted against basic ideological assumptions. Yet in an analysis of the national situation, it is important to note that those assumptions lead to similar ideas and point to a similar goal—capitalist democracy—even though some emphasize democracy as a road to socialism and others see it as an end in itself.

Someone might say that in order to make this dialogue complete it is necessary to include the "democrats," who propose a dictatorship, or the "Marxists," who consider another revolution an immediate necessity. Both are agitating for dictatorship and revolution, respectively. We should reply that our dialogue is aimed at revealing their intellectual and political inconsistency. Some call themselves democrats when they are really fascists, and some call themselves Marxists when they are really adventurers. Both the Marxist and the sociological analyses here are conceptualized on the basis of the most typical or orthodox authors. I have attempted to paraphrase as faithfully as possible these two currents of thought.[1]

1. Even though since recent times we may speak of a Marxist sociology, here we shall maintain the traditional division between Marxism and sociology.

10

The Marxist Analysis

Codes of laws and constitutions do not determine a society; rather, they are its direct or indirect expression. The Napoleonic Code did not produce modern civil society: "On the contrary, the civil society which emerged in the eighteenth century and continued developing in the nineteenth century, merely finds its legal expression in the Napoleonic Code." [1] National and class struggle in Mexico that was characteristic of a semi-colonial and semi-feudal State reproduced legal forms that were the expression of more advanced structures. Those structures did not appear in Mexico, simply because of the establishment of their legal expression.

The class ideological struggle conducted in Mexico after the downfall of the usurper Huerta led to a compromise between factions and classes. This compromise enabled the struggle to continue but now there was an advanced liberal constitution which included various social rights. The Constitution operated as an instrument of the emerging bourgeoisie, who were allied with the organized workers and armed peasants struggling against latifundism and imperialism. National

1. Karl Marx, *An die Kölner Geschwornen* (1849), par. 14. As cited in Stanley W. Moore in *The Critique of Capitalist Democracy: An Introduction to the Theory of the State in Marx, Engels and Lenin* (New York: Paine-Whitman Publishers, 1957).

and working-class leadership was in the hands of the bourgeoisie and petty bourgeoisie, depending on the power structure, and the articles of the constitutional pact were more or less honored. The exhausted masses of the people, particularly the most disorganized and primitive, were outside the pact and excluded from the Constitution. For them the Constitution had neither direct nor indirect utility.

The Constitution was thus the instrument and expression of an emerging bourgeoisie allied with the organized workers in their struggle against latifundism and imperialism. It was an instrument for the development of capitalism and for the development of the country within the capitalist system. Yet because the country did not fully develop capitalism, those institutions characteristic of capitalist democracy did not develop either.

Engels refers to democracy as the "logical form of bourgeois government," [2] and Lenin says that a "democratic republic is the best political shell for capitalism, and therefore once capital is in possession . . . of this excellent shell, it establishes its power so firmly that no change of individuals, institutions, or parties in the democratic-bourgeois republic can shatter it." [3] Both statements confirm the fact that Mexico has not yet reached a fully bourgeois government, a bourgeois democracy, because it has not yet fully established a capitalist system. Thus Mexico is pre-capitalist and therefore pre-democratic.[4]

Mexico's structure is pre-capitalist largely because the system of production characteristic of capitalism is close to the system of production characteristic of imperialism, a fact which can be observed in both the domestic and international spheres. The forms that persist in the most backward regions of the country, which resemble a condition of internal coloni-

2. Engels to Bernstein, November 24, 1884, par. 2 (6). As quoted by Moore, *op. cit.*
3. Lenin, *The State and the Revolution.* Chapter 1 and Section 3, *ibid.*
4. The term "democratic" is used here to refer to bourgeois democracy exclusively.

alism, are a symptom of the pre-capitalist form of Mexico's development as a national State. Another factor, the existence of imperialism, was absent among the first nations that developed capitalism. "Democracy corresponds to free competition. Political reaction corresponds to monopoly. In both domestic and foreign policy, imperialism struggles for the violation of democracy and for reaction." [5]

In Mexico, typical European capitalism and typical European democracy do not exist. For one thing, Mexican capitalism is not so firmly established or powerful that a change of individuals, institutions, or parties might not shatter it. For another, Mexican capitalism cannot establish democracy in its own "colonies"; capitalism has never established democracy either in its colonies or with its colonies.

"Metropolitan" Mexico itself suffers from the anti-democratic effects of colonialism, and the democratic difficulties of the Mexican "metropolis" are even greater because these are the effects of United States imperialism and of the political reaction of United States monopolies. Thus, Mexico finds itself faced with a contradiction: as capitalism becomes more firmly established, there is a corresponding strengthening of its logical superstructure, which is democracy, the logical form of bourgeois government; but imperialism exists in both domestic and foreign policy, and it struggles for the violation of democracy, for reaction. This contradiction is clearly evident in voting patterns.

In Mexico, insofar as bourgeois domination is limited, universal voting is likewise limited, and the Constitution is limited. The broadening or limitation of voting depend on the broadening or limitation of bourgeois development.

> The real meaning of the bourgeois constitution is bourgeois domination, both as the product and the result of the universal vote being considered to express the sovereign will of the people. But since the content of the vote, of the sovereign

5. Lenin, *Caricature of Marxism.* Sec. pars. 17–18, *ibid.*

will, is no longer the domination of the bourgeoisie, does the Constitution have another meaning? Is it not the duty of the bourgeoisie to regulate the voting in such a way as to achieve what is reasonable, its own domination? [6]

In those regions where the development of the bourgeoisie is less, and in which pre-capitalist forms of production predominate, there is also less voting. In all cases, there is a bourgeois or pre-bourgeois regulation of voting. Voting becomes a ritualistic activity because of internal colonialism and the dangers which imperialism poses for the Mexican bourgeoisie.

Under these conditions, to think that there might be a party system as is formally provided for in the Constitution, a division of powers, a federal government, a municipal regime, is to forget that the capitalist structure—which would make these forms of government the logical forms of a bourgeois government—is not present. For another thing, these juridical forms are the best way to mislead the bourgeoisie itself in terms of formal and absolute goals. The development of the bourgeoisie in a semi-colonial nation with problems of internal colonialism cannot occur under the traditional forms of constitutions that are prior to the appearance of imperialism.

Insofar as a fully capitalist development does not take place in Mexico, the *traditional* juridical forms of the Constitution are not fulfilled, nor will they be. As long as there is internal colonialism and Mexico does not attain a relative level of equality with the United States—improbable as long as imperialism continues—there will be no political parties peacefully succeeding each other in power, nor will there be sovereign state governments. As long as internal colonialism exists, there will be no universal voting or municipal independence.

The bourgeoisie has made use of the predominant party, the centralization of power, the pre-democratic limitation of voting, the control of governors and municipal presidents as

6. Marx, *Class Struggle in France*. Part 3, pars. 94–95, *ibid.*

caciques for the development both of capitalism and of the semi-colonial country. They are aware of these facts, and it is unlikely that they would attempt to alter the system of government to produce the typical forms of capitalist democracy.

It is equally unlikely that the country should revert to earlier forms of government characteristic of the stage of national and anti-feudal struggles. In an earlier period, Mexico's system of government brought about a policy of anti-imperialist national unity which was led by the bourgeoisie and supported by the people. The Cárdenas regime was the climax of presidentialist and single-party forms of government, as well as the high point of economic and political democratization. This was the stage of the closest revolutionary relationship between the bourgeois State and the people in dealing with latifundism and imperialism. There are those who think of a return to the Cárdenas-style forms of semi-capitalist democracy as a way of achieving national democratization. Yet, such a return is impossible.

Conditions have changed. Pre-capitalist latifundism has practically disappeared from the scene, and national and foreign capital have become increasingly interrelated. Under these conditions, it would be utopian to think in terms of an alliance between the bourgeoisie and the workers and peasants against capitalist latifundism and imperialism, in order to establish a democracy of the Cárdenas variety imposed from above. This brings us to the following question: What type of democracy is possible, and what might be its dialectics?

Here we must point out two problems related to the class struggle in Mexico. One concerns the working class and its possible evolution into a politically aware and organized social class using a given strategy. The other concerns a possible political strategy of the bourgeoisie—or of certain sectors of the bourgeoisie—which might enable it to organize a democratic-bourgeois government in which working-class political liberties would be a reality, within the limits of the Mexican capitalist structure.

Let us begin by studying the problems concerning the actual and ideological situation of the working class.

> As long as the domination by the bourgeoisie was not fully organized and had not acquired its pure political expression, neither could the opposition of other classes achieve a pure expression. It was thus unable to take that crucial turn which makes of every struggle against the government a struggle against capital.[7]

In Mexico the domination of the bourgeoisie is not fully organized and does not have a pure political expression. This is confirmed by the following facts: internal colonialism proves that there are limitations to the national market, to salaried labor, and to the full development of the bourgeoisie; the overt or covert struggles against imperialist super-exploitation are another proof of the limitations of capitalist development in Mexico. The political effects of internal colonialism and imperialism—insofar as they prevent class struggle from achieving a pure expression—are obvious, even though they have not been sufficiently studied. Here we shall merely present a few observations on a complex problem.

In Mexico internal colonialism and the absence of a pure expression of the class struggle are closely linked to a phenomenon indicated by Marx: "the more a dominant class is able to absorb the best men from the oppressed classes, the more solid and dangerous is their domination." [8] In the development of Mexican capitalism, class opposition has been obscured by the transformation of large sectors of the population from a semi-colonial to a proletarian status, by a transformation from an unskilled to a skilled proletariat, by a change from working-class and peasant leadership to bourgeois government. Thus there has evolved a structure of political control of the semi-colonial population by the semi-colonialist population, led by the bourgeoisie. Even though the proletar-

7. Marx, *The Eighteenth Brumaire of Louis Bonaparte, ibid.*
8. Marx, *Das Kapital,* 12, III, *ibid.*

iat and its class consciousness and organizations are in opposition to capital, they do not yet constitute a "class for themselves," and their struggles have not yet achieved a pure expression. For another thing, the government itself, busy with "everyday business," and the different sectors of the progressive bourgeoisie—that is, the bourgeoisie seeking to achieve full economic development under capitalism—have directed working-class and peasant struggles against either political groups of the commercial bourgeoisie and of imperialism or against those national and foreign enterprises most resistant to social reform. It has never been possible that a struggle against the government should be a struggle against capitalism and for the establishment of socialism. At the most, there has been a struggle against the present pre-capitalist and pre-democratic constitutional system, which might result in an open victory for imperialism. This phenomenon has also obscured the pure expression of the class struggle. Mexico's situation does not correspond to that of semi-colonial and semi-feudal countries in which the revolutionary conditions of an anti-imperialist and anti-feudal national struggle are present, in which the landless peasantry is mobilized against a government representing the relationships of production typical of imperialism and semi-feudalism. In Mexico there was an anti-imperialist national revolution, led by the bourgeoisie, which put an end to semi-feudal relationships of production and initiated a national policy of capitalist development. Thus it has the contradictions characteristic of any capitalist or semi-capitalist regime in the new nations. But it also has the characteristics of those new nations in which there has been a national and agrarian revolution led by the bourgeoisie, in which the working class does not constitute an independent force, and in which a socialist type of revolution is not likely.

The union leaders and peasants allied to the progressive bourgeoisie, as well as the leaders of the proletariat, have recognized that present conditions in Mexico are not those of highly developed countries, and that goals and tactics cannot be the same. Lenin wrote:

> In advanced countries—such as Great Britain, France, and Germany, the national problem was resolved long ago; national unity has fulfilled its purpose; objectively there are no "national tasks" to fulfill. Therefore only in those countries is it now possible to break national unity and establish class unity. In underdeveloped countries—on the contrary— in the whole of Eastern Europe and in the colonial and semicolonial countries, the situation is entirely different. In those places, as a general rule, we still have oppressed and underdeveloped nations, from a capitalist point of view. Objectively these nations still have national tasks to fulfill, namely, *democratic* tasks, the task of throwing out foreign oppression.[9]

These observations by Lenin on the goals and tactics of underdeveloped countries describe the actual Mexican situation and are generally and *abstractly* accepted by all left-wing parties and movements. Yet since the tactics of "national unity" and the "anti-imperialist popular front" are those which bring about the most bitter struggles within the working class and the Left, we must analyze them in order to understand the framework within which the problems of strategy and tactics of the working class are being posed and the possibility of working-class participation in the development of a bourgeois democracy or a socialist revolution.

We must objectively analyze such problems as the notion that the alliance with the national bourgeoisie against imperialism is a fiction, because a national bourgeoisie no longer exists but is really a pretext used by opportunistic politicians and reformers to continue serving the bourgeoisie and postponing the socialist revolution; and the notion that historical experience reveals that it was precisely in the underdeveloped countries in which the first socialist regimes were established, and

9. Lenin, *Caricature of Marxism, op. cit.*

that it is high time to begin the Socialist Revolution. These are the main subjects of debate within Marxist and pseudo-Marxist groups, and they particularly concern the tactics of the working class. How should these problems be objectively analyzed?

First, we shall state our goals precisely. When Lenin mentions the need to fulfil national tasks, democratic tasks, the task of eliminating foreign oppression, without breaking national unity in order to establish class unity, he is pointing to various facts. In confronting imperialism, there is a national task and a democratic task, and they postpone the moment of achieving class unity. The national task has historically led to the establishment of socialist governments, of popular democracies, of bourgeois democracies of a new type. In the case of Mexico, it led to the establishment of a bourgeois democracy of the new type, and the problem is to find out whether the notion of a national struggle is still valid, and whether it should be directed toward overthrowing the present government and establishing a socialist regime or toward accelerating the development of national capitalism, in which case the democratic task would be a democratic task within capitalism. Left-wing parties and the representatives of the proletariat have implicitly recognized that their immediate struggles must be in terms of an anti-imperialist national front, and implicitly or explicitly for the development of national capitalism, of democracy within capitalism, of an independent foreign policy, of national sovereignty and peace, of increasing working-class rights and grants, of solving agrarian issues, and of actively defending democratic liberties within capitalism. Such are the short-range goals they have set themselves as a road toward socialism. But acceptance of a social and historical situation has led to sins of opportunism and social democracy, and it has led to the "punishment" of these sins, spoken of by Lenin, "anarchist radicalism," adventurism, spontaneous movements. There is thus in Mexico a structural opportunism, which is characteristic of the alienation of the proletariat; its counterpart, a pseudo-theoretical sectarianism, is characterized by the notion of "overcoming stages," in which left-wing students "fall prey to the infantilism of promoting an independent struggle by the working class," and in which the more advanced sectors, isolated from the working class and the students, "forget Marx's famous warning that without the peasant chorus, the solo of the proletarian revolution can turn into a funeral song. . . ." [10] It is in this framework that theoretical, tactical, and strategic problems are discussed; thus it is always necessary to refute both sectarians and opportunists, and to define the dialectical method precisely in order to overcome disagreements theoretically and politically. It must be made clear that it is impossible to think of a socialist revolution in the near future, and that, since it is impossible to expect the class struggle to achieve its pure expression, the worst way to fight opportunism is through sectarian speeches or actions. They are two complementary forms which weaken the working class in the fulfilment of the national task and in the struggle for its political rights.

Here we shall specify the ideological differences between the two main subjects of discussion: the notion of the sectarians, which flourishes in the most insignificant political crisis, is that another revolution is possible; the notion of the opportunists, which prospers in times of stability, is of unrestricted national unity.

One of the most difficult problems is the timing of a socialist revolution. Trotsky said that while Herzen accused Bakunin of mistaking the second month of pregnancy for the ninth, Herzen mistook the ninth for the second. Trotsky himself erred similarly in his belief that the time was ripe for world revolution.[11] Today we witness a similar debate among the Communist parties, with the Soviet and European parties on

10. Rodney Arismendi, "Acerca del papel de la burguesía nacional en la lucha anti-imperialista," in *El movimiento contemporáneo de liberación y la burguesía nacional* (Prague: Ed. Paz y Socialismo, 1961).
11. Leon Trotsky, *Histoire de la Révolution Russe* (Paris: Editions du Seuil, 1962), p. 912.

one side and the Chinese, Albanian, and Korean on the other.
In the case of Mexico, owing to its structure, there is always a wavering from opportunism to sectarianism, from reformism to verbal radicalism and "the revolutionary phrase."
In this wavering there are shifts from the Soviet line (petty
bourgeois in Mexico) to the Albanian line (also petty bourgeois in Mexico), with attempts to imitate the Cuban Revolution or admiration for super-Trotskyism. But there is no attempt to establish whether objective and subjective conditions
for a socialist revolution are present. Eventually, left-wing
groups or leaders who have entertained the idea of another
revolution emerged. Such groups forget the most elementary
notions of any revolutionary process. They forget that one
cannot issue an invitation to participate in a revolution as one
might issue an invitation to have a cup of tea, as Mao says.
They even forget what Trotsky said, that "the fundamental
premise of a revolution is that the existing social structure
should have become obsolete in terms of resolving the urgent
problems of a nation's development." They also forget what
Che Guevara said: "Wherever a government has come to power
through some form of popular dialogue, be it fraudulent or
otherwise, and where at least an appearance of constitutional
legality is maintained, a guerrilla upsurge is impossible because the possibilities of civil struggle have not been
exhausted." [12] These groups do not carry on any kind of research; they do not know that the situation in Mexico is precisely that described by these thinkers. There is no premise for
a revolution, and the possibilities of civil action for the proletariat and the peasantry have not been exhausted, so neither a
violent revolution nor guerrilla actions are possible, and these
bases will not be brought about because of a small economic
recession. Neither will internal strife between groups of the
bourgeoisie or the imperialists provoke a revolution. Marxists
should not see in each conflict or strike movement, important

12. Ernesto (Che) Guevara, *La guerra de guerrillas* (Havana: Instituto Nacional de la Reforma Agraria, s.a.), p. 13.

as it may be, a sure sign that the time is ripe for another revolution. There will not be another revolution in Mexico until the social structure proves obsolete in terms of resolving the country's *urgent* problems of development and until the possibilities of civil action have been exhausted.

In this respect two important facts must be noted. First, no country that has undergone a democratic-bourgeois revolution of either the old or the new type, that has seen it become consolidated, and that has lived through some years of capitalist development *has ever had* a socialist revolution. Very likely, countries of the above type should be the ones to make a peaceful shift to socialism. Marx suggested the possibility of such a shift for Great Britain, the Netherlands, and other European countries, and Moscow recently confirmed this declaration for all those countries in which the political rights of the working class are brought about within capitalism. The Mexican working class and the revolutionary leadership therefore should not fall prey to adventurist attitudes promoting a socialist revolution as long as the necessary pre-conditions have not become fully apparent. They appear at times of acute and permanent crisis, and are coupled with the revolutionary dissatisfaction of the masses. In the meantime the leaders must set their goals at the level of the national and democratic tasks, aware that in the long run a peaceful or violent revolution will come about, according to internal and international conditions and the policy followed by the bourgeoisie. They should also be aware that the bourgeoisie, not the working class, will have the role of unleashing violence, of proving their incapability to work for the development of the nation, and of violating constitutional legality. The immediate mission of the working class is to fight for the Constitution, for the solution of the urgent problems of the masses, and for the political rights of the workers within the capitalist system. To avoid falling prey to sectarianism and opportunism, the workers and their leaders "must be prepared to use a double tactic, that is, while preparing for the peaceful development of the revolution, they must be sufficiently prepared for the non-peaceful development of the revolution." [13]

The second subject of bitter debate among the Mexican Left is the question of national unity and the class struggle. This problem is posed in an anguished and extreme manner both among those who underrate the role of the national bourgeoisie, and those who "exaggerate the extent of its anti-imperialist and democratic combativeness." [14] We recognize the truth of Lenin's thesis that national unity is necessary to eliminate foreign oppression; and we likewise recognize the existence of a major contradiction and a secondary contradiction referred to by Mao. But the different left-wing groups violently oppose each other and call each other sectarians and opportunists; they do not analyze the method sufficiently to formulate objectively dialectical tactics and strategies. Under these conditions, "opportunism" means suggesting the possibilities of alliance with the bourgeoisie and making apologies for its anti-imperialist struggles or social reforms without indicating that these are *necessarily* contradictory. They suggest fear of imperialism and open class struggle toward the proletariat and the peasantry. The masses must be warned during the ascendant phases of bourgeois policy that the fall of bourgeois policies is foreseeable. They must fight side by side with the bourgeoisie in their ascendant phases without failing to organize the proletariat at the same time. The rights of the proletariat must be defended when the class struggle becomes heightened to remind the bourgeoisie of their agreement to establish a class alliance against imperialism and for the goal of capitalist democracy and peaceful development.

Under present conditions in Mexico the main task of sectarians has been to downgrade the opportunists. They have not organized and struggled with the proletariat in peaceful pursuit of its rights, salaries, grants, and political culture.

13. "Nuestras Diferencias," in *Diario del Pueblo* (Peking: Foreign Language Editions), 1961.
14. Rodney Arismendi, *op. cit.*

Among some, sectarianism is verbal radicalism, the use and abuse of "revolutionary phrases" without political and ideological communication with the proletariat. In the case of both opportunism and sectarianism, the problem is that the leadership of the proletariat remains predominantly petty bourgeois and never takes roots among the proletariat. This is clearly apparent from the lack of internal democracy of working-class and political organizations within the Left.

From this perspective, the problem of opportunism and sectarianism can be dealt with and the possibilities for bourgeois democracy in Mexico and the role of the working class can be analyzed.

It is true, as Marx said, that

> while the proletariat does not develop enough to become organized as a class, while the struggle of the proletariat with the bourgeoisie does not acquire a political character, the theoreticians (of the proletariat) are mere utopians who invent systems to satisfy the needs of the oppressed classes.[15]

It is also true, as Lenin wrote, that

> no economic struggle can bring a stable improvement for the workers, it cannot even be effected in a large scale, unless the workers have the right freely to organize their assemblies and trade unions, to publish their own newspapers, to send their leaders to those institutions which are representative of the people, as was the case in Germany in 1899 and in all the other European states (with the exception of Turkey and Russia). And in order to achieve these rights, it is necessary to effect a *political struggle*. . . . The first and foremost objective of such a struggle must be the achievement of political rights, the achievement of political freedom.[16]

Because the proletariat has not developed sufficiently to become organized as a class, the struggle for the political free-

15. Karl Marx, *Das Elend der Philosophie*. Berlin, p. 142. As quoted by Dahrendorf.
16. Lenin, "Our Program," in *On Tradeunionism* (Moscow: Foreign Language Editions, 1958), pp. 40–41.

dom of the proletariat in Mexico today both allies itself with and clashes with the aims of the political groups of the progressive bourgeoisie. It is unlikely that this situation should change so long as a pre-capitalist structure such as we have described prevails. There is no reason to expect anything but failure so long as there are semi-capitalist structure, internal colonialism along with a considerable mobilization of the marginal population, and continuing absorption of peasant and working-class leaders into the political leadership of the bourgeoisie in Mexico. At the same time, imperialism and the ultra-reactionary bourgeoisie can always lead the country to fascism.

In a pre-capitalist society—which absorbs the best men from the oppressed classes—class consciousness and the concept of "a class for itself" do not hold true. Left-wing leadership becomes atomized, permanently polarized into the ruling centers of the different groups of the bourgeoisie. The development of class consciousness and of a class for itself— the integration of a true proletarian organization—can be realized only through the tactics of alliance and struggle with the national bourgeoisie and of internal democratization of working-class and peasant organizations. There must be a struggle for the immediate objectives of the working class: salaries, grants, social rights, work contracts. There must be a permanent confirmation of the anti-imperialist pact with the bourgeoisie, continuous education of the working class about the forms of struggle, and recognition that the working class has a national task to fulfil—namely, a democratic task. One of the main objectives of this task must be the organization and defense of the super-exploited workers of the countryside and the city, for they are the mainspring of a revolutionary political organization struggling toward national democratization.

One can foresee in the immediate future a limited role for the working class especially if, because of the structure of the society, it does not evolve into a class organization that might, in turn, bring about the creation of a powerful independent party of the working class. But if the working class does follow the tactic of alliance and struggle which will win for the workers their political rights—the rights freely to organize their assemblies and trade unions, to organize the super-exploited workers, to publish their own newspapers, to send their leaders to institutions representative of the people— the role of the class will be an important one.

If the Mexican situation does permit the working-class realization of the democratic task of alliance and struggle with the national bourgeoisie, what role would the Mexican bourgeoisie then fulfil in the development of a bourgeois democracy, and what are the chances for its fulfilment? The problem is to find out which of the groups of the bourgeoisie can succeed, and whether the government can take a path leading to the development of capitalism and of capitalist democracy. Engels said that political power either

> works in harmony with and in the direction of development in agreement with economic laws—in which case there is no conflict between the two and economic development becomes accelerated—or it works against economic development, and in that case, with a few exceptions, it usually succumbs. These exceptions are isolated cases of conquest in which the barbarian conquerors have exterminated or expelled the population of a country and destroyed or allowed for the deterioration of the productive forces that they were unable to use.[17]

The political problem of the direction of the development of capitalism in Mexico is a problem of the conflict among different groups of the bourgeoisie to determine the direction of that development. There are many distinctions made among those groups, but the traditional distinction between national bourgeoisie and commercial bourgeoisie is not valid for understanding the problem, since the two are increasingly

17. Engels, *Anti-Dühring*, par. 2, c. 4.

related. But in Mexico there is an obvious political difference between the public-sector bourgeoisie and the private-sector bourgeoisie. Indeed, a large sector of the bourgeoisie is aware of the fact that it must either work in the direction of development or succumb, and it is aware that in order to work in the direction of development it must maintain and increase its capacity for negotiation with foreign monopolies, limit the greed of private initiative, and democratize and liberalize Mexican politics. This group runs the ideological gamut. It holds managerial, technical, administrative, production, and mass leadership positions. These positions range from the highest posts in the executive, through enterprise managers and technicians, to rural teachers and other members of the petty bourgeoisie. In the *sui generis* combination of Mexican politics, such people can even be the leaders of progressive groups of the opposition which comprise the Left of the Mexican bourgeoisie, some of whom claim to be Marxists-Leninists.

The sensitivity of these leaders of the bourgeoisie to the idea that the government must be in harmony with the requirements of development or must succumb naturally varies, for strategic or ideological reasons: the types of links that they have with private initiative, with the government, or with the working class and peasant masses; the extent to which their revolutionary ideology is linked to nationalism, to the social liberalism of the Mexican Revolution, or to Marxism. But they make up the leadership of capitalist development, and they are placed in contradictory relationships—in the government party, in the government itself, or in the so-called revolutionary family. These relationships set the standard for their domestic political actions and for their struggles against the more backward groups of the national and foreign bourgeoisie.

The most brilliant political leader of this type was General Lázaro Cárdenas. He was keenly aware of the situation and of the only possible road toward economic and political development. During his presidency he accelerated agrarian reform and nationalized oil, and was the most forceful leader of a developmental movement within capitalism in Mexico. With him, other less decisive and forceful leaders of the bourgeoisie combined to make a large number of progressive leaders who fashioned capitalist development in Mexico. In high- medium- and low-echelon positions in the government a large number of functionaries and politicians have fought in the legislative, administrative, and technical fields for the development of capitalism. Sometimes they believed themselves to be in opposition to what General Cárdenas represented, whereas at other times they were supported by his power. They were cautious in their speech, and even careful not to expound socialist or Marxist ideas (which the more aggressive leaders of the bourgeoisie, along with the discontented masses or the proletariat in the process of achieving political independence, do expound). The fact that this political leadership of the bourgeoisie may declare itself in support of the ideology of the Mexican, nationalist, or Marxist revolution does not prevent it from guiding the direction of the capitalist development of the country. The fact that many of its members, aside from their public functions, have private interests and are economically involved in private enterprises does not prevent them from being aware that the best way to develop capitalism in Mexico is to produce an economic, cultural, and political democratization. It does not prevent them from viewing the questions of strategy and democratization as the main problem facing the government and the development of capitalism in Mexico.

Nevertheless, such awareness on the part of this sector of the bourgeoisie and the ability to carry out this idea are two different things. Both favorable and adverse conditions are in full play. Among the favorable conditions, there has been an expansion of the public sector and of its possibilities for action; there has been a contraction of private investment, leaving the leadership of development increasingly to the public sector. Yet, public power can operate in forms increasingly similar to those of a capitalist or neo-capitalist democracy as the country becomes more developed and as peace becomes more widespread in the international field.

To these conditions, which are relatively favorable to the process of democratization within capitalism, must be opposed the unfavorable conditions of imperialism and the unstabilizing effects of the Cold War and of internal colonialism and moderate and anti-democratic reformism, with their reactionary impact and their pressures, threats, demands, and fears.

The growth of the proletariat—the peasant and industrial workers—of their class consciousness, of their trade unions and political organizations, and the demands of their leaders, who can threaten revolutionary mobilization, have influence in those times of crisis when the class struggle is emphasized. These factors will most certainly be relevant in the immediate future, so the progressive sector of the bourgeoisie should accelerate the processes of democratization and development.

The public-sector bourgeoisie—with its differing and even opposing groups—has taken the first steps from the electoral reform of the Constitution to the strengthening of the left-wing groups and parties. Nonetheless, the speed and the style of this process of national democratization is the subject of serious disagreement—tactical and ideological—within the public-sector bourgeoisie. The disagreements have centered on such subjects as the needs to introduce reforms in the government party, to establish a plan for development, and to reform the electoral law. It is difficult to predict what the outcome of this conflict will be; it depends to a large extent on the nature of international and domestic economic conditions in years to come.

Whatever happens, the program for the Mexican working class in the near future is the formation of cadres and the democratic organization of the organized and the super-exploited workers. They must study the conditions for such an organization concretely and objectively. They must plan for civil struggle, taking a stand for alliance and struggle with the progressive bourgeoisie, in order to eliminate pre-capitalist relationships of production and to consolidate a class society (in the political sense of the term) which might subsequently lead to the peaceful development of socialism. This national and political struggle must be carried out with the conviction that another revolution is impossible unless the development of capitalism is suspended, the democratic organization of the working class and peasantry is permanently impeded, and imperialist and domestic reaction triumph. If that should be the case, Mexico will not be one of the countries to achieve socialism peacefully.

11

Sociological Analysis

Sociology has come a long way since Tocqueville. Even though it still relies on the ideas of the end of the eighteenth and the beginning of the nineteenth centuries, it has abandoned its taste for philosophical reflection and has leaned toward a type of generalization called "middle-range theories." In the post-World War II period, North American trends with their field research techniques and quantitative analysis, terminology, and research subjects have been predominant in sociology. In the area of political sociology, two main figures stand out today: Seymour Martin Lipset and Ralf Dahrendorf. The first is North American, the second is West German but has been particularly influenced by North American sociology. Here we shall refer mainly to Lipset and Dahrendorf, though we could quote the works of many other scholars who would confirm our statements—T. H. Marshall, Deutsch, Germani, Lerner, Hoselitz, for example.[1]

1. Cf. T. H. Marshall, *Citizenship and Social Class and Other Essays* (Cambridge: Cambridge University Press, 1950); Karl W. Deutsch, "Toward an Inventory of Basic Trends and Patterns in Comparative International Politics," *The American Political Science Review,* Vol. LIV, No. 1, March 1960, pp. 34–57; Gino Germani, *Política y Sociedad en una Epoca de Transición* (Buenos Aires: Editorial Paidós, 1962); Bert Hoselitz, *Sociological Aspects of Economic Growth* (Glencoe: The Free Press, 1962); Daniel Lerner, *et al., The Passing of Traditional Society: Modernizing the Middle East* (Glencoe: The Free Press, 1962).

The compulsory starting point of a sociological analysis of the possibilities for democracy in Mexico is Tocqueville. From a methodological point of view, his generalizations are neither too abstract nor too philosophical; he uses those based upon field research and quantitative analysis, and enunciates a series of hypotheses which deserve further field research and more accurate statistical analysis. Here we shall only outline a sociological analysis which would respect these rules or caution us when they are not sufficiently respected.

When studying the possibilities of democracy in Mexico from a sociological perspective, we must define what is understood by "democracy" in sociology. There are different resources, and the first is that of traditional definitions.

Democracy, according to Max Weber, includes two postulates: the prevention of the development of a closed group of official functionaries in order to allow for the universal possibility of access to public positions, and the reduction of official authority in order to increase the sphere of influence of public opinion.[2] Lipset supplies the following definition, which is an attempt to sum up earlier definitions by other sociologists:

> Democracy may be defined, in a complex society, as a political system which provides constitutionally and regularly the possibility of changing the rulers, and as a social mechanism which enables the largest possible sector of the population to influence main decisions by choosing their representatives among those competing for public office.[3]

These definitions clearly lend themselves to equivocal interpretations. Many of the terms they use in turn require new definitions. They serve to provide an approximate idea; they correspond to intuitive concepts, which are only useful at the first stage of research.

2. H. H. Gerth and C. Wright Mills, eds., *From Max Weber: Essays in Sociology* (London: Routledge and Kegan Paul, 1947), p. 226.
3. S. M. Lipset, *Political Man: The Social Basis of Politics* (New York: Doubleday, 1959), pp. 45–46.

Another way of defining democracy is to point out some of its characteristic institutions: freedom of the press and of dissent, freedom to meet and associate, and peaceful change of rulers through elections.

These institutions or variables can be analyzed in their structure and trends. A critical structural analysis leads to the study of rational components and of prejudice toward social strata; analysis of freedom of the press and freedom to meet and associate leads to the study of journalists and their readers, of the pressure groups that meet or associate, also regarding social strata; analysis of political mobility and the structure of voting is performed with respect to social status and standards of living and culture. The analysis of trends is done with various types of adjustments; but in principle, analysis seeks secular trends and, within them, ups and downs, cycles, and increases and decreases.

The variables are quantified and used by studying a multitude of negative or positive indicators (frequency of jailing of journalists, of repression of assemblies, of protests of voting irregularities, of jailing opposition leaders; the number of newspapers advocating different ideologies; the amount of criticism of authority not leading to repression; the number of associations, pressure groups, and parties legally recognized and politically respected; etc.). Using these indications, one can arrive at very accurate definitions of democracy, and of the postulates in each definition. Thus it is possible to predict in any given situation the likelihood that certain variables which typify the syndrome of democracy will appear. Thus, one arrives at a series of probabilistic conclusions, which political scientists can use as hypotheses for future research and politicians can use as points of reference to reflect on short- and long-range action. These conclusions indicate that the probabilities for democracy in Mexico have increased, even though from a structural point of view serious obstacles exist and cannot be ignored.

Other factors being equal, the higher the per capita income, the greater the degree of democracy; the larger the part of population employed by industry, the greater the degree of democracy; the higher the rate of urbanization, the greater the degree of democracy; and the higher the rate of literacy, the greater the degree of democracy.[4] These statements, based upon the analysis of economic and political statistics and confirmed by field studies in the most diverse countries, indicate that in Mexico the probabilities for democracy are today higher than in the past.

The probability for an expansion of democracy has increased insofar as there has been an increase in the per capita income, in the population employed by industry, in urban population, and so forth. But a probabilistic increase does not mean that the phenomenon in question must necessarily take place. There can be elements in a social structure that operate against the trends and thus engender deviations.

There are several major structural obstacles to the development of democracy. One is the existence of a plural society impeding uniform political expression and a horizontal political organization in which economic, cultural, and political class differences are not very acute. The poorer the country and the lower the absolute standard of living of the lower classes, the greater the propensity of the higher strata to treat the lower strata as vulgar, inferior by nature, and the like.[5]

In Mexico, the stereotypes of the Mexican Revolution and of the way in which the people must be treated hide the paternalistic and authoritarian characteristics of politicians and rulers. Nevertheless, they are the subject of private conversations about politics or business, and they ought to be the subject of a careful study similar to the one made by Adorno in the United States on potential fascists.[6] The humble, supplicating, and courteous attitude, under which frustrations are hidden in

4. Cf. Lipset, *op. cit.*
5. Lipset, *op. cit.*, p.66.
6. T. W. Adorno, *et al., The Authoritarian Personality* (New York: Harper & Brothers, 1959).

public political expression, is the popular or indigenous counterpart of the authoritarian and creole personality. Together they are the most serious obstacle for the development of democracy, and they make an acceleration of the process of cultural, social, and economic integration mandatory, for it is the safest road to the basis of a democratic life.

In the structure of contemporary society, the poorer strata have democratic tendencies in the economic sphere and authoritarian tendencies in the political sphere. This is explained by the fact that the lower strata have a lower rate of participation in meetings and formal organizations. They read fewer books and magazines, and they are less informed regarding public affairs. They are isolated from the control of assemblies, from public debates, from organizations, and this prevents them from being aware of and practicing the norms of tolerance and causes them to feel apathy toward institutions of which they are ignorant or which they do not control. This apathy explodes into authoritarianism in times of social crisis.

The authoritarian structure of the society and irrational authoritarianism lead to an authoritarian education of the lower strata. Within every social structure there is political education. It may be either democratic or authoritarian in nature. The people are constantly being educated, and this education is authoritarian where the power structure and the attitude of the dominant strata are likewise authoritarian. Studies about these problems include research that specifically confirms the presence of authoritarianism among the lower strata in Mexico.[7] A deeper analysis would no doubt confirm that authoritarianism among the lower strata in Mexico has much to do with political apathy as a form of disillusionment with juridical institutions, as well as with the lack of internal democracy among large sectors of the population, which are the objects of manipulation from above and have nothing to lose by economic democratization with political authoritarianism. "Inter-

7. Cf. Lipset, *op. cit.,* pp. 102–3, 110–111, 112, 120–22, and 152.

views conducted by various psychologists prove that it is difficult to find among towns with 70 per cent or more illiterates, someone having conceptions similar to those of liberty, freedom of speech, etc." [8]

Fascism, a movement characterized by conservatism with progressive appearances which attacks both capitalism and communism and claims to be both traditionalist and "socialist," has a correspondingly typically authoritarian attitude. It is irrational, in the sense that traditionalism and ideas of justice are deprived of all humanistic content, and instead emphasize phobias, fears, and stereotypes, both old and new.

Adorno states that two types of fascists can be distinguished in our time, "those who profess to believe in democracy and are really anti-democratic, and those who call themselves conservative while they surreptitiously nurture subversive ideas." [9] In either case, the fascist struggles to establish a dictatorship of the economically stronger. [10]

Fascism is not an ideology, but a certain structure of the contemporary political personality which is known by this name but which has existed under different ideologies—Nazism, fascism, Francoism, Peronism, McCarthyism, Poujadism. This phenomenon implies a novelty regarding traditional political frustrations, insofar as it is linked to the modern forms of mass communication and scientific propaganda. In underdeveloped countries, personalist sado-masochist attitudes of self-hate, no less than phobias and prejudices against others, exhibit strange combinations of the most traditionalist and modern cultural forms.

Fascism, as the social outcome of a sort of political personality, is "the product of those who feel cut off from the main trends of modern society." [11] The fascist personality emerges

8. Bruce L. Smith, "Communication Research on Non-Industrial Countries," in *The Process and Effects of Mass Communication* (Urbana, Ill.: Illinois University Press, 1955), p. 175.
9. Adorno, *et al., op. cit.,* p. 680.
10. *Ibid.,* p. 685.
11. Cf. Adorno, *et al., The Authoritarian Personality.*

in decadent classes and decadent regions, among displaced small traders and rural owners, and, generally, among those groups which feel that development has cost them a loss in status. We should study the magnitude of this problem in Mexico, since it is little known. It can be roughly placed in the regions of the Bajío, which have suffered a relative loss of status and occupy a lower rank today than they did when the Bajío was the "granary of Mexico." We know that those groups with incomes from multiple sources—small producers, owners, consumers—receive an increasingly small percentage of the national income, and that among them we can notice such characteristics. We also know that this phenomenon exists in some forms in the industrial centers existing since *porfirismo,* which have had to maintain their industrial status and their level of investments by means of a paternalist and traditionalist policy—for instance, Monterrey. But the present magnitude and intensity of the process are not known, and there is no scientific study on the subject. This process represents an obstacle to the development of democracy, and it is difficult to measure its weight.

In those regions in which there is a genuinely traditionalist political culture—in which the market economy does not yet prevail; in which people are occupied from morning to night in exhausting jobs and have no leisure or energy for political action, and are powerless in the face of economic pressures and violence exercised against them by the local privileged classes—there can be no effective democratic economic and political organizations. The traditionalist resignation to traditional forms of living and submission to the existing powers prevails, hindering the development of democracy and the various political institutions which characterize it, especially in the south and center of Mexico.

The structural obstacles to the development of democracy, which were outlined earlier, have a dynamic function, and in times of socio-political crisis, they affect the constitutionality, the very legitimacy of regimes. The State maintains its legitimacy, however, when it demonstrates its effectiveness. "Effectiveness in the modern world signifies first of all constant economic development." [12] Second, there is legitimacy when extremism represents the most complex rather than the simplest solution, because the lower strata tend to oppose extremist movements and parties, becoming *dissociated* from opposition parties insofar as they are small and offer long-range and complicated solutions.[13]

Trends maintaining legitimacy break down when economic development is stopped, when opposition parties offer simpler and short-range solutions, when the status of the main conservative institutions is threatened,[14] and when the more backward and traditionalist agrarian regions "light up in flames of revolt. . . . Once they become aware and liberated from traditional values, they go to the most radical extremes." [15] In these cases there is a complete breakdown of legitimacy and constitutionality, which are replaced by violence.

Taking into account these generalizations based upon historical experience and statistical analysis, one can conclude that as long as the Mexican State can prove its effectiveness through development, and as long as extremism represents a complex and long-range solution to the problems of the State, anti-democratic threats to the structure of the State will not affect its legitimacy.[16]

The process of modernization of any country that has initiated development and accumulation of capital involves, as noted by Lipset, the solution of three main problems: the relationships between Church and State; the admission of the lower strata, particularly the working class, to full economic and political citizenship through the universal vote and the right of collective negotiation; and the continuing fight for redistribution of income.[17]

"The solution of these tensions contributes to a stable polit-

12. Lipset, *op. cit.*, p. 82.
13. *Ibid.*, pp. 122–23.
14. Lipset, *op. cit.*, p. 78.
15. *Ibid.*
16. *Ibid.*, cf. pp. 83–90.
17. *Ibid.*, p. 83.

ical system. When, on the contrary, the solutions corresponding to a previous historic period accumulate with those of the following period, there is a political atmosphere with more bitterness and frustration than tolerance and compromise." [18] The conditions of development in Mexico—cultural, political, international—have made possible only a partial solution of these problems, and have permitted what is left of past problems to accumulate along with present problems.

The solution to the problem of the relationships between Church and State, which was resolved in the eighteenth or nineteenth centuries in the democratic countries, is similar to the solution of other no less important problems: legitimacy increases when a people have a common, national, secular political culture, the same civic festivities, heroes, and nation-founders; and "insofar as religious links reinforce political alignments, the possibilities for compromise and democratic negotiation are weak." [19] Mexico is among the most advanced Catholic nations of Hispanic culture in finding the solution to this traditional problem of the modern State. Nonetheless, Mexico's secular political culture is not yet commonly shared. Many of its national heroes and many of its civic holidays are subjects of debates. And over and above the Constitution, there are certain religious loyalties. All of this hinders the task of democratization which every modern State undertakes.[20]

"The development of voting rights and of the freedom to organize and dissent evolves in many States as concessions to the lower classes or as tactical means to control them." In both cases, the democratic norms became a part of the actual institutions of those States.[21]

In underdeveloped countries, the pressure toward rapid industrialization makes it impossible to afford an open-party system. Both the leaders of these countries and North American sociologists now agree on this point. The single-party or

18. *Ibid.*
19. Lipset, *op. cit.*, p. 84.
20. *Ibid.*, pp. 127–28.
21. *Ibid.*, p. 94.

predominant-party system is no longer typical of Communist states, or of a country such as Mexico. In India the Congress party predominantes and stands far above all others; in Indonesia the government party prevails; and in Africa the new nations that have not already established the single party are moving in that direction. The solution to the problem at the higher level of development of other poor countries seems to be in the recent electoral reform of the Mexican Constitution, which allows minority parties up to twenty representatives in Congress. If this right should be respected, it will lead to a *sui generis* party system, and the dynamics of the voting process will unfold through parliamentary channels. The government party itself will have to grant full political citizenship, universal voting rights, and representative voting to its members, both in internal party struggles and in those struggles involving other parties. The entire lower strata—not only their leaders—will have to be admitted into the party with full rights. The multiple effects of such constitutional reform are foreseeable, unless the traditionalist and fearful attitudes of Mexican politics impose themselves, and the belief that it would be convenient to have, in addition to the disciplined and duly selected representatives of the government party, disciplined and duly selected representatives of the opposition does not take root. The struggle between these two currents within the ruling groups will be characteristic of Mexican political life in coming years.

In 1859 Disraeli said, "If tomorrow we should grant universal suffrage, I have no fears that the honest and courageous people of England would resort to plunder, arson, and massacre." Something similar was thought and done a few years later by Bismarck in Prussia. They both took this measure with the same idea in mind, confident that the rural areas would support them voluntarily, confident that they would control the socialist movement [22] of England and the liberal movement of Germany, which had their strongholds in the cities,

22. In England this took a legalistic, "Chartist," form.

with the votes of the countryside. In South America, the conservatives and large landowners have often been the most ardent supporters of voting rights, relying on their personal power and the paternalistic acceptance of the agrarian masses. In all of these cases, universal suffrage has been granted and it has been defended by large landowners with a conservative political orientation. Present conditions in Mexico make it difficult to predict the political behavior of the leading strata, and whether they will choose to control the city by means of the countryside or vice versa, and to control the participating population by means of the marginal population or vice versa. Two observations made by Dahrendorf may be useful to predict the behavior and the problems of the country's political leadership:

> As long as the conflicting forces remain diffuse and constitute incoherent aggregates, the regulation of social conflict is virtually impossible. Here the point of view of Coser or Simmel is highly relevant, namely, that despite the paradoxical aspects of the situation, conflict groups often seek to accelerate the unity and organization of their opponents. A unified party prefers a unified opponent. . . . I am certain that this would be emphatically confirmed by all the colonial ministers of mid-century governments. Oftentimes absence of organized opposition is what makes the regulation of disputes so difficult. . . .[23]

In Mexico, the problem consists of finding out whether the predominant situation is that of the colonies, which Dahrendorf is referring to, or that of the countries which evolved toward a party regime.

Another observation made by Dahrendorf refers to the recognition of the workers' *effective* right to negotiate collectively.

> Individuals who have agreed to bring their disagreements to the level of discussion generally do not launch into physical

23. Ralf Dahrendorf, *Class and Class Conflict in Industrial Society* (Stanford, California: Stanford University Press, 1959), p. 226.

violence. Even more, the violence of conflict seems to decrease as parliamentary institutions increase. At the same time the presence of those institutions does not in itself guarantee the control of conflicts.

In the industrial society in which development has been undertaken by private enterprise and in which democratic institutions have been created, parliamentarianism has not been sufficient for the entry of the new groups into citizenship and the polity. Workers' unions, trade unions, and the general forms of working-class democracy, which have permitted a juridical struggle and the conciliation of conflicting parties, have been at least as important as effective voting. Disraeli himself organized and attracted the workers. He imposed effective voting rights and the rights of workers' organizations, workers' democracy, and collective bargaining. That is why today manual workers cast two out of every three votes received by Tory Party candidates.

> From a sociological point of view, it is a mistake to think of eliminating or suppressing social conflict. . . . The attempt to remove conflict with ready-made ideologies of harmony and unity has the effect of increasing rather than decreasing the violence of conflicts. . . . Social conflicts can be regulated, controlled, but never suppressed, not even in a totalitarian State. . . . Recognition means that both parties accept the conflict for what it is, as an inevitable result of the authoritarian structure of the society. Any time that there is an attempt to deny the opponent's struggle by calling it "unrealistic" or by depriving him of the right to struggle, the effective regulation of the conflict is impossible. This is also true when conflicts are not recognized as such, and when there is too much emphasis on the so-called "common interests," where the only thing achieved is confusion. I believe that *The Economist* of London (a conservative journal) was right when it reproached English trade unions for their moderation, which it declared responsible for the stagnation and low level of productivity of English capitalism, and when it compared the policy of North American trade unions

and workers' unions, whose constant pressures for higher salaries have maintained the dynamics of the United States economy. . . .

For Dahrendorf, then, the first thing is to recognize conflicts, not to hide them or to attempt to eliminate them, and the second thing is to allow and even encourage the organization of interest groups—of employers and workers. The third thing is to

> accept certain rules of the game which constitute the framework of its relationships—electoral norms, procedural norms, norms of punishment to infractors, etc. It is important to add that the rules of the games fulfill their function only insofar as both parties are in a position of equality with respect to each other, and do not involve substantive stipulations which disqualify one or the other of the groups in conflict.[24]

Representative voting and parliamentarianism alone are not enough; but if they are realized and practiced, they operate as an accelerator, as a multiplier of the democratic processes within the parties, in the relationships among the parties, and in the kind of conflict characteristic of industrial society, trade unionism, and conciliation. To the autonomous conciliation of the national groups and classes by parliamentary means, we must add the conciliation of third parties, with representatives of employers, workers, and the government—effective conciliation with effective representatives.

> Conciliation, mediation, arbitration, and its normative and structural requisites are the main mechanisms to reduce the violence of class conflict. When these relationships become routinized, conflict is less acute, and it becomes institutionalized as a form of social life. In order that revolutionary (armed) movements should become transformed into evolutionary (peaceful) changes, there is no need, contrary to Marx's belief, for a classless society (that is, a utopian

24. Ralf Dahrendorf, *op. cit.*, pp. 225–27.

fiction). Toward effective regulation, class conflict is an element of stability in a world undergoing constant change. Even when the intensity of the conflict does not decrease, its manifestations can be analyzed in such a way as to protect the individual from the physical threat of a *bellum omnium contra omnes*.[25]

In Mexico's present political situation, different attitudes can be noted in the patterns of governmental policy and of the democratization of the country. The electoral reform of the Constitution is opposed by the prevailing electoral law, which prevents the control of election results, and those who promoted and supported the constitutional reforms are opposed by those who believe that no further measures should be taken in either the reorganization of institutions or a reform of the electoral law. If these reforms are not to be carried through, the multiplying and accelerating effects of democracy contained in the constitutional reform will necessarily come to a stop, and the traditional policy will continue operating under new forms.

The leading classes and strata hold different attitudes regarding the workers and peasants. Some propose to solve conflicts by means of public relations experts. Others, in the name of a ready-made type of national "unity" or "harmony," seek to annul any reorganization of political working-class or peasant forces, and describe their leaders as unrealistic and immature and even deprive them of their right to debate, by a sort of ideological warfare in which they use anti-Communist stereotypes to disqualify any leader attempting to change the prevailing structure. Others yet, in the name of the crime of social dissolution, accuse and incarcerate the leaders of workers' and peasant movements, thereby removing them from political competition. All these traditionalist attitudes are opposed by more audacious and reformist attitudes, characteristic of the modern State. Should the latter trends win over the

25. *Ibid.,* p. 230.

former, they would accelerate the democratization of the country, and protect Mexicans from the sterile threat of a *bellum omnium contra omnes.*

With what we know, based on judgment, historical experience, and sociological laws, we are not in a position to predict with scientific accuracy the outcome of this struggle. Any prediction claiming to be scientific would smack strongly of charlatanry. Sociological analysis can tell us only that the development of democracy in Mexico is within the realm of the probable, owing to the over-all level of development in the country, and that effective democracy is the indispensable prerequiste for continued peaceful development.

12

The Immediate Future

The coinciding conclusions of opposing ideologies bring us closer to the scientific ideal. For this reason it is important that in the midst of the Cold War and of ideological struggles we should be able to conclude today, together with any ideology, that the immediate future of the country depends on effective democratization and development, and that the advance in democratization will have positive effects upon development and vice versa. It is important to arrive at this conclusion at a time in which the democratization of the country is a possibility, even a probability, even though the obstacles are many, and at a time in which development advances with minimum rates of security and demands great effort. The similarity of conclusions arrived at through different types of analysis and the precision and objectivity of concepts can accelerate and specify joint political action, especially when these facts are functional to the interest of large sectors of the population which have come together through an objective "national task" to be fulfilled.

But this coincidence, this precision, this objectivity of the enunciated concepts do not prevent it from being equally functional for the different classes—their members and organizations—to hide these concepts and obscure them by means of rationalizations and demagogic acts, rhetoric and half-baked truths, to satisfy other kinds of immediate aspirations, crossed interests, or ideological passions. For this reason we believe it necessary to state synthetically the main conclusions which weaken political alienation in Mexico and which are very simple truths and necessary prerequisites for the development of the country. The problem lies in that, although we are in possession of very simple truths and know which are the *sine qua non* prerequisites for the development of the country, those truths will nonetheless remain obscured and those prerequisites hidden, owing to the political struggle and conflicting interests. The major struggle must be to maintain the clarity of those concepts, to keep in mind the prerequisites for development, and to apply the relevant measures. This will be one of the most important battles for the co-ordination of political action among groups and countries in the nation, and the clarity and awareness of what is *necessary* for development and democratization will be significant insofar as these are genuine collective acts representative of political forces.

Development is both an increase of the national product and a *redistribution of the national product;* without the presence of these two processes there is no development. There are only two kinds of development, capitalist and socialist. All the developed capitalist countries have increased the power of negotiation and organization of the working class, and thanks to that power those countries achieved their present income redistribution which is higher than that of underdeveloped countries. In those countries the democratization of the parties and trade unions was the key to development, and that democratization—in terms of a higher participation of the masses in political decisions—is higher than that of underdeveloped countries. It is not enough to establish democratization formally in the underdeveloped countries in order to accelerate development, nor to imitate all the specific forms of classic democracy in order to have democracy: democracy exists to the extent that the people share the income, culture, and power; anything else is democratic folklore or rhetoric.

The conditions for a socialist revolution are not present in Mexico. The conditions for a fascist *coup d'état,* however, could appear. The country's margin of security is very low, and without an acceleration of the processes of democratization and development, in a situation of crisis the dominant classes might recur to a dictatorial government in order to retain power. Under these conditions, if development is sought it must be a peaceful development and, in Marxist terminology, it must be a bourgeois development and a bourgeois democracy. This situation makes of any *consistent* Marxist a necessary and potential ally of the processes of development and democracy, even though his long-range goal is the achievement of socialism.

It is not only this perspective which provides a national task. A national task exists because the forms of a semi-colonial situation subsist. This coincidence and this alliance will not prevent struggles and conflicts. These may be similar to the ones which took place in the European countries, different only insofar as the national task compels to an emphasis of the peaceful and institutional character of struggles and conflicts. In this sense the extreme Left cannot be unaware that if Mexico suffers from internal colonialism and a permanent absorption of the proletariat, a *"structural opportunism,"* a semi-capitalist development, the goal must be to put an end to internal colonialism and semi-capitalist development, to achieve the political rights and liberties of the marginal, semi-colonial population, to emphasize civic struggle and political organization in the rural areas and indigenous regions, and to form, in the cities, leading cadres composed of the most aware and radical workers. As long as Mexico does not fully develop under capitalism and internal colonialism is not removed, it will remain a single-party system, without the conditions for a proletarian mass party or a class struggle in its pure form.

The ruling class must be aware of the fact that democratization is the basis of and indispensable prerequisite for development, and that the possibilities for democracy have increased insofar as there has been an increase of the per capita income, urbanization, and literacy. Serious and all-important obstacles subsist, such as a plural society, so that the foremost objective must be national integration. The pre-fascist condition of those regions which have suffered a loss of status calls for special plans for development. Regions that have a traditionalist culture and lack political liberties and functional political organizations are the breeding grounds of violence; in order to avoid it, special efforts must be made toward the democratization and political representation of the marginal and indigenous population, as well as legislative, political, and economic tasks to ensure the admission of that population into civic life, the admission and integration of the marginal strata to full economic and political citizenship. It is necessary to emphasize the unity of Mexico's secular political culture, and maintain the constitutional principle that political alignments must not be linked to religious affiliation. There must be a redistribution of income and both the maintenance and organization of popular pressures and national discipline. The predominant party must be both democratized and maintained, while the democratic play of the other parties must be intensified, which would compel the internal democratization of the party as a primary goal, coupled to a respect and encouragement of the opposition parties by means of an immediate revision of the electoral law. The democratization of the party must be linked to a trade union democratization and to the reform of many labor laws and institutions. A constant economic development is the minimum guarantee for public peace, and in order to achieve these goals, the personality of the President, the technical character of the plan, and the democratization of the party are indispensable prerequisites, in a country in which the President holds an extraordinary concentration of power, at a time when it is not possible either to mistrust technical plans or to use them demagogically, and at a stage in which popular pressure must be channelized in order to unify the country for the continuity and acceleration of its development, allowing for the free expression and organization of dissent toward democratic play and the peaceful solution of conflicts.

Tables

TABLE 1. PRESIDENTIAL ELECTIONS IN THE UNITED STATES OF MEXICO (1910–64)

Years and candidates	Number of votes	Per cent of votes
1910 *	18 826	100.00
Díaz	18 625	98.93
Madero	196	1.04
Limantour	1	0.00
Resendis	2	0.01
Dehesa	1	0.00
Sánchez G.	1	0.00
1911 *	20 145	100.00
Madero	19 997	99.26
L. de la Barra	87	0.40
Vázquez Gómez	16	0.07
others	45	0.12
1917	812 928	100.00
Carranza	797 305	98.07
González	11 615	1.43
Obregón	4 008	0.49
1920	1 181 550	100.00
Obregón	1 131 751	95.78
Robles D.	47 442	4.01
others	2 357	0.19

(TABLE 1. *continued*)

Years and candidates	Number of votes	Percent of votes
1924	1 593 257	100.00
Calles	1 340 634	84.14
Flores	252 599	15.86
others	24	0.00
1928	1 670 453	
Obregón	1 670 453	100.00
1929	2 082 106	100.00
Ortiz Rubio	1 947 848	93.55
Vasconcelos	110 979	5.32
Triana	23 279	0.11
1934	2 265 971	100.00
Cárdenas	2 225 000	98.19
Villarreal	24 395	1.07
Tejeda	16 037	0.70
Laborde	539	0.03
1940	2 637 582	100.00
Avila Camacho	2 476 641	93.89
Almazán	151 101	5.72
Sánchez Tapia	9 840	0.37
1946	2 293 547	100.00
Alemán	1 786 901	77.90
Padilla	443 357	19.33
Castro	29 337	1.27
Calderón	33 952	1.48
1952	3 651 201	100.00
Ruiz Cortines	2 713 419	74.31
Henríquez	579 745	15.87
González Luna	285 555	7.82
Toledano	72 482	1.98

(TABLE 1. *continued*)

Years and candidates	Number of votes	Per cent of votes
1958	7 483 403	100.00
López Mateos	6 767 754	90.43
Alvarez	705 303	9.42
others	10 346	0.13
1964	9 422 185	99.98
Díaz Ordaz	8 368 446	88.81
González Torres	1 034 337	10.97
others	19 402	0.20

* In 1910 and 1911 elections were indirect.

Source: Diario de Debates de la Cámara de Diputados.

TABLE 2. VOTES BY THE CHAMBER OF REPRESENTATIVES
ON PROJECTS OF THE EXECUTIVE BRANCH
(1935–64)

Years	No. of approved projects	Average no. of representatives present	Unanimously approved projects		Projects approved by majority			
			Absolute	Relative	No. of absolute projects	No. of relative projects	Opposing votes absolute *	Opposing votes relative
1935	39	95	39	100.00	—	—	—	—
1937	23	86	23	100.00	—	—	—	—
1941	56	96	56	100.00	—	—	—	—
1943	24	78	22	91.66	2	8.34	6	3.87
1947	57	89	42	73.68	15	26.32	41	2.80
1949	65	98	50	76.92	15	23.08	51	3.18
1953	49	100	29	59.18	20	40.82	63	3.00
1955	37	112	23	62.16	14	37.83	84	5.34
1959	39	102	37	94.86	2	5.13	8	4.37
1960	32	108	28	87.50	4	12.50	12	2.79
1961	28	137	23	82.14	6.5	17.85	20	2.88
1962	25	132	22	88.00	3	8.00	13	3.58
1963	31	124	30	96.77	1	3.23	4	3.03
1964	20	172	17	85.00	3	15.00	60	12.07

Note: In the average of Representatives present only those who had answered the roll call on time were considered.
* Total opposing votes in projects approved by majority.
Source: Diario de Debates de la Cámara de Diputados.

TABLE 3. PUBLIC TREASURY (THOUSANDS OF PESOS) (1929–62)

Year	Total	Federal	Per cent	States	Per cent	Federal District	Per cent	Munici- palities	Per cent
1929	452,574	322,335	71	62,663	14	33,261	7	34,315	8
1930	418,411	288,863	69	62,760	15	33,399	8	33,389	8
1931	382,310	256,088	67	61,917	16	33,260	9	31,045	8
1932	331,420	212,347	64	56,926	17	33,066	10	29,081	9
1933	358,674	222,900	62	60,478	17	46,400	13	28,896	8
1934	439,830	295,277	67	69,846	16	42,388	10	32,319	7
1935	462,891	313,074	68	72,675	16	44,035	9	33,107	7
1936	552,479	385,174	70	78,024	14	55,327	10	33,954	6
1937	625,873	451,110	72	85,797	14	52,500	8	36,466	6
1938	632,407	438,328	69	92,399	15	63,395	10	38,285	6
1939	748,727	535,812	71	104,109	14	67,494	9	41,312	6
1940	808,094	577,004	72	115,455	14	72,639	9	42,996	5
1941	936,447	664,919	71	127,575	14	96,487	10	47,466	5
1942	1,049,116	745,596	71	151,197	14	99,192	10	53,131	5
1943	1,443,055	1,091,597	76	172,874	12	109,221	8	69,365	4
1944	1,690,939	1,295,338	77	195,922	11	120,132	7	79,547	5
1945	1,857,992	1,404,025	76	214,662	11	137,530	7	101,775	5
1946	2,526,157	2,011,502	80	254,116	10	175,049	7	85,490	3
1947	2,624,473	2,054,694	78	289,710	11	181,300	7	98,769	4

(TABLE 3. *continued*)

Year	Total	Federal	Per cent	States	Per cent	Federal District	Per cent	Munici-palities	Per cent
1948	3,330,038	2,654,642	80	338,746	10	227,141	7	109,509	3
1949	4,687,623	3,891,216	83	409,904	9	257,450	5	129,053	3
1950	4,583,560	3,640,807	79	487,862	11	303,225	7	151,666	3
1951	6,116,513	4,883,666	80	703,737	11	356,834	6	172,276	3
1952	7,796,786	6,338,083	81	793,613	10	457,873	6	207,217	3
1953	6,458,871	5,023,106	78	799,262	12	409,250	6	227,253	4
1954	9,477,003	7,713,833	81	968,449	10	525,444	6	269,307	3
1955	11,149,312	9,023,531	81	1,166,678	10	631,939	6	327,164	3
1956	12,789,420	10,193,522	80	1,414,793	11	797,747	6	383,358	3
1957	13,676,722	10,869,859	80	1,541,595	11	816,704	6	448,564	3
1958	16,119,787	13,183,250	82	1,480,751	9	937,323	6	518,463	3
1959	18,460,213	14,163,433	77	1,825,432	10	1,879,845	10	591,503	3
1960	24,767,648	19,457,602	78	2,172,848	9	2,434,571	11	702,627	3
1961	25,687,670	19,941,051	77	2,267,707	9	2,714,077	12	764,835	3
1962	26,750,830	20,397,949	76	2,595,563	10	2,962,715	11	794,607	3

SOURCE: *Anuario Estadístico de los Estados Unidos Mexicanos.*

TABLE 4. STATE INCOME AND FEDERAL INCOME
(1950–63)

Year	1 Total income	2 Federal contribution	2/1	Participation in federal taxes	Federal subsidies	Loans *
1950	967,565,415	268,354,202	27.73	235,659,344	4,105,988	28,588,870
1951	1,149,050,021	332,159,256	28.90	276,246,264	6,150,957	49,762,035
1952	1,349,087,628	458,554,888	33.98	331,000,034	17,451,786	110,103,068
1953	1,302,055,463	284,299,583	21.82	208,479,900	14,709,796	61,109,887
1954	1,605,802,289	378,555,227	23.57	246,752,630	25,353,839	106,448,758
1955	2,003,363,066	496,109,068	24.76	314,118,265	33,693,741	148,297,062
1956	2,481,616,449	590,718,292	23.80	368,950,014	34,174,623	187,593,655
1957	5,001,663,135	578,118,161	11.55	372,685,963	33,757,429	171,674,769
1958	2,957,579,969	469,057,290	15.85	392,554,709	38,230,747	38,271,834
1959	5,528,220,666	507,901,976	9.18	435,179,282	46,028,168	26,694,526
1960	7,187,671,108	565,732,751	7.87	491,643,088	31,847,564	42,262,099
1961	7,671,883,003	699,017,749	9.11	350,722,189	44,435,598	294,859,962
1962	9,198,142,715	835,410,789	9.08	508,291,548	45,687,914	281,431,327
1963	10,347,184,982	1,024,678,709	9.90	559,233,480	67,559,776	391,885,453

* Includes loans and advances from the Federal Government, official banking institutions, and other official institutions.
Source: Dirección General de Estadística.

TABLE 5. FEDERAL STATE INCOME
(1963)

State	Total	Federal contribution	Per cent	Participation in federal taxes	Federal subsidies	Loans
Aguascalientes	14,843,609	3,507,927	23.63	3,459,555	—	48,372
Baja California	182,129,603	42,928,771	23.57	16,116,145	—	26,812,626
Baja Calif. (T)	22,085,140	13,394,048	60.65	4,703,858	8,192,515	497,675
Campeche	48,230,232	17,765,437	36.83	5,215,437	2,400,000	10,150,000
Coahuila	66,947,835	13,394,048	20.00	13,875,699	—	—
Colima	23,350,385	4,078,077	17.46	2,578,077	1,500,000	—
Chiapas	127,034,360	10,321,590	8.12	6,095,781	2,263,099	1,962,710
Chihuahua	368,712,327	107,848,272	29.25	62,849,766	6,004,860	38,993,646
Distrito Federal	7,100,677,463	168,952,067	2.37	117,415,318	—	51,536,797
Durango	50,267,628	26,693,493	53.10	12,272,531	14,420,962	—
Guanajuato	110,049,655	41,675,807	37.87	14,797,277	—	26,878,530
Guerrero	81,623,993	8,701,720	10.66	8,701,720	—	—
Hidalgo	37,860,516	22,894,706	60.47	22,894,706	—	—
Jalisco	169,341,095	26,117,528	15.42	22,891,697	—	3,225,831
México	267,552,317	72,712,875	27.18	22,016,307	—	50,696,568

(TABLE 5. continued)

State	Total	Federal contribution	Per cent	Participation in federal taxes	Federal subsidies	Loans
Michoacán	191,117,764	18,592,533	9.72	13,721,506	—	4,871,027
Morelos	41,697,177	9,004,227	21.59	3,860,000	944,227	4,200,000
Nayarit	29,006,930	6,974,122	24.04	4,124,122	1,000,000	1,850,000
Nuevo León	183,840,326	24,594,589	13.37	24,139,516	—	455,073
Oaxaca	83,148,300	14,610,249	17.57	7,376,992	—	7,233,257
Puebla	136,427,749	22,296,394	16.34	15,956,816	408,673	5,930,905
Querétaro	20,000,000	4,772,941	23.86	4,772,941	—	—
Quintana Roo	30,872,514	26,411,857	85.55	791,566	25,620,291	—
San Luis Potosí	59,697,650	26,411,857	85.55	20,044,413	—	6,925,728
Sinaloa	92,095,844	17,764,958	19.29	17,764,958	—	—
Sonora	232,575,265	27,354,911	11.76	24,778,822	—	2,576,089
Tabasco	74,965,884	9,636,939	12.85	8,550,857	103,838	982,244
Tamaulipas	85,498,297	16,907,584	19.77	16,907,584	—	—
Tlaxcala	21,642,695	8,991,355	41.54	7,941,475	50,000	999,880
Veracruz	191,067,580	35,375,142	18.51	35,375,142	—	—
Yucatán	185,796,536	62,337,466	33.55	8,486,893	2,792,078	51,058,495
Zacatecas	37,028,313	10,615,236	28.66	8,756,003	1,859,233	—

Source: Dirección General de Estadística.

TABLE 6. EXPENDITURES OF THE FEDERAL GOVERNMENT DESTINED
TO THE ARMY (thousands of pesos) (1924–63)

Years	Expenditures of the federal government	Expenditures destined to the Army	Per cent of expenditures for the Army
1924	261,519	114,510	43.78
1925	302,164	82,853	27.41
1926	314,322	86,155	27.40
1927	310,081	86,379	27.85
1928	287,244	85,452	29.74
1929	275,541	90,021	32.67
1930	279,121	73,490	26.32
1931	226,478	58,875	25.99
1932	211,624	55,030	26.00
1933	245,950	54,381	22.11
1934	264,740	54,210	20.47
1935	300,822	62,740	20.85
1936	406,098	70,412	17.33
1937	478,756	83,052	17.34
1938	503,764	84,303	16.73
1939	582,227	91,868	15.77
1940	631,544	120,488	19.07
1941	681,869	130,247	19.10
1942	836,848	154,331	18.44
1943	1,075,539	194,358	18.07
1944	1,453,334	213,088	14.66
1945	1,572,804	234,316	14.89
1946	1,770,543	252,892	14.28
1947	2,142,961	277,299	12.93
1948	2,773,364	306,314	11.04
1949	3,740,587	330,003	8.82
1950	3,463,290	346,331	10.00
1951	4,670,088	380,353	8.14
1952	6,464,230	467,739	7.23
1953	5,490,401	509,233	9.27
1954	7,916,807	640,867	8.09
1955	8,883,120	709,046	7.98
1956	10,270,112	774,742	7.54
1957	11,303,248	903,697	7.99
1958	13,287,707	968,668	7.28
1959	14,163,433	942,125	6.65
1960	20,150,330	1,086,067	5.38
1961	20,362,040	1,132,785	5.56
1962	20,219,158	1,240,196	6.13
1963	20,294,906	1,249,175	6.15

Source: *Anuario Estadístico de los Estados Unidos Mexicanos.*

TABLE 7. POPULATION PER RELIGIOUS AFFILIATION
(1930–60)

	1	2		3	4	5
Year	Total population	Catholic	2/1	Protestant	Jewish	Other
1930	16,552,722	16,179,667	97.74	130,322	9,072	56,696
1940	19,653,552	18,977,585	96.56	177,954	14,167	35,758
1950	25,791,017	25,329,498	98.21	330,111	17,574	113,834
1960	34,923,129	33,692,503	96.47	578,515	100,750	137,208

	6		7		8	9	
Year	3+4+5	3+4+5/.01	None	7/1	Not indicated	None + not indicated	9/1
1930	196,090	1.18	175,180	1.05	1,785	176,965	1.06
1940	227,879	1.15	443,671	2.25	4,417	448,088	2.27
1950	461,519	1.78	. . . . .		. . . . .	. . . . .	
1960	816,473	2.33	192,963	.55	221,190	414,253	1.18

TABLE 8. POPULATION PER RELIGIOUS AFFILIATION
(1960)

State	None and not indicated	Ratio *	None	Ratio *	Catholic
1 Aguascalientes	4,182	1.75	1,024	.43	237,820
2 Baja California	10,999	2.24	5,241	1.06	490,719
3 Baja California (T)	551	.68	216	.26	80,429
4 Campeche	3,822	2.45	1,565	.99	156,626
5 Coahuila	13,629	1.57	4,316	.49	866,547
6 Colima	3,959	2.47	402	.25	159,656
7 Chiapas	27,403	2.44	10,967	.97	1,122,908
8 Chihuahua	28,692	2.49	5,823	.50	1,151,351
9 Distrito Federal	56,953	1.21	24,915	.53	4,677,685
10 Durango	6,602	.89	3,734	.50	739,310
11 Guanajuato	7,649	.44	5,203	.30	1,717,189
12 Guerrero	9,979	.86	4,738	.40	1,158,334
13 Hidalgo	9,334	.96	7,266	.75	963,408
14 Jalisco	74,906	3.18	4,094	.17	2,350,221
15 México	5,228	.28	2,794	.15	1,859,825
16 Michoacán	15,167	.83	11,995	.66	1,816,062
17 Morelos	4,672	1.27	2,401	.65	367,571
18 Nayarit	3,396	.89	2,072	.54	381,356
19 Nuevo León	5,642	.54	4,624	.41	1,037,830
20 Oaxaca	17,466	1.03	5,383	.31	1,687,379
21 Puebla	10,916	.56	7,875	.41	1,916,588
22 Querétaro	641	.18	393	.11	353,240
23 Quintana Roo (T)	693	1.50	633	1.37	46,099
24 San Luis Potosí	9,233	.90	8,012	.78	1,018,012
25 Sinaloa	10,565	1.29	9,883	1.21	814,489
26 Sonora	7,552	.99	4,555	.60	758,234
27 Tabasco	7,714	1.72	7,164	1.60	447,008
28 Tamaulipas	8,535	.87	7,269	.74	970,999
29 Tlaxcala	3,070	.92	1,371	.41	333,558
30 Veracruz	33,663	1.28	29,539	1.12	2,618,266
31 Yucatán	5,387	.91	3,001	.50	591,225
32 Zacatecas	5,953	.75	4,525	.56	802,459
Republic	414,153	1.22	192,963	.57	

* With respect to the total Catholic population.

TABLE 9. FEDERAL ENTITIES ACCORDING TO THE PROPORTION
OF THE POPULATION WITH NO RELIGIOUS AFFILIATION
(1960)

0.00–0.20	0.21–0.40	0.41–0.60	0.61–0.80	0.81–1.00	More than 1.00
Jalisco	Baja California (T)	Aguascalientes	Chihuahua	Campeche	Baja California
México	Colima	Coahuila	D. F.	Chiapas	Quintana Roo
Querétaro	Guanajuato	Nayarit	Durango		Sinaloa
	Guerrero	Nuevo León	Hidalgo		Tabasco
	Oaxaca	Puebla	Michoacán		Veracruz
		Sonora	Morelos		
		Tlaxcala	San Luis Potosí		
		Yucatán	Tamaulipas		
		Zacatecas			

TABLE 10. 400 LARGEST ENTERPRISES

	Number of enterprises	Income (millions of pesos)	Per cent	Per cent of national total *
100 Largest				
1. Total	100	28 038	100.00	49.63
2. Foreign control	39	9 340	33.31	16.50
3. Strong foreign participation	17	4 756	16.96	8.42
4. Total of (2)+(3)	56	14 096	50.27	24.92
5. Government	24	10 153	36.21	17.97
6. Independent private sector	20	3 789	13.52	6.74
200 Largest				
1. Total	200	35 370	100.00	62.61
2. Foreign control	83	12 639	35.73	22.37
3. Strong foreign participation	39	6 449	18.23	11.41
4. Total of (2)+(3)	122	19 088	53.96	33.78
5. Government	28	10 436	29.51	18.47
6. Independent private sector	50	5 846	16.53	10.36
300 Largest				
1. Total	300	40 077	100.00	70.94
2. Foreign control	126	14 695	36.64	25.99
3. Strong foreign participation	54	7 166	17.87	12.69
4. Total of (2)+(3)	180	21 861	54.51	38.68
5. Government	32	10 608	26.45	18.78
6. Independent private sector	87	7 668	19.04	13.48
400 Largest				
1. Total	400	43 643	100.00	77.26
2. Foreign control	161	15 788	36.20	28.00
3. Strong foreign participation	71	7 796	17.86	13.80
4. Total of (2)+(3)	232	23 584	54.06	41.80
5. Government	36	10 844	24.85	19.19
6. Independent private sector	132	9 215	21.09	16.27

* Two thousand greatest enterprises with an income of 56,000 million pesos.
Source: José Luis Ceceña, *Los monopolios en México,* México, 1962 (Professional Thesis).

TABLE 11. DIRECT FOREIGN INVESTMENTS IN MEXICO: VALUE OF INVESTMENT PER COUNTRY (thousands of pesos)

Year		U.S.A.	Canada	Sweden	England	France	Other*	Total
1938	Total	1,267,448	448,454	96,297	194,155	49,626	916	2,056,896
	Per cent	62	22	5	9	2	0	
1939	Total	1,384,635	582,643	119,278	161,491	49,478	1,058	2,298,853
	Per cent	60	25	5	7	2	0	
1940	Total	1,441,183	473,821	100,196	194,093	51,363	1,193	2,261,849
	Per cent	64	21	4	9	2	0	
1941	Total	1,391,360	477,574	107,533	221,255	37,354	1,637	2,236,713
	Per cent	62	21	5	10	2	0	
1942	Total	1,522,655	498,116	111,235	225,704	39,101	3,336	2,400,147
	Per cent	63	21	5	9	2	0	
1943	Total	1,604,450	474,673	112,013	224,900	39,942	4,398	2,460,376
	Per cent	65	19	5	9	2	0	
1944	Total	1,708,355	472,491	121,781	231,962	44,193	4,641	2,583,423
	Per cent	66	18	5	9	2	0	
1945	Total	1,946,972	470,255	123,518	239,045	46,021	5,421	2,831,232
	Per cent	69	17	4	8	2	0	
1946	Total	1,972,782	396,454	151,025	231,959	62,877	9,330	2,824,427
	Per cent	70	14	5	8	2	0	
1947	Total	2,207,218	425,287	184,521	153,222	60,417	9,937	3,040,602
	Per cent	73	14	6	5	2	0	
1948	Total	2,599,979	571,138	182,898	179,359	62,659	24,186	3,620,219
	Per cent	72	16	5	5	2	0	

(TABLE 11. continued)

Year		U.S.A.	Canada	Sweden	England	France	Other *	Total
1949	Total	3,150,808	630,603	227,256	153,638	33,960	37,549	4,233,814
	Per cent	74	15	5	4	1	1	
1950	Total	3,371,452	743,357	446,640	257,217	45,087	32,164	4,895,917
	Per cent	69	15	9	5	1	1	
1951	Total	4,061,180	884,645	491,663	308,915	40,822	53,504	5,840,729
	Per cent	70	15	8	5	1	1	
1952	Total	4,769,789	893,082	308,124	239,712	31,908	59,520	6,302,135
	Per cent	76	15	5	4	1	1	
1953	Total	4,989,508	1,002,303	356,804	283,239	42,878	154,330	6,829,062
	Per cent	73	15	5	4	1	2	
1954 **	Total	7,353,482	1,603,474	620,455	455,744	58,902	337,099	10,429,156
	Per cent	71	15	6	4	1	4	
1955	Total	8,173,175	1,688,657	760,498	490,286	48,789	329,185	11,490,590
	Per cent	71	15	7	4	1	3	
1956	Total	10,388,575	1,789,175	133,112	567,688	—	376,950	13,255,500
	Per cent	78	14	1	4		3	
1957	Total	11,756,613	2,024,800	150,562	642,388	—	426,512	15,000,875
	Per cent	78	14	1	4		3	

The value of investments is composed of the following elements: (a) social goods; (b) capital reserves; (c) surplus; (d) long-term matrix debt; (e) short-term matrix debt; (f) profits of the fiscal year.   * Includes Germany, Argentina, Cuba, Italy, Holland, Brazil, Denmark and Belgium.   ** The investment increase of 1954 was mainly due to the revaluation of assets effected by the enterprises.
Source: Banco de México, 33rd General Assembly of Shareholders, Mexico, 1955, pp. 80–81; and for 1954–55, 34th General Assembly, Mexico, 1956.

TABLE 12. PERCENTAGE OF MEXICAN IMPORTS AND EXPORTS FROM AND TO THE UNITED STATES (1925–65)

Year	Imports			Exports		
	Total	U.S.	Per cent	Total	U.S.	Per cent
1925	390,996,172	274,495,561	70.20	682,484,832	516,862,614	75.73
1926	381,263,040	268,622,421	70.46	691,753,935	491,094,975	70.99
1927	346,387,272	232,835,157	67.22	633,658,850	417,221,320	65.84
1928	357,762,358	241,612,651	67.53	592,444,048	404,072,355	68.20
1929	382,247,637	264,010,226	69.07	590,658,605	358,697,206	60.73
1930	350,178,416	239,055,226	68.27	458,674,489	267,512,914	58.32
1931	216,585,416	144,559,186	66.74	399,711,314	244,430,942	61.15
1932	180,912,211	115,430,644	63.80	304,697,177	199,011,710	65.31
1933	244,475,056	146,544,913	59.94	364,967,039	174,871,105	47.91
1934	333,973,908	202,704,614	60.69	643,710,297	333,604,147	51.83
1935	406,136,234	265,348,342	65.33	750,292,490	471,203,337	62.80
1936	464,142,705	274,457,269	59.13	775,313,330	471,100,740	60.76
1937	613,755,448	381,479,268	62.15	892,388,563	501,762,858	56.23
1938	494,118,125	284,933,491	57.67	838,127,957	564,846,430	67.39
1939	629,708,225	415,834,280	66.04	914,289,882	678,820,342	74.24
1940	669,016,462	527,285,017	78.81	960,041,432	858,758,744	89.45
1941	915,110,234	771,232,177	84.28	729,515,609	665,211,845	91.19
1942	753,038,993	655,222,929	87.01	989,725,173	904,635,714	91.40
1943	909,583,302	805,472,811	88.55	1,130,228,780	991,908,929	87.76
1944	1,895,198,265	1,699,169,910	89.66	1,046,984,709	890,487,830	85.05
1945	1,604,404,468	1,321,544,074	82.37	1,271,878,431	1,061,955,385	83.50
1946	2,636,786,960	2,204,432,101	83.60	1,915,260,677	1,366,120,065	71.33

(TABLE 12. continued)

Year	Imports			Exports		
	Total	U.S.	Per cent	Total	U.S.	Per cent
1947	3,230,294,498	2,856,287,306	88.42	2,161,848,416	1,655,329,792	76.57
1948	2,951,495,442	2,560,382,223	86.75	2,661,271,063	2,005,066,771	75.34
1949	3,527,320,760	3,068,414,052	86.99	3,623,081,194	2,850,719,965	76.68
1950	4,403,368,452	3,716,377,104	84.40	4,339,404,924	3,747,284,135	86.35
1951	6,773,170,062	5,520,358,915	81.50	5,446,912,749	3,836,927,755	70.44
1952	6,394,192,667	5,292,602,812	82.77	5,125,772,448	4,027,372,479	78.57
1953	6,560,934,365	5,386,077,970	82.09	5,689,544,100	3,494,868,998	61.43
1954 *	8,926,339,720	7,183,451,268	80.48	6,936,145,910	4,165,803,033	60.06
1955	11,045,729,280	8,762,295,849	79.34	9,484,266,903	5,753,146,812	60.67
1956	13,395,320,855	10,490,925,355	78.26	10,670,695,237	5,985,029,891	56.09
1957	14,439,413,499	11,120,969,792	77.02	8,729,248,868	5,617,500,871	64.35
1958	14,107,468,513	10,861,597,184	76.99	8,846,057,978	5,441,993,063	61.52
1959	12,582,614,469	9,174,087,130	72.91	9,006,862,690	5,468,842,551	60.70
1960	14,830,598,081	10,688,851,545	72.07	9,247,354,640	5,684,598,411	61.47
1961	14,232,912,483	9,938,536,377	69.83	10,044,312,880	6,268,527,609	62.41
1962	14,287,500,895	9,749,670,586	68.24	11,243,592,537	6,905,669,349	61.42
1963	15,496,087,175	10,614,174,414	68.50	11,699,030,584	7,450,953,257	63.69
1964	18,661,697,095	12,779,090,059	68.48	12,780,611,402	7,608,976,186	59.54
1965	18,055,105,635	11,584,967,390	64.16	11,558,007,531	8,295,416,578	71.77

* That corresponding to free areas is included.
Source: Anuarios de Comercio Exterior.

TABLE 13. COPIES SOLD OF MEXICAN AND FOREIGN MAGAZINES
(1961 and 1964)

Mexican magazines			Foreign magazines		
	Copies sold			Copies sold	
Name	1961	1964	Name	1961	1964
Hoy	15 000	30 000	Life en español	170 204	88 000
Impacto	35 000	37 000	Selecciones	220 320	412 000
Jueves de Excélsior	38 686	29 861	Visión	44 000	46 000
Mañana	25 600	27 920			
Política	21 000	25 000			
Revista de Revistas	35 000	10 000			
Siempre!	54 200	70 000			
Sucesos	70 000	70 000			
Tiempo	17 421	18 030			
Todo	21 000	21 000			
Total per issue	332 907	338 811		434 524	546 000
Average per issue	33 290	33 881		144 841	182 000

Source: *Medios Publicitarios Mexicanos*, August–November 1965.

TABLE 14. LITERACY IN URBAN AND RURAL POPULATION
(1960)

Urban—Rural (by sex)	Population aged five or over	Per cent	Literate	Per cent	Illiterate	Per cent
United States of Mexico	27,987,838	100	17,414,675	62.23	10,573,163	37.77
Men	13,886,456	100	9,102,747	65.56	4,783,709	34.44
Women	14,101,382	100	8,311,928	58.95	5,789,454	41.05
Urban	14,176,078	100	10,749,345	75.84	3,426,733	24.16
Men	6,813,561	100	5,387,722	79.09	1,425,839	20.91
Women	7,362,517	100	5,361,623	72.84	2,000,894	27.16
Rural	13,811,760	100	6,665,330	48.26	7,146,430	51.74
Men	7,072,895	100	3,715,025	52.54	3,357,870	47.46
Women	6,738,865	100	2,950,305	43.79	3,788,560	56.21

Source: Dirección General de Estadística.

TABLE 15. CHARACTERISTICS REGARDING FOOD AND FOOTWEAR IN THE URBAN AND RURAL POPULATION (1960)

Urban—Rural (by sex)	Population aged one or over	Per cent	Eat wheat bread		Eat one or more of: meat, fish, milk and eggs		Percentage of people who usually		
			Yes	No	Yes	No	wear shoes	wear sandals	go barefoot
United States of Mexico	33,778,942	100	68.57	31.43	75.89	24.11	62.28	23.43	14.29
Men	16,829,298	100	67.94	32.06	75.51	24.49	58.90	29.00	12.10
Women	16,949,644	100	69.20	30.80	76.28	23.72	65.63	17.91	16.46
Urban	17,125,650	100	87.25	12.75	87.42	12.58	84.35	9.38	6.27
Men	8,307,760	100	87.11	12.89	87.27	12.73	82.91	11.49	5.60
Women	8,817,890	100	87.39	12.61	87.56	12.44	85.72	7.39	6.89
Rural	16,653,292	100	49.36	50.64	64.04	35.96	39.58	37.89	22.53
Men	8,521,538	100	49.25	50.75	64.05	35.95	35.50	46.07	18.43
Women	8,131,754	100	49,47	50.53	64.04	35.96	43.86	29.32	26.82

Source: General Demographic Census, 1960.

TABLE 16. MARGINAL AND PARTICIPATING POPULATION (1930–1960)

Concepts	1930 Absolute	Per cent	1940 Absolute	Per cent	1950 Absolute	Per cent	1960 Absolute	Per cent
Total population	16,552,722	100	19,653,552	100	25,791,017	100	34,923,129	100
Urban	5,540,631	33.5	6,896,669	35.1	10,983,483	42.6	17,705,118	51.0
Rural	11,012,091	66.5	12,756,883	64.9	14,807,534	57.4	17,218,001	49.0
Literacy Younger than six	3,010,147	100	3,433,236	100	4,752,275	100	6,935,291	100
Six or over	13,542,575	100	16,220,316	100	21,038,742	100	27,987,838	100
Literate	4,525,035	33.4	6,770,359	41.7	11,766,258	55.9	17,414,675	62.2
Illiterate	9,017,540	66.6	9,449,957	58.3	9,272,484	44.1	10,573,163	37.8
Education Aged 6–14	3,479,400	100	4,662,900	100	6,002,400	100	8,516,800	100
With schooling	1,789,300	51.3	2,113,900	45.3	3,031,700	50.5	5,401,500	63.4
Without schooling	1,693,100	48.7	2,549,000	54.7	2,970,700	49.5	3,115,300	36.6
Food and Footwear Younger than one	261,346		535,899		814,314		1,144,187	
One or over	16,291,372	100	19,117,653	100	24,976,703	100	33,778,942	100
Eats wheat bread	—		8,322,071	43.5	13,592,780	54.4	23,160,216	68.6
Does not eat wheat bread	—		10,795,582	56.5	11,383,923	45.6	10,618,726	31.4
Wears shoes	—		9,264,450	48.5	13,567,203	54.3	21,038,595	62.3
Does not wear shoes	—		9,853,203	51.5	11,409,500	45.7	12,740,347	37.7
Language Younger than five	2,510,521	100	2,864,892	100	3,969,991	100	4,776,747	100
Five or over	14,042,201	100	16,788,660	100	21,821,026	100	30,146,382	100
Spanish-speaking	11,791,258	83.9	14,297,751	85.1	19,373,417	88.8	25,968,301	89.95
Indian monolingual	1,185,273	8.5	1,237,018	7.4	795,069	3.6	1,104,955	3.66
Indian bilingual	1,065,670	7.6	1,253,891	7.5	1,652,540	7.6	1,925,299	6.38
Monolingual-bilingual	2,250,943	16.1	2,490,909	14.9	2,447,609	11.2	3,030,254	10.05

TABLE 17. PERCENTAGE OF VOTING POPULATION
IN THE UNITED STATES AND MEXICO
(1888–1956)

Years	U.S. per cent	Years	Mexico per cent
1888	18.81	1910	—
1892	18.34		
1896	19.48	1911	—
1900	18.35	1917	5.36
1904	16.45		
1908	16.78	1920	8.20
1912	15.76	1924	10.60
1916	18.17		
1920	25.08	1928	10.50
1924	25.43	1929	12.90
1928	30.60		
1932	31.89	1934	12.70
1936	35.64	1940	13.34
1940	37.75		
1944	36.19	1946	10.06
1948	33.42	1952	13.38
1952	39.51		
1956	37.09	1958	23.14

Sources: Diario de Debates de la Cámara de Diputados and *Statistical Abstract of the United States.*

TABLE 18. PRESIDENTIAL ELECTIONS: MARGINALITY AND PARTICIPATION
(1917–64)

Years	Male population aged twenty or over	Voted	Per cent	Did not vote	Per cent
1917	3,219,887	812,928	25.25	2,406,959	74.75
1920	3,396,083	1,181,550	34.79	2,214,530	65.21
1924	3,631,010	1,593,257	43.88	2,037,753	56.12
1928	3,872,848	1,670,453	43.13	2,202,395	56.87
1929	3,938,489	2,083,106	52.89	1,855,383	47.11
1934	4,227,250	2,265,971	53.60	1,961,279	46.40
1940	4,589,904	2,637,582	57.46	1,952,322	42.54
1946	5,379,367	2,293,547	42.64	3,085,820	57.36
1952	6,306,631	3,651,201	57.89	2,655,430	42.11
1952 *	6,306,631	3,651,201	57.89	2,655,430	42.11

Years	Total population aged twenty or over	Voted	Per cent	Did not vote	Per cent
1917	6,814,593	812,928	11.93	6,001,665	88.07
1920	7,162,876	1,181,550	16.50	5,981,326	83.50
1924	7,627,251	1,593,257	20.89	6,033,994	79.11
1928	8,117,660	1,670,453	20.25	6,447,207	79.75
1929	8,248,312	2,083,106	25.25	6,165,206	74.85
1934	8,830,265	2,265,971	25.66	6,564,294	74.34
1940	9,561,106	2,637,582	27.59	6,923,524	72.41
1946	11,170,817	2,293,547	20.53	8,977,270	79.47
1952	13,035,668	3,651,201	28.01	9,384,467	71.99
1958 *	15,152,440	7,485,403	49.40	7,667,037	50.60
1968 *	17,455,071	9,434,687	54.05	8,020,163	45.95

* Men and women voted.
Sources: Diario de Debates de la Cámara de Diputados; Dirección General de Estadística; Comisión Nacional Electoral; Dirección del Registro Nacional de Electores.

TABLE 19. DISTRIBUTION OF THE NATIONAL INCOME, PER FACTORS
(millions of pesos)
(1939–60)

Year	Total	Work *	Per cent	Capital **	Per cent	Mixed †	Per cent
1939	5,737	1,744	30.4	1,974	34.4	2,019	35.2
1940	5,207	1,510	29.0	1,906	36.6	1,991	34.4
1941	7,366	2,048	27.8	2,828	38.4	2,490	33.8
1942	9,255	2,443	26.4	3,748	40.5	3,064	33.1
1943	11,791	2,936	24.9	5,011	42.5	3,844	32.6
1944	15,551	3,670	23.6	6,920	44.5	4,961	31.9
1945	18,522	4,167	22.5	8,891	48.0	5,464	29.5
1946	24,118	5,161	21.4	12,421	51.5	6,536	27.1
1947	26,300	5,786	22.0	13,360	50.8	7,154	27.3
1948	28,800	6,595	22.9	14,227	49.4	7,978	27.8
1949	31,700	7,513	23.7	15,279	48.2	8,908	28.1
1950	37,500	8,925	23.8	17,775	47.4	10,800	28.8
1951	46,800	10,483	22.4	22,604	48.3	13,713	29.3
1952	52,000	11,596	22.3	25,116	48.3	15,288	29.4
1953	50,200	12,801	25.5	23,343	46.5	14,056	28.0
1954	59,180	16,866	28.5	26,335	44.5	15,979	27.0
1955	74,760	19,737	26.4	34,240	45.8	20,783	27.8
1956	84,000	21,756	25.9	38,724	46.1	23,520	28.0
1957	92,000	25,576	27.8	41,308	44.9	25,116	27.3
1958	101,800	30,438	29.9	44,385	43.6	26,977	26.5
1959	109,000	33,572	30.8	46,870	43.0	28,558	26.2
1960	120,200	37,743	31.4	51,205	42.6	31,252	26.0

* Includes wages and other payments for work.
** Includes profits, interest, dividends and sales.
† Mixed income derived from work and capital. Includes allocations to owners who work.
Sources: Comisión Mixta, *El desarrollo económico de México y su capacidad para absorber capital del exterior.* Mexico, 1953; and Nacional Financiera, S. A., Dirección de Investigaciones Económicas.

TABLE 20. LAND GRANTS AND BENEFICIARIES, BY PRESIDENTIAL PERIODS

Presidents	Term of office	Extension in hectares	Bene- ficiaries
Venustiano Carranza	5.1.17 to 5.21.20	132,639-87-02	59,846
Adolfo de la Huerta	6.1.20 to 11.30.20	33,695-73-24	17,355
Alvaro Obregón	12.1.20 to 11.30.24	971,627-34-82	158,204
Plutarco E. Calles	12.1.24 to 11.30.28	3.088,071-57-03	302,432
Emilio Portes Gil	12.1.28 to 2.4.30	1.173,118-91-40	155,826
Pascual Ortiz Rubio	2.5.30 to 9.3.32	1.468,745-27-41	84,009
Abelardo L. Rodríguez	9.4.32 to 11.30.34	798,982-41-09	161,327
Lázaro Cárdenas	12.1.34 to 11.30.40	17.889,791-78-78	774,009
Manuel Avila Camacho	12.1.40 to 11.30.46	5.518,970-17-30	112,447
Miguel Alemán	12.1.46 to 11.30.52	3.844,744-96-94	85,026
Adolfo Ruiz Cortines	9.1.52 to 11.30.58	3.198,780-95-82	55,929
Adolfo López Mateos	12.1.58 to 11.30.64	16.004,169	245,803
Gustavo Díaz Ordaz	12.1.64 to 1965	1.214,162	27,773

Sources: Memorias de Labores, Departamento de Asuntos Agrarios y Coloniza-ción, 1964, and Diario de Debates de la Cámara de Diputados.

TABLE 21. GROSS NATIONAL PRODUCT, POPULATION AND PER CAPITA PRODUCT
(1940–64)

Year	Gross national product (millions of pesos, 1950) A	Population (millions) B	Production per capita (pesos, 1950) A / B
1940	22.6	19 654	1 150
1941	24.8	20 332	1 220
1942	26.3	20 866	1 260
1943	27.5	21 418	1 284
1944	29.7	21 988	1 351
1945	30.5	22 576	1 351
1946	32.3	23 183	1 393
1947	33.5	23 811	1 407
1948	35.0	24 461	1 431
1949	37.1	25 132	1 476
1950	40.6	25 79.1	1 574
1951	43.6	26 544	1 643
1952	45.4	27 287	1 664
1953	45.6	28 056	1 625
1954	50.4	28 853	1 747
1955	54.8	29 679	1 846
1956	58.2	30 538	1 906
1957	62.7	31 426	1 995
1958	66.2	32 348	2 046
1959	68.1	33 304	2 045
1960	73.5	34 923	2 105
1961	76.0	36 091	2 106
1962	79.7	37 233	2 141
1963	84.7	38 416	2 205
1964	93.2	39 642	2 351

Source: *La economía mexicana en cifras* (Mexico: Nacional Financiera, S. A., 1965).

TABLE 22. RATES OF GROWTH OF THE GROSS NATIONAL PRODUCT
(PER ACTIVITIES)
(1940–65)

Year	GNP	Agri-culture	Manu-factures	Oil	Elec-tricity	Trans-ports
1940-1945	8.7	6.3	9.5	3.3	4.1	7.4
1945-1950	5.4	9.8	5.9	8.5	7.5	7.4
1950-1955	4.8	5.6	4.8	8.8	9.6	6.1
1940-1950	7.2	8.0	7.8	5.9	5.8	7.9
1956	6.7	1.5	9.8	9.8	11.9	8.8
1957	3.6	4.0	6.3	9.9	7.7	7.2
1958	4.5	9.1	4.8	14.3	7.7	2.4
1959	4.6	2.5	7.4	16.7	7.4	3.4
1960	5.7	0.4	8.6	6.5	9.8	8.2
1961	3.5	3.0	3.5	15.0	9.5	0.1
1962	4.8	5.3	6.4	1.9	6.5	0.2
1963	6.3	1.5	9.2	6.2	9.6	4.3
1964	10.0	8.1	14.2	9.1	14.9	6.2
1965	5.1	3.0	7.0	4.2	9.5	4.7

Source: Banco de México, S. A., Annual Reports.

TABLE 23. DEMOGRAPHIC MOVEMENTS (THOUSANDS OF PERSONS)
(1940–64)

Concept	1940	1950	50/40	1960	60/50	1964	64/60
Productive population	6,055	8,272	3.7	11,332	3.7	13,216	4.2
Primary activities	3,831	4,824	2.6	6,114	2.7	6,909	3.3
Secondary and tertiary activities	2,240	3,448	5.5	5,188	5.0	6,307	5.4
Population of the main cities *	2,777	4,121	4.8	7,951	9.3		

* Includes the population of the 14 largest cities.
Source: *La economía mexicana en cifras* (Mexico: Nacional Financiera, S. A., 1965).

TABLE 24. DISTRIBUTION OF THE LABOR FORCE PER ACTIVITIES
(1940–64)

Activity	1940 Thousands of workers	Per cent	1950 Thousands of workers	Per cent	1960 Thousands of workers	Per cent	1964 Thousands of workers	Per cent
Agriculture *	3 831	65.1	4 824	61.0	6 144	54.7	6 909	52.7
Industries	747	12.7	1 319	15.9	2 008	16.9	2 652	20.2
Extractive **	107	1.9	97	1.3	142	1.3	174	1.3
Transforming	640	10.9	972	12.3	1 556	13.9	1 923	14.7
Construction	106	1.7	225	2.9	408	3.7	499	3.8
Electricity	56	1.0	25	0.4	41	0.4	56	0.4
Commerce and Finance	552	9.4	684	8.7	1 075	9.6	1 288	9.8
Transports and communications	149	2.6	211	2.7	357	3.2	437	3.3
Services †	450	7.7	879	11.2	1 527	13.6	1 812	13.8
Total:	5 891		7 917		11 250		13 098	

* Includes cattle-breeding, forestry, and fishing.
** Includes mining and oil.
† Includes government and private services and unspecified occupations.
Source: *La economía mexicana en cifras* (Mexico: Nacional Financiera, S. A., 1965).

TABLE 25. AGRICULTURAL WORKERS ADMITTED
TO THE UNITED STATES AND WETBACKS APPREHENDED
(1942–57)

Year	Workers on contract admitted [a]	Wetbacks apprehended [b]	Total [d]
1942	4,203	c	4,203
1943	52,098	c	52,098
1944	62,170	c	62,170
1945	49,454	c	49,454
1946	32,043	c	32,043
1947	19,632	c	19,632
1948	33,288	180,000	213,288
1949	143,455	280,000	423,455
1950	76,519	466,000	542,519
1951	211,098	500,000	711,098
1952	187,894	800,000	987,894
1953	198,424	1,000,000	1,198,424
1954	310,476	1,000,000	1,310,476
1955	390,846	242,000	632,846
1956	444,581	72,000	516,581
1957	436,290	44,000	480,290
	2,652,471	4,584,000	7,236,471

a. Data from House Committee on Agriculture. *Mexican Labor Hearings,* 1958.

b. Approximate data.

c. There are no data available.

d. In some cases there is a duplication of data by addition of *a* and *b,* or because the same wetback is caught a few times. Nonetheless the total of *b* is conservative, because many wetbacks were able to avoid being caught.

Source: Richard H. Hancock, *The Role of the Bracero in the Economic & Cultural Dynamic of Mexico. A Case Study of Chihuahua* (Stanford: California Hispanic-American Society, 1959).

TABLE 26. AGRICULTURAL WORKERS HIRED
IN THE UNITED STATES AND
SELECTED AT THE MIGRATORY STATIONS
ESTABLISHED IN THE COUNTRY
(1952–64)

Year	Total	Repatriated
1952	197,100	148,542
1953	201,380	172,408
1954	309,033	243,261
1955	398,650	360,787
1956	432,916	424,677
1957	436,049	405,315
1958	432,802	436,353
1959	444,418	426,536
1960	319,412	325,999
1961	296,464	292,520
1962	198,322	217,761
1963	189,528	188,520
1964	179,298	179,535

Sources: *Anuario Estadístico de los Estados Unidos Mexicanos* and Oficina Documentadora de Trabajadores Emigrantes.

TABLE 27. THE OCCUPATIONAL STRUCTURE AND PERCENTAGE
OF UNIONIZED WORKERS
(1964)

Sector	Workers (thousands)	Unionized * (thousands)	Per cent
Primary activities **	6,909	130	1.9
Industries	2,652	810	30.6
Extractive	174	103	59.2
Transforming	1,923	494	25.7
Construction	499	164	32.9
Electricity, gas, etc.	56	50	88.8
Transports and communications	437	249	57.0
Commerce and financial	1,288	115	8.9
Unspecified services and labor	1,930	82	4.2
Totals	13,216	1,388	

* Approximate estimate based on the trend of the past five years.
** Agriculture, cattle-breeding, forestry and fishing.
Sources: Occupational structure: *La economía mexicana en cifras* (Mexico: Nacional Financiera, S. A., 1965). Unionized workers: *Anuario Estadístico de los Estados Unidos Mexicanos,* 1962–63. Dirección General de Estadística, Mexico, 1965.

230

TABLE 28. UNIONIZED AND NON-UNIONIZED WORKERS *
(1939–63)

Years	1 Unionized	2 Non-Unionized	Ratio of 2 / 1
1939	605,433	5,190,000	8.6
1940	547,063	5,400,000	9.9
1941	803,379	5,610,000	7.0
1942	656,079	5,820,000	8.9
1943	684,190	6,030,000	8.8
1944	669,256	6,240,000	9.3
1945	712,668	6,450,000	9.0
1946	727,222	6,660,000	9.2
1947	737,806	6,870,000	9.3
1948	783,812	7,080,000	9.0
1949	802,856	7,290,000	9.1
1950	817,381	7,454,712	9.1
1951	835,735	7,677,806	9.2
1952	852,023	7,899,863	9.3
1953	864,656	8,134,029	9.4
1954	967,684	8,286,649	8.6
1955	979,991	8,539,266	8.7
1956	1,000,462	8,794,190	8.8
1957	1,013,311	9,066,199	8.9
1958	1,202,917	9,172,154	7.6
1959	1,277,000	9,404,873	7.4
1960	1,298,025	9,700,000	7.5
1961	1,324,682	10,734,123	8.1
1962	1,353,742	10,891,258	8.0
1963	1,364,877	11,267,123	8.3

* The figures for 1939–49 and for 1960 are estimated.
Source: *Anuario Estadístico de los Estados Unidos Mexicanos.*

TABLE 29. REGISTERED CITIZENS AND CITIZENS WHO VOTED
IN THE ELECTIONS OF 1964

State	(1) Registered	(2) Voted	(3) Abstained	Per cent 3 / 1
Aguascalientes	100,551	73,791	27,360	27.21
Baja California	257,984	181,894	76,090	29.49
Baja California (T)	35,025	26,894	8,183	23.36
Campeche	69,833	59,205	10,628	15.22
Coahuila	340,419	265,021	75,398	22.15
Colima	68,902	39,587	29,315	42.54
Chiapas	433,770	335,923	97,847	22.56
Chihuahua	498,502	282,302	216,200	43.37
Distrito Federal	2,080,465	1,424,857	655,608	31.51
Durango	312,512	229,361	83,151	26.60
Guanajuato	627,364	419,624	207,740	33.11
Guerrero	519,622	397,369	122,253	23.53
Hidalgo	399,751	345,377	54,374	13.60
Jalisco	992,016	590,290	401,726	40.49
México	704,174	505,355	198,819	28.23
Michoacán	671,327	393,287	278,040	41.42
Morelos	184,322	117,273	67,049	36.38
Nayarit	157,343	76,400	80,943	51.44
Nuevo León	452,648	261,418	191,230	42.25
Oaxaca	576,228	448,606	127,622	21.15
Puebla	762,202	554,010	208,192	27.31
Querétaro	142,834	111,742	31,092	21.77
Quintana Roo	17,829	17,484	345	1.94
San Luis Potosí	406,639	284,932	121,707	29.93
Sinaloa	297,960	214,121	83,839	28.14
Sonora	273,594	157,798	115,796	42.32
Tabasco	175,442	147,592	27,850	15.87
Tamaulipas	414,023	302,339	111,684	26.97
Tlaxcala	127,126	102,578	24,548	19.31
Veracruz	988,387	683,116	305,271	30.88
Yucatán	259,261	206,901	52,360	20.19
Zacatecas	241,539	178,513	63,026	26.09
Total	13,589,594	9,434,908	4,154,686	30.57

Source: Comisión Nacional Electoral. Registro Nacional de Electores.

Table 30. Probable Voters, Registered Voters, and Voters (1964)

State	Rank	Per cent 2/1	(1) Probable voters	(2) Registered citizens	Increase of Registrations with Respect to 1958			(3) Total of votes	Per cent 3/1	Per cent 3/2
					Citizens	General per cent	Direct per cent			
Jalisco	6	84.01	1,180,767	992,016	326,768	11.89	49.11	590,290	49.99	59.50
Michoacán	5	78.50	885,165	671,327	252,743	9.20	60.38	393,287	45.98	58.58
México	18	77.95	903,356	704,174	242,805	8.84	52.62	505,355	55.94	71.76
Veracruz	24	76.65	1,289,499	988,387	238,234	8.67	31.75	683,116	52.97	69.11
Puebla	14	81.38	936,576	762,202	230,669	8.40	43.39	554,010	59.15	72.68
Guanajuato	12	77.79	806,465	627,364	159,112	5.79	33.97	419,624	52.03	66.88
Chihuahua	15	82.73	602,518	498,502	110,326	4.02	28.42	282,302	46.85	56.63
Nuevo León	19	81.96	552,255	452,648	99,362	3.62	28.12	261,418	47.33	57.75
Zacatecas	29	66.59	362,731	241,539	93,398	3.40	40.23	178,513	49.21	73.90
Chiapas	17	80.34	539,905	433,770	89,752	3.27	26.08	282,302	46.85	56.63
Hidalgo	22	88.91	449,575	399,751	89,614	3.26	28.89	345,377	76.82	86.39
Guerrero	21	94.70	548,726	519,622	83,011	3.02	19.01	397,369	72.42	76.47
Sinaloa	11	79.07	376,825	297,960	79,536	2.89	36.41	214,121	56.82	71.86
Durango	4	91.56	341,325	312,512	75,990	2.77	32.12	229,361	67.19	73.39
Baja California	10	86.55	298,049	257,984	72,092	2.62	38.78	181,894	61.02	70.50
Sonora	13	70.91	385,808	273,594	68,652	2.50	33.49	157,798	40.90	57.67
Coahuila	23	78.37	434,377	340,419	61,126	2.22	21.88	265,021	61.01	77.85
Morelos	3	94.94	194,142	184,322	59,061	2.15	47.15	117,273	60.40	63.62
Tamaulipas	26	81.09	510,523	414,023	58,716	2.14	16.52	302,339	59.22	73.02
Tabasco	8	81.42	215,455	175,442	53,309	1.94	43.64	147,592	68.50	84.12

(TABLE 30. continued)

State	Rank	(1) Probable voters	Per cent 2/1	(2) Registered citizens	Increase of Registrations with Respect to 1958			(3) Total of votes	Per cent 3/1	Per cent 3/2
					Citizens	General per cent	Direct per cent			
San Luis Potosí	28	482,988	84.19	406,639	32,613	1.19	8.71	284,932	58.99	70.07
Oaxaca	30	829,731	69.45	576,228	32,453	1.18	5.96	448,606	54.06	77.85
Aguascalientes	2	114,875	87.53	100,551	25,905	.94	34.70	73,791	64.23	73.38
Nayarit	32	180,325	87.24	157,343	25,235	.92	19.10	76,400	42.35	48.55
Tlaxcala	27	161,616	78.66	127,126	20,660	.75	19.40	102,578	63.47	80.69
Yucatán	9	302,035	85.84	259,261	17,555	.64	7.26	206,901	68.50	79.80
Campeche	7	81,807	85.36	69,833	15,844	.58	29.34	59,205	72.37	84.78
Colima	31	79,738	86.41	68,902	12,559	.46	22.29	39,587	49.64	57.45
Baja California (T)	20	38,506	90.96	35,025	8,619	.31	32.64	26,842	69.70	76.63
Querétaro	25	163,741	87.23	142,834	6,388	.23	4.68	111,742	68.24	78.23
Quintana Roo	1	24,866	71.70	17,829	5,368	.19	43.07	17,484	70.31	98.06
Total states		14,244,304	80.79	11,509,129	2,747,475	100.00	23.87	8,010,051	56.28	69.66
Federal District		2,672,548	77.84	2,080,465	482,654		30.20	1,424,857	53.51	68.48
Republic		16,916,852		13,589,594	3,230,129			9,434,908	55.77	69.42

TABLE 31. POPULATION AGED TWENTY OR OVER, POPULATION WHICH VOTED, DID NOT VOTE, AND VOTES OF THE OPPOSITION PER STATES (1960–61)

States	Population* aged twenty or over	Voted	Per cent	Population (July 1961) Did not vote	Per cent	Opposition votes
Aguascalientes	96,121	58,183	60.5	37,938	39.5	7,493
Baja California	234,594	136,322	58.1	98,272	41.9	44,999
Baja California (T)	36,581	27,431	74.9	9,150	25.1	117
Campeche	76,855	39,359	51.2	37,496	48.8	3,398
Coahuila	414,966	239,007	57.5	175,959	42.5	6,821
Colima	74,123	38,298	51.7	35,825	48.3	4,564
Chiapas	525,062	291,153	55.4	233,909	44.6	2,118
Chihuahua	559,528	202,868	36.2	356,660	63.8	36,705
Distrito Federal	2,389,231	817,682	34.2	1,571,549	45.8	288,789
Durango	334,180	168,426	50.4	165,754	49.6	4,399
Guanajuato	768,064	337,785	44.0	430,279	56.0	15,533
Guerrero	527,385	287,878	54.6	239,507	45.4	21,226
Hidalgo	448,491	256,699	57.2	191,792	42.8	3,208
Jalisco	1,102,604	420,441	38.1	682,163	61.9	42,085
México	851,868	285,666	33.5	566,202	66.5	6,388
Michoacán	815,048	274,456	33.7	540,592	66.3	34,994
Morelos	179,399	46,720	26.0	132,679	74.0	12,570
Nayarit	171,600	82,670	48.1	88,930	51.9	1,766
Nuevo León	510,463	193,951	38.0	316,512	62.0	11,453
Oaxaca	819,227	410,358	50.0	408,869	50.0	21,226

(TABLE 31. *continued*)

States	Population * aged twenty or over	Population (July 1961)				Opposition votes
		Voted	Per cent	Did not vote	Per cent	
Puebla	902,882	412,137	45.6	490,745	54.4	23,571
Querétaro	158,619	88,151	55.6	70,468	44.4	5,298
Quintana Roo (T)	21,764	11,861	54.5	9,903	45.5	—
San Luis Potosí	469,638	200,937	42.8	268,701	57.2	27,321
Sinaloa	361,881	112,117	31.0	249,764	69.0	6,261
Sonora	352,608	104,433	29.6	248,175	70.4	8,268
Tabasco	205,494	110,343	53.7	95,151	46.3	825
Tamaulipas	474,454	338,230	71.3	136,224	28.7	8,069
Tlaxcala	156,594	95,591	61.0	61,003	39.0	258
Veracruz	1,238,019	509,763	41.2	728,256	58.8	77,578
Yucatán	295,146	206,009	69.8	89,137	30.2	25
Zacatecas	350,268	140,901	40.2	209,367	59.8	10,084

* Includes that not indicated (1960 Census).
Sources: Dirección General de Estadística and Registro Nacional de Electores.

TABLE 32. POPULATION AGED TWENTY OR OVER,
POPULATION WHICH VOTED, DID NOT VOTE, AND VOTES OF THE OPPOSITION (1964)

State	Population aged twenty or over	Voted	Per cent	Did not vote	Per cent	Opposition votes
Aguascalientes	117,832	73,791	62.6	44,041	37.3	6,453
Baja California	323,684	181,894	56.2	141,790	43.8	38,946
Baja California (T)	39,648	26,842	67.7	12,806	32.3	827
Campeche	84,426	59,205	70.1	25,221	29.9	2,394
Coahuila	444,321	265,021	59.6	179,300	40.3	17,436
Colima	82,834	39,587	47.8	43,247	52.2	4,967
Chiapas	555,527	335,923	60.5	219,604	39.5	3,682
Chihuahua	625,144	282,302	45.1	342,842	54.8	58,332
Distrito Federal	2,799,555	1,424,857	50.9	1,374,698	49.1	355,798
Durango	347,747	229,361	66.0	118,386	34.0	22,490
Guanajuato	827,964	419,624	50.7	408,340	49.3	85,350
Guerrero	562,582	397,369	70.6	165,213	29.4	11,867
Hidalgo	456,609	345,377	75.6	111,232	24.4	5,407
Jalisco	1,220,670	590,290	48.3	630,380	51.6	76,328
México	931,389	505,355	54.2	426,034	45.7	41,700
Michoacán	877,840	393,287	44.8	484,553	55.2	54,116
Morelos	200,934	117,273	58.4	82,727	41.2	6,740
Nayarit	185,732	76,400	41.1	109,332	58.9	5,679
Nuevo León	573,243	261,418	45.6	311,825	54.4	40,733
Oaxaca	845,954	448,606	53.0	397,348	47.0	15,036

(TABLE 32. *continued*)

State	Population aged twenty or over	Voted	Per cent	Did not vote	Per cent	Opposition votes
Puebla	954,749	554,010	58.0	400,739	42.0	34,275
Querétaro	167,248	111,742	66.8	55,506	33.2	9,725
Quintana Roo	26,453	17,484	66.1	8,969	34.9	526
San Luis Potosí	492,712	284,932	57.8	207,708	42.2	24,757
Sinaloa	387,326	214,121	55.3	173,205	44.7	4,084
Sonora	402,536	157,798	39.2	244,738	60.8	2,424
Tabasco	222,224	147,592	66.4	74,632	33.6	914
Tamaulipas	528,780	302,339	57.2	226,441	42.8	10,185
Tlaxcala	164,802	102,578	62.2	62,224	37.7	1,740
Veracruz	1,327,259	683,116	51.5	644,143	48.5	21,759
Yucatán	307,196	206,901	67.3	100,295	32.6	29,106
Zacatecas	370,151	178,513	48.2	191,638	51.8	36,942
	17,455,071	9,434,908	54.0	8,020,163	46.0	1,030,718

Source: Comisión Federal Electoral. Dirección del Registro Nacional de Electores. Presidential Elections of July 5, 1964.

TABLE 33. DELINQUENTS SENTENCED AT PRIMARY COURTS
OF CLAIMS PER OCCUPATIONAL ACTIVITY
(1951–62)

Year	Total labor force	Agricul- tural labor force	Sentenced	1000	Farmers	1000
1951	8,513,541	4,964,693	19,509	2.29	8,970	1.80
1952	8,751,886	5,103,685	22,096	2.52	9,900	1.93
1953	8,998,685	5,247,605	27,943	3.10	11,831	2.25
1954	9,254,333	5,396,688	30,554	3.30	12,850	2.38
1955	9,519,257	5,551,179	30,731	3.22	13,949	2.51
1956	9,794,652	5,711,776	30,796	3.14	13,947	2.44
1957	10,079,510	5,877,892	32,111	3.18	14,418	2.45
1958	10,375,071	6,050,249	30,827	2.97	13,617	2.25
1959	10,681,873	6,229,161	31,039	2.90	13,920	2.23
1960	11,873,000	6,342,000	32,284	2.71	14,783	2.33
1961	11,563,440	6,510,330	33,723	2.73	15,426	2.35
1962	11,886,920	6,667,190	35,305	2.98	15,644	2.35

Source: Dirección General de Estadística. *Anuario Estadístico de los Estados Unidos Mexicanos.*

TABLE 34. URBAN AND RURAL ECONOMICALLY ACTIVE POPULATION, PER INCOME LEVELS. ABSOLUTE AND RELATIVE FIGURES (1961–62)

Monthly income levels per working person	Republic	Per cent	Urban	Per cent	Rural	Per cent
Up to 300	4 462 627	41.49	1 182 445	20.64	3 280 182	65.25
301–500	2 809 059	26.12	1 719 690	30.01	1 089 369	21.67
501–750	1 343 904	12.49	1 025 174	17.89	318 730	6.34
751–1,000	1 020 197	9.48	822 403	14.35	197 794	3.93
1,000–2,000	812 901	7.56	689 231	12.03	123 670	2.46
More than 2,000	307 674	2.86	290 617	5.07	17 057	.34
Total	10 756 362	100.00	5 729 560	99.99	5 026 802	100.02

NUMBER AND PERCENTAGE OF FAMILIES PER INCOME LEVELS AND URBAN AND RURAL POPULATION (1961–62)

Family monthly income levels	Republic	Per cent	Urban	Per cent	Rural	Per cent
Up to 300	1 752 106	26.00	355 256	9.68	1 396 850	45.52
301–500	1 610 038	23.89	755 904	20.60	854 134	27.83
501–1,000	1 832 552	27.19	1 254 522	34.18	578 030	18.84
1,001–3,000	1 333 878	19.79	1 106 298	30.14	227 580	7.42
More than 3,000	210 031	3.12	197 837	5.39	12 194	.40
Total	6 738 605	99.99	3 669 817	99.99	3 068 788	100.01

(TABLE 34. *continued*)

NUMBER AND PERCENTAGE OF PERSONS PER INCOME
LEVELS AND URBAN AND RURAL POPULATION (1961–62)

Family monthly income levels	Republic	Per cent	Urban	Per cent	Rural	Per cent
Up to 300	8 338 848	22.48	1 292 457	6.65	7 046 391	39.90
301–500	8 699 565	23.45	3 686 108	18.96	5 013 457	28.39
501–1,000	10 309 857	27.79	6 563 421	33.77	3 746 436	21.21
1,001–3,000	8 425 791	22.71	6 660 675	34.27	1 765 116	9.99
More than 3,000	1 323 819	3.57	1 235 047	6.35	88 772	.50
Total	37 097 880	100.00	19 437 708	100.00	17 660 172	99.99

Name Index *

241

Subject Index

agrarian reform, 48-49
army, power, 36-38, 67-69
authoritarianism: and democracy, 182-83; and fascism, 183; lower-class, 182-83

bilingualism, vs. monolingualism, 79-83
bourgeoisie: and democracy, 160-77; and socialist revolution, 173-77

caciquismo, 32-36, 67-69
capitalism: and colonialism, 159-77; and democracy, 159-77
caudillismo, 32-36, 67-69
church (*see* clergy)
class: entrepreneurial, 48-55, 67, 160-77; struggle, 163-77; working, 14-17, 163-77, 182-83
clergy, 38-48; policies of, 46-48; power, 38-48, 67-69
colonialism (*see also* domination): and capitalism, 159-77; and democracy, 159-77; internal, 71-103
control: of popular organizations, 121-23; of unorganized population, 121-23
culture, and United States influence, 59-64

decision-making, and development, 143-51
democracy: and the bourgeoisie,

160-77; and capitalism, 159-77; and colonialism, 159-77; and Marxism, 158-77; and the sociological approach, 178-92; sociological definitions of, 179-80
development (*see also* economic development), 3-6, 111-12; and decision-making, 143-51; and foreign policy, 140-43; and marginality, 71-79
disconformity: and civic struggle, 120-34; and marginality, 124-34; and paternalism, 128-34; and violence, 126-27; and voting patterns, 124-26
domination (*see also* colonialism): vs. subjugation, 71-103; United States, 56-64

economic development (*see also* development), 3-6; and political decisions, 137-51
elections, 12-13; and shifts in power, 12-13

fascism: and authoritarianism, 183; and democracy, 183-84
foreign policy, and development, 140-43

government (*see also* power structure *and* State): control, 121-25; federation and states, 24-28; local, 28-30, 32-36; models of, 6, 11;

243